ANTI-JUDAISM AND
EARLY CHRISTIAN IDENTITY

STUDIA POST-BIBLICA

GENERAL EDITOR

DAVID S. KATZ (Tel Aviv)

VOLUME 46

ANTI-JUDAISM AND EARLY CHRISTIAN IDENTITY

A Critique of the Scholarly Consensus

BY

MIRIAM S. TAYLOR

E.J. BRILL
LEIDEN · NEW YORK · KÖLN
1995

The paper in this book meets the guidelines for permanence and durability of the Committee on Production Guidelines for Book Longevity of the Council on Library Resources.

Library of Congress Cataloging-in-Publication Data

Taylor, Miriam S.
    Anti-Judaism and early Christian identity : a critique of the
scholarly consensus / by Miriam S. Taylor.
        p.   cm. — (Studia post-Biblica, ISSN 0169–9717 ; v. 46)
    Slight revision of the auhtor's thesis (doctoral)—Oxford
University, Nov. 1991.
    Includes bibliographical references and index.
    ISBN 9004101861 (alk. paper)
    1. Judaism (Christian theology)—History of doctrines— Early
church, ca. 30–600. 2. Christianity and other religions—Judaism.
3. Judaism—Relations—Christianity. 4. Simon, Marcel, 1907–
Verus Israel. 5. Church history—Primitive and early church, ca.
30–600. 6. Judaism—History—Talmudic period, 10–425. I. Title.
II. Series.
BT93.T38   1994
261.2'6'09015—dc20   94-35320
                                                                      CIP

Die Deutsche Bibliothek – CIP-Einheitsaufnahme

Taylor, Miriam S.:
Anti-Judaism and early Christian identity : a critique of the
scholarly consensus / by Miriam S. Taylor. – Leiden ; New
York ; Köln : Brill, 1994
    (Studia post-biblica ; Vol. 46)
    ISBN 90–04–10186-1
NE: GT

ISSN 0169-9717
ISBN 90 04 10186 1

PRINTED IN THE NETHERLANDS

In Memory

of

ALBA ROMER TAYLOR

April 30, 1931 - August 14, 1990

TABLE OF CONTENTS

Typology

ACKNOWLEDGEMENTS

This book is a slightly edited version of my doctoral dissertation, submitted to Oxford University in November 1991. I am grateful to the F.C.A.R. (Québec) and the S.S.H.R.C.C (Canada), as well as to the Lady Davis Fellowship in Israel for doctoral fellowships that made research for this study possible. I would like to thank my supervisor, Dr. Martin Goodman, for his consistent support and faith in my work. Thanks also to Professor Guy Stroumsa for his encouragement and positive feedback during my stay in Israel. Sharon Helfer helped prepare the manuscript for publication, and my sister, Wanda, was, as always, a useful resource on editorial matters.

Many thanks to all the members of my family and close friends for their love and support through the difficult years in which my thesis came into being. I am grateful to Avriel Butovsky (ז״ל), who inspired my original interest in this area of research. I am thankful to my father, who rescued me from innumerable practical and intellectual snags, and whose enthusiasm for my work was a constant source of inspiration. My husband, Steven, was my mainstay over the years this work was written, and my daughter Alba came along at the end.

This book is dedicated to the memory of my mother, Alba Romer Taylor, whose spirit continues to inspire me in my life and work.

INTRODUCTION

Since the Second World War, the Christian past and its relationship to Judaism have come under new scrutiny. The Holocaust raised with urgency the question of the role of Christian teaching in the history of Western anti-Semitism, and led to a reevaluation of the origins and nature of Christian anti-Judaism. Flowing from this, the contribution of the patristic age to the tradition of anti-Judaism within the church has become the focus of renewed scholarly interest. Although anti-Jewish sentiments in the church had their origins in the early tensions that led to the eventual separation of church and synagogue, it was after the church became fully conscious of its own autonomy and independent mission that the main lines of a Christian theology of Judaism were drawn. In the period leading up to the transformation of Christianity into a dominant religion, enjoying imperial sponsorship, church and synagogue lived side by side as minority religious groups in a pagan empire. Scholars interpreting the works of the Christian authors who wrote throughout this critical time (150-312 C.E.) have been intrigued by the church's relationship with the religious tradition from which it sprang, and, in their attempt to uncover the principles that governed this relationship, they have sought to trace the formation and development of Christian teaching on Judaism. In this book, I will examine the consensus view of the patterns of Jewish-Christian interaction in the early patristic period, and the hypotheses that this view has generated about the sources of and motivations for anti-Judaism within the church. I propose to challenge the current approach adopted by modern scholars on historical, hermeneutical and theological grounds.

First published shortly after the Second World War, and now widely cited as the foundational work in this area, is Marcel Simon's *Verus Israel*, a study of relations between Christians and Jews in the early centuries of Christian expansion (135-425).[1] Simon's model of Jewish-Christian relations and his thesis about the impetus behind the early church's opposition to the synagogue, now forms the basis of a widespread consensus in modern scholarship on the subject of Christian anti-Judaism. According to Simon, "the most compelling reason for Christian anti-semitism was the religious vitality of the Jews" (Simon 1986: 232). Indeed, Simon's study might be characterized as an attempt to account for the origins of the church's anti-Judaic teachings through a defence of the vigour and vitality of ancient Judaism. In his interpretation of the Christian anti-Jewish references, Simon

---

[1] On the contribution of Simon see Wilken 1967: 313; Efroymson 1980: 25; Gager 1983: 20; Gager 1986: 101.

constructs an historical and hermeneutical model which I call the "conflict theory" of Jewish-Christian relations. It holds that the vitality of the synagogue inevitably resulted in a collision with the church, "for if Judaism did continue for some time to play a part, or to attempt to play a part, in the ancient world, Christianity must necessarily have come into collision with it" (Simon 1986: xi). Simon presumes that Jews and Christians in the second and third centuries of the Common Era were involved in a fierce rivalry for converts in the pagan world, and that this conflict or competition defined the way the two groups interacted with one another.

In a postscript to a later edition of his work (1964), Simon congratulated himself on the fact that the validity of his central thesis had not been contested (Simon 1986:385). Indeed, Simon's main premise, Jewish vitality, and his central thesis, Jewish-Christian conflict as a source of Christian anti-Judaism, have remained virtually unchallenged to this day. It is my aim to undertake such a challenge.

Simon's approach must be understood against the background of the position he sought to refute when he made his vehement defence of Jewish vitality, for some of the weaknesses of the "conflict theory" flow directly from its refutational stance. Describing his book as a challenge to some of the traditionally held views in the study of religion (Simon 1986: x), Simon's aim in *Verus Israel* was to expose and refute the theological biases underlying the historical analysis of the traditional "doctrinal historians" of the church.[2] These theologians, the most famous of whom was Adolf von Harnack, interpreted the history of Christian growth and expansion according to the categories of dogmatic theology, and viewed the emergence and eventual triumph of the Christian movement as a natural function of Christianity's inherent superiority. If the exponents of this traditional view assumed that Christian success was assured, even predetermined from the outset, it was because they adopted the theological myth of Christian supersession over Judaism as historical fact. Christianity was said to flourish at Judaism's expense, and in the unfolding story of the church's growth and expansion, Judaism was portrayed as a religion in decline whose fate had less and less relevance to the church as it retreated into isolation (cf. Harnack 1908; 44-71).

That Simon felt the need to correct some of these blatant theological prejudices is understandable. In taking the Christian "conversion" of the empire for granted, and in assuming that the "triumph" of Christianity was self-explanatory, the traditional theologians had failed to address one of the most challenging questions faced by religious historians of the Roman Empire. In addition, Harnack's deprecatory, even condescending portrayal of Judaism, so obviously rooted in theological preconceptions, was no doubt distressing to a scholar who set store by the standards of critical historical investigation. Accordingly, Simon set out to rescue the Jews from the obscurity and isolation to

---

[2] See Simon 1986: ix-xi; Wilken 1971: 222ff.

which they had been relegated by Harnack. He insisted on granting them an active role in the life of the empire and sought thereby to rescusitate Judaism, while at the same time giving a more plausible historical account of the challenges faced by the church on its road to "victory". In general, Simon sought to move away from the abstract theological preoccupations of the dogmatic historians towards a greater sensitivity to the polemical and apologetic concerns that gave rise to the early Christian writings. His revival of Judaism also afforded him a ready-made explanation for the church's expressed opposition to the Jews during the course of the early Christian mission to the gentile world.

Simon's work has been praised as an important corrective to a long tradition of scholarship shaped by anti-Jewish biases. In place of a theologically predetermined view of Christian expansion which assumed that Judaism was of no real consequence to the Christians, the "conflict theory" claims to interpret the sources of Christian anti-Judaism in terms of wider social realities, and to account in a more credible way for the vehemence and persistence of the anti-Jewish arguments in the writings of the church fathers. Though the "conflict theory" appears to offer a more plausible explanation for anti-Judaism, this approach is problematic in its own right.

The "conflict theory's" central idea of Christian-Jewish rivalry has served in the development of a number of hypotheses seeking to account for the anti-Judaism expressed in the writings of the early church. Priding themselves on the adoption of a more sophisticated, nuanced approach than the traditional theologians, and clearly aspiring to meet the standards of critical historical scholarship, the conflict theorists aim to present us with a well rounded, global explanation for early Christian anti-Judaism. Scholars have theorized about the religious, social, political and environmental dimensions of what is conceived of as a complex phenomenon rooted in conflict. While it is not explicitly stated, the unspoken assumption seems to be that these various sources of anti-Judaism complement one another, that together, they provide a comprehensive picture of the negative attitudes to Jews found among the early Christians, and that they unlock the key to the patterns of Jewish-Christian interaction. It follows from this, though again it is not explicitly stated, that the more factors one can identify, the more complete an explanation one can offer.

However, while these hypotheses are all defended in one form or another by Simon, and while they appear selectively and in different combinations in the works of other scholars, nowhere are they clearly identified or distinguished in the secondary literature. To that end, this book takes the form of a typology of anti-Judaism. In the chapters which follow, I identify and categorize the hypotheses put forward by modern scholars. While these theories all have a superficial air of plausibility that has contributed to their widespread acceptance, their presuppositions have never been fully questioned, and their real implications remain unexplored. The result is an approach ensnared in confusions and contradictions. Indeed, when these theories are carefully scrutinized, they reveal themselves to be based on dubious historical assumptions that lead to hasty and unjustified conclusions.

In addition, while the "conflict theory" challenges some of Harnack's theological presuppositions, it does not accomplish this task fully. As will be argued in Chapter One, the notion of Jews as proselytizers, on which the "conflict theory" is based, stems from the imposition of the Christian model of development on ancient Judaism. Consequently, the strength and "vitality" the conflict theorists attribute to Judaism, and that is so central to their main assumption about conflict between the two groups, ultimately proves to be a pseudo-vitality which, as we shall see in the concluding chapter, contains within it the seeds of Jewish defeat, and hidden presumptions about Jewish inferiority vis-à-vis the church.

As a result of its conceptual weaknesses, and its susceptibility to Christianizing preconceptions, the "conflict theory" fails as a hermeneutical theory, in other words, in its stated aim of accounting for the anti-Judaism expressed in the early Christian writings. The problem, as we shall see, is in part that the dichotomy established by Simon between dry, abstract theological concepts and social reality has confined scholars in their attempts to identify the Jews who are opposed by the authors of the early church. Against Harnack's view that the Jews depicted in the Christian writings were artificial stereotypic figures adopted for purely literary purposes, Simon argues that these Jews are the contemporary members of an active and dangerous rival group (Harnack 1883: 56-91; Simon 1986: 136, 271). While the "conflict theory" succeeds in accounting for the evident importance attached to the Jewish question by church thinkers, it removes the references to Judaism from the theoretical context in which they appear, underemphasizes their coherence and consistency, and translates them out of the scriptural language in which they are couched. I will argue that where close attention is paid to the context, substance, spirit, tone and orientation of the Christian texts, the inward rather than outward apologetic focus of the anti-Jewish passages is revealed. To the fathers fell the task of interpreting salvation history, and of defining the movement to which they belonged, and the anti-Jewish argumentation of the church formed part of this endeavour.

The Jewish question was certainly an issue of pressing urgency, but it was not the pressures of a living Judaism that made it so. The patristic writers were preoccupied, rather, with Judaism on a symbolic level, and more specifically, with the internal theological questions raised by the church's supersessionary claims vis-à-vis Judaism, and by its attempts to forge a *via media* between appropriation and rejection of different elements of the Jewish tradition. This book aims to demonstrate that the Jews in the writings of the fathers are neither the men of straw envisaged by Harnack, nor Simon's formidable rivals, but symbolic figures who play an essential role in the communication and development of the church's own distinctive conception of God's plans for His chosen people, and in the formation of the church's cultural identity.

In important respects, this is a preliminary study. It operates in the realm of concepts and ideas, and is strictly speaking, a theoretical rather than an textually interpretive work. It aims to establish some conceptual clarity in a field marred by confusions and contradictions, by exposing the implications of the historical and hermeneutical choices made by modern scholars. It seeks to suggest an alternative approach to understanding the references to Jews in the early patristic writings, and to prepare the way for a much needed thorough and systematic reexamination of the early Christian texts on Judaism.

The first chapter, "Competitive Anti-Judaism", focuses on theories about a supposed religious rivalry for converts between the church and synagogue, and begins with a reappraisal of the common assumption that the Jews were proselytizers on the Christian model. The second chapter, entitled "Conflictual Anti-Judaism", seeks to identify the various theories that have been generated from assumptions about the socio-political underpinning of the supposed conflict between Christians and Jews. The third chapter, under the heading "Inherited Anti-Judaism", explores the notion that anti-Jewish ideas in the early church were a) absorbed by the church fathers from their pagan environment, or b) adopted from established traditions of biblical interpretation.

In the fourth chapter, entitled "Symbolic Anti-Judaism", I will defend the theory that the Judaism opposed in the writings of the fathers was not a living Judaism connected to Jewish contemporaries, but a symbolic Judaism which served a vital function in the formation of Christian identity. I will explore the reasons for the reluctance among scholars to take this dimension of anti-Judaism seriously, and will show how, though divorced from social reality, this "theological" anti-Judaism is by no means removed from life altogether. I will then defend its relevance to our understanding of the mind-set and preoccupations of the early Christians, as well as its ability to make sense of the nature of early Christian anti-Judaism.

Finally, the theological implications of the hypotheses generated by the "conflict theory" shall be examined in the concluding chapter. In virtue of its historical and hermeneutical failings, the "conflict theory" also proves inadequate as a theory of theological explanation. Not only does it contain inherently denigrating ideas of ancient Judaism, but it obscures the role of anti-Judaism in Christian theology, fails to understand it as a phenomenon of enduring significance, and fails in its supposed aspirations to address the questions so essential to any genuine attempt at theological reevaluation.

CHAPTER ONE

COMPETITIVE ANTI-JUDAISM

The consensus in support of Marcel Simon's thesis is indeed impressive. Writing in 1967, Robert Wilken urged church historians to pay heed in their interpretive work to Simon's characterization of Judaism: "Judaism, far from coming to an end, was a real, active and often effective rival and competitor of Christianity" (Wilken 1967: 313; repeated in Efroymson 1976: 56). Like Simon, Wilken also sees the so-called competition between church and synagogue as the main source of Christian hostility toward the Jews: the "virulence of Christian anti-Semitism is a sign of the vitality of Judaism in the later empire" (328). In a study of Jews and Christians in Ancient Antioch, Wilken and Wayne Meeks speak of the necessity of recognizing Judaism as "a vital social and religious force during the early centuries of the Common Era" (Meeks & Wilken 1978: vii), and they characterize the relations between "the parent community and its somewhat unnatural offspring" as one of "active" competition "for the social as well as religious favours of the larger society" (Meeks & Wilken 1978: 1-2). Citing Simon in his work on Origen, J.W. Trigg writes: "Historians have only recently become aware of how vital and aggressive a missionary religion Judaism was in Origen's time" (Trigg 1983: 183). Here, the "aggressive" behaviour of the Jews helps account for, make sense of, and even excuse anti-Judaism: "Although such remarks have today the ring of anti-Semitism, we must bear in mind that they were uttered in the midst of an intense rivalry between groups on an *equal* footing and that Jews *gave as well as they got*" (my emphasis, Trigg 1983: 185). The model of two parallel groups vying for the same prize is also found in the work of John Gager: "It is now clear that Judaism and Christianity were regular competitors for the religious loyalties of the gentiles. Literally as well as figuratively, they faced each other in the marketplace" (Gager 1983: 154; cf. also Gager 1986: 104). The "intense" competition is characterized by Jack Lightstone as one between "two expressions of Yahwism" "engaged in the same game in the same ball park" (Lightstone 1986: 129-32).

Not only have Simon's insights become universally accepted but it seems that scholars have also adopted Simon's "refutational" stance. Harnack still looms large as an opponent in modern scholarship. As late as 1986, in a "Retrospect" following a five-year seminar on "Anti-Judaism in Early Christianity", Lloyd Gaston reiterates Simon's refutation of Harnack, challenging anew the assumption "that second century Judaism was moribund and obso-

lescent and that the Greco-Roman world was ripe for the church's plucking"
(Gaston 1986b: 165). In sum, modern scholarly references supporting the
"conflict theory" of Jewish-Christian relations, both in detailed studies and in
passing statements, are innumerable.[1] Still busy combatting the abstract, confessional model denounced by Simon, modern scholars have not paused to
question the model constructed by Simon himself to take its place.

Christianizing Presuppositions

As has already been stated, that Simon's theory has gained such widespread
acceptance and continues to hold sway, is no doubt due in part to the fact that
it appears to fit in with the general move towards deconfessionalization and
contextualization in the study of biblical and post-biblical Christian literature
(see Introduction). Indeed, Simon's attempt to break free from theological
presuppositions, seems on the surface to conform to recent trends in modern
scholarship. The basis of my historical critique of the "conflict theory" is that
it does not *fully* accomplish this task. In what follows, I propose to show that
the foundation of the "conflict theory" is based on Christianizing preconceptions carried over from the traditional, confessional approach to the study of
early church history, the very approach, in other words, that Simon so vehemently criticizes. These preconceptions are Christianizing in that they impose
the Christian model of development on the other religions of antiquity, and in
particular on ancient Judaism. Before we launch into a discussion of
"competitive" anti-Judaism proper, some of these preconceptions need to be
examined more thoroughly.

One of the central premises of Simon's argument, as we have seen, is that
Judaism remained active as a proselytizing movement throughout the early
centuries of the common era, and that the effectiveness of this proselytizing
activity provoked the creation of the early Christian anti-Jewish polemical literature. Indeed, Simon identifies "the problem that the anti-Jewish polemical
literature presents us with" as "nothing other than the whole problem of Jewish-Christian relations, and more narrowly, the problem of Jewish proselytizing" (Simon 1986: 146). The belief that Judaism was a missionary religion in
the early centuries of the Common Era is widely held among modern schol-

---

[1] See also Grayzel 1946: 85; Williamson 1982: 89; Langmuir 1963: 234; Flannery 1985:
42, 46; Fiorenza 1976:2; Remus 1986:66; Wilson 1986c: 95; Poliakov 1965: 37; Lovsky 1955:
114-15; Grosser and Halperin 1983: 52; Donahue 1973: 1.

ars.[2] In this important respect, therefore, Simon's portrayal of Judaism reflects generally accepted views about the people of the synagogue found in wider scholarship.

Recently, however, a small number of scholars have begun to question the assumptions underlying this view, and to point to the faulty preconceptions that have perpetuated it. Their general critique of the notion that ancient Judaism was an actively missionary religion, is a critique of the unidimensional vision of ancient religion on which this notion is based. They demonstrate that the idea of Jews as proselytizers is founded on faulty assumptions about Christianity's emergence from Judaism, as well as on more general misconceptions about the nature of ancient religion. This recent critique raises some important questions about the consensus view of ancient Judaism, and it obviously has very important implications for the study of relations between Christians and Jews in the period leading up to the Christianization of the empire. Indeed, it allows us to see Simon's refutation of Harnack in a new light. Perhaps Simon is not quite as successful in deconfessionalizing Harnack as many modern scholars seem to assume.

Simon challenges one important aspect of Harnack's vision of early Judaism, but he accepts some of its most central underlying principles. Against Harnack, Simon defends the "vitality" of second and third century Judaism but in this defense he accepts, even adopts, the *measure* of religious "vitality" as it was defined by Harnack. Like Harnack, Simon measures a religion's strength and vigour by its expansionist drive and by the success of its missionary activity. The difference between the two scholars lies not in their assumptions about the nature of Jewish vitality, but about the periodization of that vitality. Harnack believed that the Jews were active proselytizers prior to the destruction of their sacred temple, but he assumed that their missionary activity gradually waned from the second century onwards. Simon's attempt to prove against Harnack that Judaism remained strong and vigorous throughout the early centuries of the church's expansion is essentially an argument for the *continued* effectiveness of the synagogue as a proselytizing movement. Without acknowledging it, Simon carries over into his own work some of the presuppositions central to Harnack's outlook. These preconceptions about Christianity's emergence from Judaism, and about the nature of religion in general, are only coming to light now that they can no longer be taken for granted without justification. Let us examine them:

---

[2] Among scholars of Jewish-Christian relations, the idea that the Jews were active proselytizers is often taken as a given. See Gager 1983: 20; Donahue 1973: 5; Ruether 1974: 123; Flannery 1985: 35, 42, 45; Parkes 1969: 106-7, 120; Blumenkrantz 1946: 85, 165; Grosser & Halperin 1983: 52; Grayzel 1946: 85; Poliakov 1965: 37-8; Williamson 1982: 89; Fredouille 1972: 254. Slightly more nuanced views are found in Efroymson 1976: 57; Moore 1927: 323-353; cf. also Baron 1952: I. 388 n. 27.

(1) The notion of Jews as proselytizers is partly rooted in the assumption that "the idea of a mission to convert was inherited by the early Jesus movement from contemporary Judaism" (Goodman 1992:53). This assumption is stated quite plainly in the work of Harnack: the church's "missionary zeal was inherited by Christianity from Judaism". Indeed, in Harnack's view "the amount of the debt is so large, that one might venture to claim the Christian mission as a continuation of Jewish propaganda" (Harnack 1908: 9,15). Though Simon doesn't study in depth the formative period when the mission of the church first took shape, he too assumes that Christianity took over the model of the Jewish mission, that both groups operated on the "same grounds" (Simon 1986: 64), and that the synagogue even supplied the church with a ready made clientèle (Simon 1986: 69). Paul Donahue, in his study of Justin's *Dialogue*, describes the church as seeking to wrest away from the Jews their gentile mission (Donahue 1973: 251; cf. also Lovsky 1955: 159).[3]

(2) Alongside and reinforcing this belief is the premise that proselytizing is a "natural religious instinct". Unfortunately, both these presumptions have little basis in historical fact. They clearly use Christianity as a measure of what is "natural", and ignore the "rarity of missionary behaviour in other religious movements in the ancient world" In fact, "the notion that existing worshippers should put effort into attracting others to their cult was rarely, if ever, found outside Christianity before the third century" (Goodman 1989: 183). The preconception that proselytizing was a natural religious drive leads to a third assumption which is fundamental to both Harnack's and Simon's vision of Judaism, and which is the most objectionable of the Christianizing preconceptions examined here.

(3) Although Simon ostensibly objects to Harnack's view that the triumph of the church was a function of Christianity's inherent superiority, in adopting Harnack's measure of a religion's "vitality", Simon also accepts Harnack's definition of a religion's superiority. Judaism and Christianity stood out in the ancient world as monotheistic religions with universalistic aspirations. In as much as they are also assumed to have been proselytizing movements, it is in terms of the progress of their so-called missions that the strength and vitality of these movements inevitably comes to be judged. By extension, the relative success of these supposed missions to convert the world also becomes a measure of the relative ability of both movements to live up to their religious ideals, a measure, in other words, of their *worth* as religious movements.

Harnack interpreted what he saw as the Jewish retreat and disinterest in the gentile world after 70 C.E. as a decline, and as an indication of the inherent

---

[3] This notion finds its most tenacious and most thorough exponents in the area of New Testament studies, where there is a natural interest in Christianity's emergence out of Judaism. See, for example, D. Georgi 1986, and J. Jeremias 1958.

inferiority of Judaism vis-à-vis Christianity. Against Harnack, Simon supposedly makes himself a champion of Judaism. He sets out to prove the dynamism of Judaism, arguing that the Jews continued to play a significant role in the religious development of the gentile world beyond the first century. In order to counter Harnack's view that the victory of the church was virtually predetermined from the outset, however, Simon has to argue that the Jews challenged the Christians on their own turf, and he maintains, therefore, that the Jews remained active and effective as proselytizers throughout the early centuries of the Common Era. In other words, Simon accepts the *terms* as defined by Harnack, and he sets out to prove that Judaism hadn't failed according to the *standards* set by Harnack. For both of these scholars, indeed for most modern scholars, the only acceptable model of an active religion is an actively missionary religion.[4]

In his evaluation of the state of Judaism in the years of Christian expansion, Simon outlines the alternatives in very limited terms. Either Judaism was alive, vital, dynamic and evangelistic or it was dead, withdrawn, on the decline and inwardly turned. These are the only options envisaged. Either Judaism withdrew into itself, and "no longer really confronted the Church but restricted itself to a conflict in the realm of theory, to a bookish, sterile controversy around the sacred texts" or it was "still a proselytizing movement", and "then it was a real and dangerous rival" (Simon 1986: 271).

Revision of the Consensus View

As was mentioned above, very recently a small number of scholars have begun to recognize that many fundamental uncertainties remain in this field of study, and have called for a serious reappraisal of commonly held views. Two scholars interested in Jewish-Christian interaction in the Roman world initiated this revision in the early 80s. A.T. Kraabel numbers the view of Jews as proselytizers among six "questionable assumptions" about ancient Judaism in modern scholarship. He argues that the biased Christian sources, in particular the New Testament, have been given "inordinate weight" in determining this issue, with the result that passages clearly carrying a "heavy burden of their author's theology" have been accepted as "solid historical evidence" (Kraabel 1982: 451-2).[5] David Rokeah also casts doubt on the assumption that the an-

---

4 Interestingly, Scot McKnight points out that some Jewish scholars have also been motivated by apologetic concerns in efforts to prove the inherent missionary nature of Judaism. McKnight describes the work of Bernard Bamberger 1939 and William Braude 1940 as rooted in a defence against late nineteenth-and early twentieth century German scholars who portrayed Judaism as an inferior religion (McKnight 1991: 2).

5 One of the key New Testament passages assumed to provide evidence of Jewish proselytizing is Matthew 23.15: "Woe to thee, scribes and Pharisees, that you cross land and sea to make one proselyte". Goodman proposes an alternative explanation, suggesting that the logion can be traced back to the earliest tradition about Jesus, and that the term "proselyte" here need

cient Jews were proselytizers.[6] He points not only to the scarcity of corroborating evidence, but argues that where evidence relating to the question is to be found, much of it is contradictory, and he laments the fact that scholars seek to "explain away" this "uncomfortable fact" (Rokeah 1982: 32-44).

Indeed, the presuppositions underlying the view that Jews were proselytizers are so firmly entrenched that most scholars remain convinced of the idea even where they themselves must recognize the inadequacy of the available evidence. Simon, for instance, admits that the information on the proselytizing activity of the Jews is "scarce and not very exact", and that "direct evidence is difficult to discover". The rabbinic sources, he acknowledges, remain divided on the issue of the mission to the gentiles.

> We seek in vain in the Talmud for any uniformity of attitude toward proselytism, or any consistent teaching concerning it. What we do find there represents no more than a collection of individual opinions. These opinions are varied and often contradictory. They vary from scholar to scholar according to the individual's temperament, and they vary from time to time and place to place according to circumstances (Simon 1986: 274).

Simon also concedes that the pagan sources are not as plentiful as he would have liked. He tries to account for the meagerness of evidence by suggesting that the church's "dangerous rival", though formidable, was outdone in its efforts by the church. "The pagan authors, in so far as the religious situation of their day interests them, are struck most by the missionary activity of the Christians, which was doubtless not only livelier but infinitely more efficacious" (Simon 1986: 278-79). Paul Donahue, who follows Simon's lead in his study of Justin's *Dialogue* (arguing that Justin combatted the "vigorous propaganda activity" of the Jews in his work), also admits that the rabbinic attitude to proselytism is "difficult to determine", because "they differed among themselves on this issue as on many others" (Donahue 1973: 79).

Ultimately, Simon and Donahue both base their judgements about Jews as proselytizers on the a priori assumption that Judaism had an inherently missionary nature. Though Simon acknowledges that the rabbinic arguments "are not enough to establish that real missionary activity did go on" (Simon 1986:

---

not be interpreted in the conventional sense, but may well refer to the conversion of *Jews* to Pharisaism (Goodman 1992:60-2; cf. McKnight 1991: 106-8). This logion also appears in Origen's commentary on the gospel of Matthew (*Commentarium* series 16). Though Simon assumes that this passage provides evidence of continuing proselytizing activity among the Jews (Simon 1986: 286), it is judaizing among Christians that Origen is condemning here, and not conversion. As shall be argued in the discussion of "defensive" anti-Judaism (Typology I.2), the connection of these "judaizing" practices to a living Judaism is extremely tenuous. They do not necessarily presuppose direct Jewish influence, let alone an active attempt on the part of Jews themselves to encourage such practices.

[6] Rokeah is one of the only scholars to challenge some of the premises underlying Simon's views (Rokeah 1982, 1983).

278), he remains firm in his presumption that it did, because his preconceptions predetermine his approach to, and interpretation of, the evidence. Any evidence which appears to lend credence to the notion that Jews were proselytizers is automatically accepted as a genuine reflection of Jewish inclinations, while evidence to the contrary is either ignored or dismissed.

But the problem here goes beyond the reliance on scanty and insubstantial evidence. In the last few years, two scholars, Martin Goodman and Scot McKnight, have shown that the confusions and uncertainties in this area of study are due in large part to the inadequacy of the very criteria used in the evaluation of proselytizing activity. Confirming the existence of a proselytizing religion is not as straightforward as many scholars seem to assume. The imposition of the Christian model on Judaism has severely limited the options open to scholars in the interpretation of evidence that is recognized by all to be complex and contradictory. Scholars have portrayed isolationism and proselytizing as two exclusive alternatives, and have failed to consider that they might rather be seen as extremes on a continuum, opening the door to the possibility that ancient Judaism defined the relationship between insiders and outsiders in a more complex and more nuanced fashion.

Both Goodman and McKnight have called for a fundamental reevaluation of the terms and indices used in the measure of missionizing among the Jews. McKnight refers to the "lack of consistency in the use of terms" as "one of the most notable deficiencies of this advancing area of study". In his own definition of what constitutes a "missionary religion", he outlines two essential components. Firstly, a missionary religion is one who adopts "a mission to the rest of the world" as a conscious aim, and for whom this aim is integral to the "self-definition" of the movement. Secondly, a missionary religion also "practices its mission through behaviour that intends to evangelize" and convert nonmembers to the religion. This second feature is a necessary component in McKnight's definition because he recognizes that "there may be a vast chasm between one's belief system…and one's actual practice", and no religion can be properly called "missionary" unless it actively seeks out new adherents as a matter of course (McKnight 1991: 4-5).

The missionary drive, then, is built on a type of self-consciousness and on a type of action that is consistent with this self-consciousness. This definition is so simple and straightforward that it might seem self-evident. Unfortunately, however, the evidence generally presented by scholars as proof of Jewish missionizing fails to meet these minimal requirements. As we shall see, the criteria relied on in the attempt to prove the existence of proselytizing among the Jews tend to tell us more about the inclinations of gentiles than they do about the inclinations and actions of Jews. Where they do relate to the attitudes of the Jews themselves, they reveal a positive disposition rather than an active mission.

(1) Gentile Attraction to Judaism

Many scholars seem to assume that wherever there are signs that Judaism held some attraction to gentiles, there is confirmation of proselytizing activity among the Jews. When Simon turns to the Christian sources in order to find corroboration for his assumption that the Jews were active missionaries, he appeals among other texts to Tertullian's *To the Nations (Ad Nationes)* I.13, which he claims "bears particular witness to the hold Jewish rites had over the pagan masses".

> It is you, at all events, who have even admitted the sun into the calendar of the week; and you have selected its day, as the most suitable in the week for either an entire abstinence from the bath, or for its postponement until the evening, or for taking rest from banqueting. By resorting to these customs, you deliberately deviate from your own religious rites to those of strangers. For the Jewish feasts are the Sabbath and the meal of purity, and Jewish also are the ceremonies of the lamps, and the fasts of unleavened bread, and the open-air prayers, all of which are, of course, foreign to your gods (I.13).

Although Simon himself recognizes that this "diffuse influence...cannot properly be called a form of proselytism", he remains convinced that "it is a side effect of proselytism, and presupposes its existence" (Simon 1986: 286). One might well wonder how Simon justifies the claim that one reference by a Christian author to the gentile adoption of certain Jewish practices presupposes *any* kind of attitude on the part of the Jews themselves, let alone an active pursuit of converts.

In addition, it is questionable that the passage even provides evidence of Judaism's "diffuse influence". The aim of *To the Nations* is to show that heathen prejudices against the Christians are based on "culpable ignorance" (I.1), and the purpose of chapter 13 is to prove that Christian practices are not so strange or so distant from Roman customs as some Romans seem to assume. "You who reproach us with the sun and Sunday should consider your proximity to us. We are not far off from your Saturn and your days of rest" (I.13). The fact that Christians have chosen Sunday as their day of worship does not mean that they worship the sun, Tertullian states. In order to illustrate this point, he refers to the similarity of some Roman customs to Jewish practices and argues that no one would claim these similarities as evidence that the Romans were opting for Judaism. The analogy is meant to be provocative; had there been an acknowledged attachment among Romans to Judaism, the analogy would lose much of its force.

I agree with J. Nolland, then, that "there is certainly no case here of Jewish sympathizers". For Tertullian's audience "Judaism is something "over there" of which they know little, but which they nevertheless firmly dislike. The ignorance of Judaism seems to Tertullian to be so great that he can 'prove' from this ignorance that the Judaism-like practices of the Romans cannot indicate any kind of attachment to Judaism" (Nolland 1979: 11).

The assumption that gentile attraction to Judaism is a measure of Jewish proselytizing is also found in the work of Paul Donahue. Because of the complexity and contradictory nature of the rabbinic sources on the question of proselytizing, Donahue decides to restrict his investigation to what he describes as a "question of judgement": "Were rabbinic statements, and more importantly, rabbinic rulings likely to increase or diminish the number of converts to Judaism?" (Donahue 1973: 79). Donahue seems to assume that proving the existence of proselytizing activity amounts to little more than establishing that the rulings of the rabbis would have been more likely to attract than repel non-Jews.

(2) The Existence of Converts

Several scholars appeal to evidence for the existence of proselytes as proof of Jewish missionary activity in the period under study here. Alongside earlier references,[7] Simon, Gager and Donahue refer to Justin's mention of proselytes (*Dialogue with Trypho the Jew*) 122-123), as confirmation of the persistence of "effective proselytism in this period" (Simon 1986: 282-83), and as corroboration of the "successful proselytizing activity" of Roman Jews (Gager 1983: 61; cf. Donahue 1973: 174-179). Simon also sees significance in Tertullian's identification of the Jewish discussant in the dispute supposedly recorded in his *Against the Jews (Adversus Judaeos)* as a proselyte (*Against the Jews* 1). Simon seems to assume that Tertullian would not have drawn attention to the fact that the Jew in his dialogue was a convert from paganism if this had not been a common occurrence.[8] But even if we assume that Tertullian was alluding in his *Against the Jews* to the large number of Jewish proselytes in Carthage at this time, it still remains that conversions to Judaism indicate more about the inclinations and actions of some gentiles than they do about the actions and intentions of Jews. Even "the existence of numerous converts" does not in itself reveal a mission to win them (Goodman 1989: 181). Interestingly, Goodman points out that "the etymology of the word 'proselyte' implies movement by the gentile concerned...and not a bringing in

---

[7] From *Acts of the Apostles* (2.11; 6.5; 13.43); Josephus, on attraction to Judaism among the masses (eg. *Against Apion* 2.282); Juvenal, on full conversion of son whose father was only a sympathizer (*Satires* 14); Seneca, on "influence" of Jewish customs (preserved by Augustine *City of God* 6.11); Dio Cassius, on the execution of prominent Romans, on charges of "atheism" (Dio *History* 67.14.1-3). cf. Simon 1986: 278-288; Gager 1983: 59-61; Donahue 1973: 6-37).

[8] Tertullian may have had other reasons for identifying the Jewish opponent in this way. Rokeah suggests that this was a deliberate strike at the "Jewish claim to election" (Rokeah 1982:43 n.10).

by the body of the Jews as the model of mission would require" (Goodman
1992:72).

(3) The Welcome of New Converts

So far, we have seen evidence of gentile attraction and even conversion to Judaism. Where they were regarded with sympathy among gentiles, the Jews
were admired for their rigorous ethical standards and for their monotheism.
The Jewish response to this admiration is, of course, relevant to our discussion. It seems that they were not loathe to encourage respect and to inculcate
their values among the gentiles. Indeed, "the notion of a proselyte was well
established in Judaism long before the end of the Second Temple era"
(Goodman 1989: 175; cf. Goodman 1992:54-5). Wherever converts were discussed in the Jewish writings, "it was usually with sympathy and sometimes
with admiration", and gentiles who wished to come to the God of Israel were
generally welcomed (Goodman 1992:71). So "the dominant view of proselytes was positive in that Jews generally accepted any who would assume the
'yoke of the Torah'" (McKnight 1991: 45), and many texts seem to take for
granted that prospective converts will normally offer themselves" (Goodman
1989: 176).

It is important to note, however, and this is stated by both Goodman and
McKnight, that the Jewish openness to prospective converts provides no
measure of proselytizing activity among the Jews. Goodman succinctly makes
this point in the opening lines of his article on "Proselytizing in Rabbinic Judaism". "Members of a community who accept that suitable outsiders should
be welcomed into their society do not imply by their acceptance that a positive
search for such newcomers is appropriate". Certainly for the ancient Jews,
"the impetus for conversion was expected to come from the worthy gentile
concerned, not from the Jews whom he or she wished to join" (Goodman
1989: 175). "The role of the Jews was simply passively to bear witness; how
the gentiles reacted was up to them" (Goodman 1992:72). Indeed, "there is
almost no evidence that Jews were involved in evangelizing gentiles and ag-
gressively drawing gentiles into their religion. Jews were not in the business
of hawking their wares" (McKnight 1991: 48). It is the failure of scholars to
make this important distinction between passive acceptance and active pursuit
that is, in part, responsible for all the confusion in this area of study.[9]

So the evidence generally appealed to in the attempt to establish missionary activity among the Jews falls far short of demonstrating the existence of a
conscious and active bid to win over non-Jews. But apart from their negative
critique of the current approach to this issue, Goodman and McKnight also go

---

[9] See references to proselytizing activity collected in Bamberger 1939; Braude 1940; Juster
1914: I. 253-337.

further to suggest that there are positive reasons to deny the existence of an active mission among the Jews. The commonly used indices, outlined above, reveal nothing about a Jewish mission to the gentiles. But Goodman and McKnight also put forward new indices which provide a more genuine measure of proselytizing. According to these new more exacting standards, it becomes even more clear that the impetus for an active mission was lacking in ancient Judaism. Let us examine these:

(1) Entrance Requirements and the Status of New Members

In order to encourage the absorption of new converts without thereby blurring the boundaries between members and non-members, a missionary religion must be preoccupied with questions relating to the status of new converts, and to the definition of firm and consistent entrance requirements. Yet "Jewish terminology about the status of gentiles who accreted to their community" remains vague (Goodman 1989: 176). "Diaspora Judaism seems to have accepted a wide range of gentile behaviour (from superficial interest to full conversion)", but it was "not too greatly concerned to establish the specific points at which one became eligible for salvation" (Collins 1985: 184). This lack of attention to entrance requirements would surely not have been tolerable "had Judaism been a missionary religion in any centralized sense" (McKnight 1991: 88), and so the "ambiguous status of proselytes" is in itself evidence that the Jews did not see the winning of new converts as a "religious duty" (Goodman 1992:71).

(2) The Equality of Members New and Old

Essential to ensuring the attraction of converts is the notion that all members of a religious group, whether they be veterans of the movement or newly accepted converts, are members in equal measure. This principle of equality before God was an important one in the early church. This is not to say that Christians eliminated all social distinctions. Far from it, but certainly no orthodox Christian, whether new or old, was thought to have a greater or lesser claim to the Christian heritage. In the immortal words of Paul, "there is neither Jew nor Greek, there is neither slave nor free, there is neither male nor female; for you are all one in Christ Jesus. And if you are Christ's, then you are Abraham's offspring, heirs according to the promise" (*Epistle to the Galatians* 3.28-9).

Yet as Goodman points out, if we compare Jewish attitudes to proselytes to those in the early church, the "limitations" of Jewish "openness to outsiders" stand out. A "proselyte to Judaism became in religious terms a member of a clearly defined, separate, and, in a few cases mostly concerned with marriage, less privileged group within the Jewish commonwealth". Goodman attributes this to the "dual function of conversion as entry into a political and social as well as into a religious entity", but the significant point, in his view is "that the distinct definition of proselytes as a particular *sort* of Jew was retained throughout antiquity" (Goodman 1992:71).

(3) Exclusivity

Essential to the Christian outlook was a belief that Christianity and Christianity alone possessed the key to salvation. The church called upon sinners to respond to Christ and implicit in its promise of eternal salvation was the claim that faith in Christ was the only way men and women could hope to save their souls. As shall be discussed in greater depth in Typology IV.1, a great emphasis was placed in the church on the exclusivity of the union in Christ, and Tertullian's statement that truth "has as many foes as there are strangers to it" (Tertullian *Apology (Apologeticum)* 7), reveals the "whoever is not with us is against us" mentality of the early church. The powerful sense of solidarity created by this exclusivity was no doubt part of what made the Christian message so attractive to some. Correspondingly, the threat of damnation which was said to hang over non-Christians no doubt created a sense among prospective converts that conversion was a matter of pressing urgency. Indeed, the belief that the "unenlightened are in some way damned" is essential to any "truly missionary philosophy". Yet it is not easy to find clear evidence of this in first century Judaism (Goodman 1992:72). In Judaism, "there is no uniformity of view on the question of whether or not the covenant is the *exclusive* soteriological category. Many rabbis were prepared to allow for salvation of "righteous gentiles" (Sanders 1976: 42). Gentiles certainly were thought to stand outside the covenant between God and Israel, and had no share in that covenant, but "no early source holds gentiles morally guilty for not being full Jews" (Goodman 1989: 175). The only duty uniformly required of gentiles, in the eyes of Jews, was a general morality (Goodman 1992:74).

As monotheists, the Jews like the Christians had universalistic aspirations. They believed that their God was the God of all humanity, and they were convinced that the truth of their ways would be proven at the end of days. Both groups possessed a kind of "triumph motif" which asserted that God would ultimately vindicate the truth.[10] While in the Christian texts, this firm conviction in the certainty of victory went hand in hand with the expansionist drive of the church, the way in which the triumph motif expresses itself in the Jewish writings actually suggests the absence of a missionizing drive among the Jews, rather than the contrary. The notion that an act of God would bring about a massive conversion of gentiles at the Last Day was an important element in Jewish references to proselytization (see references in McKnight 1991: 47). Because this theme finds expression chiefly in apocalyptic and

---

[10] For more on the Christian "triumph motif" see Typologies II.3 and IV.1.

prophetic literature, McKnight suggests that it reflects the "reality of the lack of converts to Judaism in the present" (McKnight 1991: 74 and 47), rather than constituting a present encouragement to proselytizing activity. The Jews seemed content for the present to passively bear witness to the truth, leaving the task of winning over the world in the hands of God.

It becomes clear from this brief review of the proselytizing question, that the common assumption that Judaism and Christianity operated according to the same "pattern" or model is unfounded. E.P. Sanders challenged some of the prevailing misapprehensions about first century Judaism among New Testament scholars when he demonstrated that "Paul presents an essentially different type of religiousness from any found in Palestinian Jewish literature" (Sanders 1977: 543). Unfortunately most historians of Christian-Jewish relations in the early centuries of the Common Era have failed even to consider the possibility that the religious patterns of these two minority groups could be markedly different. Yet once the evidence relating to ancient Judaism is freed from the presuppositions of the Christian model of development, then not only does the considerable diversity within Judaism emerge more clearly, but to the extent that a general orientation toward gentiles can be detected, this orientation deviates from the Christian "norm".

Certainly ancient Judaism was not isolationist, but it is now clear that we cannot thereby assume, as if by default, that the Jews were proselytizers. It is not sufficient simply to establish that Judaism had its occasional evangelists, nor to point to those few rabbinic texts that seem to condone the active pursuit of proselytes. What we are looking for, in the attempt to make sense of complex and contradictory evidence, is that which was "commonplace" in Judaism. McKnight calls on scholars to keep in mind that the "significant data" for proselytizing activity among the Jews "can be reduced to about a handful—and it strikes me as hasty to base far-reaching conclusions on such an amount of evidence" (McKnight 1991: 75). There was no "consistent consciousness" of a mission to the gentiles, nor does the evidence "permit us to infer" that missionary activity was in any way consistent or widespread (McKnight 1991: 74, 77). There can be no doubt that the Jews were convinced they were God's chosen people, and that the God of Israel was the God of all humanity. They were also generally tolerant of, and well disposed to gentiles. In bearing witness to their convictions through their piety and good deeds, they also succeeded in attracting a number of converts from the gentile world in which they lived. In his search for the distinctive religious pattern of Judaism, McKnight comes to the conclusion that the Jews were in the true sense "Yahweh's light among the nations"—" 'a light' because Judaism was fully assured that truth was on its side; 'among the nations' because Jews were thoroughly woven into the fabric of the Roman world" (McKnight 1991: 117; cf also 26,29).

Once the distinctions are made between gentile and Jewish inclinations, between passive acceptance and active pursuit, then the confusing and contradictory evidence on the proselytizing question can be examined in a new light. Martin Goodman detects a pattern of development in Jewish attitudes to proselytizing which turns the current assumption that the Christian mission had its origin in Judaism on its head. The first century Jewish authors who are most often appealed to for evidence of proselytizing, Philo and Josephus, actually "have little about proselytes and nothing about a mission to win them" (Goodman 1992:70-1). In order to find any evidence in Jewish works of a real desirability to win proselytes, we must turn to the later rabbinic writings, texts composed well after the start of the Christian mission.

Goodman perceives evidence of an interesting and curious shift some time in the second and third centuries, in which there emerged among *some* rabbis, "perhaps for the first time among any non-Christian Jews, a belief that Jews have a duty to win proselytes" (1989: 176-77). Even this new development, however, does not mark the beginning of a real missionary drive in Judaism. The notion of the desirability of a proselytizing mission only appears in a select number of rabbinic texts, and even where it is to be found, it is "implied rather than explicitly formulated", and it was never to become a "general rabbinic doctrine" (Goodman 1989: 181-2). In addition, this new approval of proselytizing developed alongside a trend to codify in the Noachide laws the behaviour that would earn for the non-Jew the title of "righteous gentile".

The espousal of precise requirements for pious gentiles, implying that gentiles could be considered worthy while remaining gentiles, would hardly have been an act of sound strategy for a religious group who identified proselytizing as one of its main goals. Indeed, such requirements would tend to "make conversion to Judaism irrelevant and any mission to win proselytes otiose" (Goodman 1989: 182). Yet the rabbis seemed able to hold these contradictory notions in "conjunction" (Goodman 1989: 183), and Goodman tells us it is important not to "shirk" this "paradox" (Goodman 1989: 181). He suggests several conceivable reasons for the new interest of Jews in the "precise boundaries" marking off their communities from the gentile world, including the possibility that the Jews may have been responding in some way or other to the Christian mission, thus reversing the common assumption about the origin of the Christian mission in Judaism.

To sum up: the evidence, when it is freed from presuppositions, does not bear out the common assumption that Judaism defined itself in terms of actively pursued missionary goals. But Judaism was no less vital or dynamic for its lack of an organized missionary drive. The Jews clearly had a somewhat different orientation toward the gentiles than did the church, and the success or failure of their movement was not seen to be dependent on their ability to win over the gentile world. We see already at this early stage that the main premise of the "conflict theory" is on extremely shaky ground. If the Jews had different goals and aspirations from the Christians, then it can no longer be assumed that they were the church's main competitor for converts. The faulty historical preconceptions of the "conflict theory" have coloured and distorted its interpretation of the church's anti-Jewish writings, resulting in further historical misapprehensions.

   In the following review of the various types of anti-Judaism that have been detected in the Christian writings, the current hermeneutical approach and its historical implications will come under scrutiny. We turn first, in this section on competitive anti-Judaism, to what are considered to be the two main settings in which the competition between church and synagogue is to have taken place.

The Two Settings of Competitive Anti-Judaism

The rivalry between Christians and Jews is thought to find expression in two main settings (cf. Gager 1983:117): first, the literary controversies between Jews and Christians, which, it is assumed, gave rise to a form of anti-Judaism referred to here as "polemical and apologetic" anti-Judaism; and second, the "judaizing" influences in the early church, which are considered to have created a form of anti-Judaism, which I call "defensive anti-Judaism". Let us examine each in turn.

TYPOLOGY I.1
POLEMICAL AND APOLOGETIC ANTI-JUDAISM

The Christian texts on Judaism take the form of exegetical dissertations, appealing to the Scriptures, and seeking to demonstrate that: (1) Jesus is the Messiah long-promised and prophesied to the Jews; (2) that the Christians, who recognized and accepted him, are the rightful successors to the Jews as the chosen people of God; (3) and that the Mosaic dispensation has been superseded by a new spiritual covenant. The supersessionary character of these commentaries on the Holy Scriptures involves a denial of all legitimacy to Judaism after the advent of Christ. This negation of Judaism is seen by the conflict theorists as a manifestation of the rivalry that is said to have characterized the relationship between church and synagogue.

Indeed some scholars have concluded that the rivalry between Christians and Jews found its main expression in a dispute over the correct interpretation of the Holy Scriptures. (Gaston 1986: 166-67; cf. DeLange 1976: 82). The competition between church and synagogue is thought to have expressed itself in disputes in which "both parties lay exclusive claim to the legitimate heritage of the divine covenant and built a case around the same documents" (Gager 1983: 154 & 134), in which both set themselves up as "rival interpreters of ancient tradition" (Wilken 1980: 467). And these disputations, it is assumed, often took the form of public debates, "a familiar feature of the Greco-Roman landscape" (Gager 1983: 154). We are encouraged to think that "the written works embody the substance of arguments used in verbal encounter" (Simon 1986: 173), that they contain "invaluable information about the issues at stake" (Stanton 1985: 378), and "serve to define the principal topics of debate" (De Lange 1976: 102). The "learned controversies", affirms Simon, are thought to "shed light on the real significance of the anti-Jewish literature" (Simon 1986: 173). The debates, it is further assumed, served both a polemical and an apologetic need for the Christians. The drive to demonstrate the truth of Christianity was thought to have been directly linked to the attempt to refute the claims of Judaism. Affirmation and refutation are seen as two sides of the same coin (Simon 1986: 156; cf. Fiorenza 1976: 2; Remus 1986: 77; Stanton 1985: 378).

The notion that Jews and Christians were involved in scriptural debates is based on the assumption that the two religious groups operated within a common arena in which both groups addressed the same issues and responded to the same objections. Yet, despite their reluctance to do so, modern scholars have had to acknowledge that the form of the Christian writings on Judaism does not encourage us to view them as reflective of genuine debates. For one thing, the themes of the anti-Jewish passages are repetitive and consistent over centuries. This is hardly what one would expect of controversial writings which, by definition, must remain sensitive to ever-changing circumstances, and responsive to new objections. The traditional character of the anti-Jewish writings shall be examined in greater depth in Typology III:2, but there is also another important respect in which the Christian references to Judaism lack the quality of live disputations.

The Judaism opposed in the Christian writings is somehow devoid of life and substance, and the Jewish disputant in the texts lacks credibility as a real opponent. This fact has not escaped the notice of modern scholars. Rosemary Ruether comments on the one-sided character of the Christian arguments against Judaism: "the Jew in the dialogue represents what the Christians thought Jews would say rather than representing an authentic dialogue where the Jew is allowed to give his own arguments in his own terms" (Ruether 1976: 165-66). Simon also concedes that the Christian authors were "not all equally able, and not all equally alive to the way in which their opponents were thinking" (Simon 1986: 173). David Efroymson points to the abstract quality of the anti-Jewish references in Tertullian's writings (Efroymson 1976: 4).

Not surprisingly, this aspect of the Christian anti-Jewish writings was stressed by Harnack. As we saw above, Harnack's assessment of the anti-Jewish literature was based not only on "external" historical assumptions about the withdrawn and indifferent character of Judaism, but also on internal evidence from the texts themselves. In other words, his judgement was founded partly on the character of the writings. Though Harnack's measure of Jewish vitality and his historical conclusions about the withdrawal and decline of Judaism have already been refuted, his hermeneutical insights bear some consideration. According to Harnack, the refutations against the Jews in the literature were "too weak and theoretical" to be based in reality. He estimated that the adversaries depicted in the texts were purely "conventional" figures, whose arguments were rendered in a standardized form, and whose outlook tied in all too neatly with Christian refutations and justifications. Speaking of Justin, Harnack stated his certainty that the church father "took liberties in the creation of his *Dialogue*, and he almost always makes his opponent say just what seems to him useful for the development of his own thought and the carrying through of his own proof" (Harnack 1883: 77-78). It is partly on this basis that Harnack concluded that the Jewish opponents in the Christian dialogues were fictitious characters, created by the Christians themselves, for their own purposes. Unfortunately, not recognizing anti-Judaism as a problem that needed addressing, Harnack did not understand the enduring significance of the fathers' "weak and theoretical" refutations. Harnack failed to see that while they are removed, strictly speaking, from contemporary reality, these "conventional" representations have a power and magnitude that does not allow us to dismiss them as lightly as he did.

Though most scholars concede that the Christian anti-Jewish writings are abstract, one-sided, traditional and insubstantial, the premises of the "conflict theory" will not allow them to take this aspect of the texts seriously. The firm belief in a pre-defined sort of Jewish "vitality", and in the inevitable confrontation between church and synagogue that is said to have stemmed from this vitality, forces scholars to view the church's anti-Jewish texts as polemical writings directed at live Jews and at real Jewish objections, in spite of all evidence to the contrary.

The "conflict theory" drastically reduces the hermeneutical options open to modern scholars even before the interpretive task is embarked upon.[11] This is because the current approach to the interpretation of the Christian references to Judaism starts out with a priori historical assumptions in which the evaluation of the actual character and substance of the anti-Jewish passages takes second place. Because it is taken as given that the early Christians were preoccupied with the threat posed by the rival synagogue, scholars come to the anti-Jewish writings with a preconceived notion of the intention behind the composition of these texts.

For the conflict theorists, the anti-Jewish writings fulfill no more than a corroborative function for an already elaborated theory. Thus the obliqueness of the writings is only taken into account to the extent that it can be made to fit in with the notion of conflict and rivalry. Ambiguities and biases in the portrayal of Jews and Judaism are automatically attributed to the church's polemical needs and apologetic techniques. The absence of direct confrontation with the Jews in the Christian texts is attributed to evasive tactics, and to the inevitable tendency of polemicists to misrepresent their opponents. Simon suspects the Christian references on Judaism of suffering from a "certain lack of objectivity", but he never questions their applicability to Judaism as such, nor their ability to reflect the topics that divided church and synagogue (Simon 1986: 116). Nicholas De Lange laments the fact that "polemical impetus and apologetics prevailed" over a genuine attempt at dialogue (De Lange 1976: 103), but he never stops to consider that the ambiguous nature of the texts might call into question their suitability as sources of historical information about Christian-Jewish interaction.

For the conflict theorists, the only real hermeneutical challenge is the need to distinguish between polemical distortions and historical fact in the church fathers' attack on Judaism. They do not pause to consider the kind of Judaism that is really being negated in the writings, nor the level on which this Judaism was thought to be objectionable. In thus narrowing their hermeneutical options, modern scholars have missed out on an essential first step in the attempt to come to grips with the origins and nature of Christian anti-Judaism.

---

[11] For a more detailed discussion of this see Typology III.2.

Surely the key to finding the impetus and direction of Christian anti-Judaism must be found in the Christian scriptural arguments themselves. If the content of these writings is traditional and their form is abstract and oblique, then before theorizing about how this might reflect some clever polemical strategy to defeat the Jews down the road, we must first determine the level on which the entire discourse is taking place. The theoretical dimension of anti-Judaism will be considered in greater depth in Typology III.2. For now what has already become clear is that the conflict theorists have missed a few important milestones on the hermeneutical journey.

TYPOLOGY I.2
DEFENSIVE ANTI-JUDAISM

There is evidence that the borrowing of certain Jewish practices and the
involvement in some forms of Jewish worship, as well as in Jewish festivals
and ceremonies, was popular among certain Christian groups. It is to such
tendencies that the condemnation of "judaizing" practices in the early Christian writings is thought to refer, and it is assumed that anti-judaizing formed
part of a defensive reaction among ecclesiastical leaders who saw such influences as a threat to the integrity of the church. Unfortunately however, misconceptions in modern scholarship about the judaizing phenomenon have led
to a fundamental misrepresentation of *anti-*judaizing in the early church, and
to a misunderstanding of the motivations behind it.

Confusions in this area of study stem from: (1) the assumption that judaizing was a by-product of the Jewish-Christian conflict; and (2) the overemphasis, in the evaluation of this phenomenon, on evidence from the post-
Constantinian era, on the unfounded assumption, in other words, that tendencies found present in the fourth century must also have existed in the preceding period. Let us consider each question in turn.

(1) Judaizing and the "Conflict Model"

The attraction of Jewish practices for some early Christians is viewed, by
modern scholars, as direct confirmation of the strength, vitality, even power
and prominence of the Jewish community in the centuries of early Christian
expansion. In other words, it is thought to lend credence to the "conflict theory", and behind the phenomenon of judaizing is believed to be the presence
of an attractive and vibrant Jewish community (Wilken 1971: 37; cf. Trebilco
1991: 29). In their discussion of Jews and Christians in Antioch, Wayne
Meeks and Robert Wilken see judaizing as a function of the strength and vitality of the synagogue (Meeks & Wilken 1978: vii, 36). Simon tells us that it
was not just the appeal of Jewish rites that attracted the Christians but a certain prestige enjoyed by the synagogue in the ancient world (Simon 1986:
321). John Gager explains judaizing in terms of Judaism's position as "the
dominant force in the world of early Christianity" (Gager 1983: 113-114). Judaizing should be seen, according to Gager, as part of an attempt by some
Christians to benefit from an attachment to a religious tradition whose vigour
and influence made it into an "obvious source of power" in the Roman world
(Gager 1983: 133). Nicholas De Lange refers to the percolation in the church
of Jewish practices as a corruptive influence that constituted one of the more
serious threats posed by *Judaism* for the early Christian community (De
Lange 1976: 84 and 87).

Because judaizing is traced directly back to the influence of a living Judaism, anti-judaizing is portrayed by modern scholars as an integral aspect of the Christian-Jewish polemic. It is seen, in other words, as one of the factors that generated the church's polemical attack on Judaism. It is simply assumed to form part of a "wider and well-ordered polemic that takes issue with the whole structure of Jewish institutions and beliefs" (Simon 1986: 321).

The Jewish response: Judaizing and Proselytizing

Though not all scholars follow his lead, Marcel Simon moves (through a subtle escalation of claims) from the affirmation that judaizing in the church was a function of the attraction and appeal of the synagogue to the claim that it was a by-product of Jewish proselytizing.[12] Simon affirms that the Jews not only sympathized with judaizers, but actually promoted their activities. The judaizing pressure, Simon states, "could not have been brought to bear against the will of the Jews, or even without their cooperation". Indeed, Simon goes on to say, the phenomenon is "only fully comprehensible if the Jews actively participated" in creating it. It follows, according to Simon, that the "judaizing influence implies the survival of a missionary, proselytizing spirit in Israel" (Simon 1986: 269-70). For Simon, then judaizing seems to provide confirmation of all the essential aspects of the "conflict theory".

In fact, Simon is so convinced of the intimate connection between judaizing and proselytizing that he is prepared to use the judaizing evidence as confirmation of his proselytizing theory. Evidence of judaizing in the early Christian writings actually constitutes a measure for Simon of the proselytizing activity of the synagogue. For "as long as the judaizing movement continued, we may legitimately infer that proselytizing continued also", for the two declined in step with one another and the "falling off of one entailed the gradual disappearance of the other" (Simon 1986: 286). Simon thus permits himself to state categorically in his conclusion that the persistence of proselytizing among the Jews was the determining factor in the attraction that Judaism held for the Christians (Simon 1986: 369), and judaizers are simply assumed to be the products of the synagogue's efforts. The fact that Jewish attempts to convert the Christians produced sympathizers rather than full converts, the fact that these sympathizers were not in any real sense a gain for Israel, is quickly dismissed by Simon. For what is important, as far as he is concerned, is that the efforts of the synagogue, though meagre from the Jewish point of view, were "nevertheless a cause of grave concern for the church" (Simon 1986: 305).

---

[12] Other scholars take a much more nuanced view, refusing to see judaizing as a mere extension or by-product of Jewish proselytizing activity. Cf. below, Meeks and Wilken 1978: 32; also Efroymson 1976: 56-7. On Jews as proselytizers refer back to beginning of this chapter, under heading *Christianizing Presuppositions*.

Because the Jewish sources make no specific references to judaizers, Simon recognizes that he can do no more than hypothesize about the "Jews' reactions to those Christians who complied with their rites". He turns, therefore, for assistance and confirmation of his theory to the imprecations of John Chrysostom. "It emerges from the homilies of Chrysostom", Simon tells us, that the Jews received the Judaizers with "enthusiasm, encouraging them to persevere" (Simon 1986: 337).[13] This reading of Chrysostom is questionable, however. So much so, that other scholars have sought to temper Simon's claim.

Wayne Meeks and Robert Wilken, for instance, argue that Simon fails to distinguish here between the real substance of Chrysostom's accusations, and the rhetorical excesses of the renowned Christian orator. Meeks and Wilken offer an alternative explanation of the church father's accusations against the Jews. They point out that references likening the Jews to "wolves", preparing "at the approach of their festivals to attack the flock" (*Homilies* 4.1) are exceptional in Chrysostom's homilies, and they suggest that such outbursts clearly tell us more about Chrysostom's rhetorical fervour, even his overzealousness, than they do about the actions and attitudes of Jews. "Chrysostom sometimes is carried away by his own metaphors" (Meeks & Wilken 1978: 32). He admits himself that he has come to lust for combat against the Jews. The real concern of the homilies, conclude Meeks and Wilken, is not with the Jews as aggressors, but with the strange Christian attraction to Judaism, which the church father seeks to curb. "The remedies which Chrysostom prescribes also support the impression that he feared Christian fascination with Judaism more than active Jewish recruitment of Christians" (Meeks & Wilken 1978: 33).

Ultimately, then, Simon's connection between judaizing and proselytizing is based not on documentary evidence of any kind, but rather on his version of the "conflict theory", and on its underlying assumption that the Jews were active missionaries, preoccupied with the need to undercut the expansive drive of the church. Simon's belief that the Jews sought out and encouraged judaizers in the Christian camp fits in so neatly with the "conflict theory" precisely because it is really an extension of his conviction that the synagogue was the church's main rival.

Simon's conclusions about Christian judaizing are certainly consistent with his premises about Jewish proselytizing, but the accuracy of these conclusions is dependent on the truth of premises which we have already shown to be

---

13. As we shall see shortly, much of the confusion in the examination of the phenomenon of judaizing stems from the fact that insights drawn from the fourth century evidence of Chrysostom in particular are read back into earlier centuries, and assumed, without justification, to represent the continuation of a generalized phenomenon. Cf. "Reading back from the fourth century".

extremely questionable. This is but one example, in my view, of the way in which the "conflict theory" generates and compounds its own historical misconceptions.

Interestingly enough, most scholars seem to be in general agreement that, on the whole, the exponents of judaizing were gentile rather than Jewish-Christians (Gager 1983: 115; Gaston 1986b: 166; Strecker 1971: 262). Strictly speaking, the anti-judaizing polemic was addressed, then, not to Jews or Christians with one foot in the Jewish camp, but to Judaizers from *within the confines of* the church (Gaston 1986b: 166). And the arguments against these judaizers were arguments offered for internal consumption (Simon 1986: 145). Simon himself confirms the internal character of the judaizing movement when he describes it as no more than a "tendency in which Christianity in some areas felt itself drawn", rather than a "sect beyond the boundaries of the church" (Simon 1986: 307). Yet even in the light of these admissions, the hold of presumptions generated by the "conflict theory" remains so strong that Simon and others continue to make the connection between judaizing and Judaism. One might well wonder why either the fact or the nature of this connection should be taken as given. Judaizing does not necessarily imply an attraction to Judaism, just as anti-judaizing does not necessarily imply a reaction to such an attraction. Indeed both seem to be directed at something quite separate from Judaism. As will be argued in the review of the Christian anti-judaizing passages below, judaizing appears to have been chiefly an internal phenomenon with no apparent connection either to the drawing power of contemporary Judaism, or to positive pressures exerted by the Jews. But before we turn to this evidence, we must consider the second factor that has stood in the way of a proper evaluation of the judaizing phenomenon.

(2) Reading Back from the Fourth Century

One of the more striking factors about the judaizing tendency is that the Christian evidence for it is most notable in the fourth century in the East of the empire. If the phenomenon of judaizing has come to the general attention of scholars, this is in no small part due to the homilies of John Chrysostom (mentioned above), and the anti-judaizing that characterizes them. Set in late fourth century Antioch, Chrysostom's harsh, almost crazed vituperations against the Jews have puzzled and troubled Christian scholars. The "violence" of his arguments, and the "coarseness" of the language that he uses are "without parallel" (Simon 1986: 217). His extreme language becomes more comprehensible, however, if we see him as fighting against a widespread phenomenon that was threatening to lure Christians away from the fold, and into the Jewish camp. Invariably, the evidence provided by Chrysostom takes centre stage in any discussion of the judaizing question. Studies either open with a review of the homilies of this "master of anti-Jewish invective" (Simon 1986: 217; Gager 1983: 118), or are a mere prelude to a consideration of his polemic (Meeks & Wilken 1978: 25).

In addition, most of the main anti-judaizers in the early church, whose writings are quoted to supplement the evidence found in Chrysostom, also date from the post-Constantinian period. The main texts are those of Aphrahat and Ephrem, fourth century Syriac Christians; the writings of Cyril, bishop of Alexandria from 412; and the canons of several fourth century church councils, including the Spanish council of Elvira, the council of Antioch in 341 C.E., and the council of Laodicea in Asia Minor in 360 C.E.[14]

Yet despite their heavy reliance on fourth and fifth century evidence, scholars make no effort at periodization in their evaluation of the judaizing phenomenon. As with all aspects of what is seen as the Jewish-Christian conflict, judaizing is assumed to be a generalized phenomenon that posed a challenge for orthodox Christians throughout the life of the church, from its inception to its ultimate triumph. The sparseness of the evidence for judaizing in the *pre*-Constantinian period has forced scholars to formulate their theories on the basis of the later evidence which is then read back and presumed to apply in the earlier period as well.

Simon, for instance, assumes the existence of an "uninterrupted tradition", whose persistance "defied all the anathemas of the Church authorities" (Simon 1986: 330). Gager also presumes that "judaizing Christians were a common feature of the Christian landscape from the very beginning" (Gager 1983:132). Gaston, too, generalizes on the basis of the writings of the later Christian fathers, claiming that their polemic reveals that "many Christians were very attracted to Judaism and Jewish practices and presumably also to Jewish persons" (Gaston 1986b: 166). Meeks and Wilken also seem to assume that the existence of fourth century judaizers in Antioch is evidence of the "*continuing* attraction of Judaism to outsiders" (Meeks & Wilken 1978: 36; my emphasis). They make this affirmation despite their admission that the lack of evidence from the earlier period severely restricts their findings, allowing them to do no more than *speculate* about active contact between Christians and Jews (Meeks & Wilken 1978: 22 & 24).[15]

---

[14] On these texts see Simon 1986: 306-338; Gager 1983: 117-133; Kraabel 1968; Neusner 1971; Wilken 1971.

[15] Interestingly, Meeks and Wilken also acknowledge the existence of contradictory evidence, though unfortunately, they don't pursue this avenue. In Theophilus' apology to Autolycus, written in 180 C.E., it is the "casual disregard for the continued existence of Judaism" that is noteworthy (Meeks & Wilken 1978: 22). In his appropriation of the Holy Scriptures, in his claim that these belonged to the church and to the church alone, Theophilus felt free to ignore the Jews altogether. "And therefore it is proved that all others have been in error; and that we Christians alone have possessed the truth; in as much as we are taught by the Holy Spirit, who spoke in the holy prophets and foretold all things" (*To Autolycus (ad Autolycum)* II. 33). That

Unfortunately these scholars fail to make any distinction, in their consideration of the judaizing evidence, between the fourth century, when Christianity began to gain ascendancy and enjoy imperial favour, and the earlier centuries when the church subsisted as a minority group in a pagan empire. In fact they assume that if Judaism still managed to exert its influence over Christianity, through the intermediary of judaizers in the fourth century, then the problem must have seemed all the more acute in the earlier period when the church was in a weaker position and the synagogue in a relatively stronger one. I would argue that, to the contrary, such a progressive, uninterrupted development in Jewish-Christian relations cannot be assumed unless it is proven and backed by solid evidence. Such evidence is lacking. If anything, there seem to be more reasons for assuming a lack of continuity in the pre-and post-Constaninian periods.

In certain important respects the Constantinian period marks a critical turning point in the history of both church and synagogue. Rosemary Ruether characterizes Judaism and Christianity as "two fourth-century religions" because it was in this period that the systems of thought of sages and theologians "found its fullest ripening" in shaping "the classical form of both Judaism and Christianity" (Ruether 1972: 1). In his study of *Judaism and Christianity in the Age of Constantine*, Jacob Neusner also describes this period as transformative in a decisive way for the two religious groups. The conversion of Constantine, and the recognition of Christianity as the religion of the Roman empire in the Theodosian code, were to give Christianity the "position of political and cultural dominance that it would enjoy until the twentieth century". It was also in this period that the flowering of the Talmudic tradition defined "Judaism as we have known it" (Neusner 1987: ix). If we accept Neusner's thesis, then the conditions which prevailed in the post-Constantinian era were unique, marked a break from what had come before, and it would be a mistake to take as given that a phenomenon attested in the fourth and fifth centuries existed in the same form at an earlier time.

Interestingly, Neusner's book touches not simply on the development of church and synagogue, but on the relationship between the two religious groups, and he affirms that the new historical circumstances in the Constantinian age also influenced the way in which Jews and Christians interacted with one another. Neusner identifies the age of Constantine as the period of the *initial* confrontation between Christianity and Judaism. It was only in the fourth century, Neusner tells us (when Christianity met the Israel of the sages,

---

Theophilus felt no need to justify his claims vis-à-vis the Jews surely casts doubt on common assumptions about the drawing power and influence of the Jewish community. This self-confident and unselfconscious appropriation of what was recognized by all as the tradition of the Jews hardly seems compatible with the prevailing view of a church ever on guard against the all-pervasive, and irresistible lure of Judaism. On Theophilus see also Typology II.1.

and when Judaism responded to the "triumph" of Christianity), that members
of the two communities entered into real dialogue with one another. This was
the "first and last moment in the history of Judaism in the context of Christianity, when both sides asked the same questions, framed the same way, in the
response to the same circumstances". This was, according to Neusner, *the*
point of intersection between the historians of the two religions" (Neusner
1987: x).

The implications of this for the judaizing evidence and for the conflict
model as a whole are major, though Neusner doesn't address these issues
specifically. If Neusner is right, then it is entirely possible that judaizing posed
a problem for *fourth* century Christians. Perhaps the increased contact between the thinkers in the two communities awakened a movement in some
circles to return to the roots of the faith, and to reintroduce some Jewish practices. But such a development would have been peculiar to the altered circumstances that governed Jewish-Christian relations in the Constantinian
world, and should in no way be viewed as the continuation of influences
prevalent in the earlier period.

An evaluation of Neusner's hypothesis is beyond the confines of this
study, but the central premise of his book raises some vital questions which
directly challenge the assumptions underlying the "conflict theory".[16] The
claim that one model of interaction applies universally to relations between
two groups over a period of centuries is a bold one. Continuity over such an
extended period would be remarkable if it could be proven, but it would need
solid proof to be convincing. Scholars defending the "conflict theory" have
not only failed to provide this proof, but seem to be unaware of the need to do
so.

A Reevaluation of the Pre-Constantinian Evidence

Let us now turn to an examination of the main passages that are thought to
provide evidence for judaizing in the second and third centuries. I suggest that
if we can free ourselves from reading these writings as a mere prelude to
Chrysostom, if we do not assume a priori that these texts necessarily relate
back to the influence and power of a living Judaism, then the judaizing phenomenon that they reveal appears in quite a new light. The two main texts to
be considered here, are some passing references to "judaizers" in the

---

[16] Indeed Neusner's assertion that the Constantinian period marks the initial time of genuine confrontation between the two communities, implicitly challenges the unproven and uncor-
roborated assumptions underlying the "conflict theory". If Christians and Jews did not ask the
"same questions", in response to the "same circumstances" before the fourth century, then we
can no longer claim that the response to the challenges and criticisms of the synagogue was
among the main preoccupations of the second and third century writers of the church.

epistles of Ignatius of Antioch, and the discussions of festivals and ritual commandments in the *Didascalia Apostolorum.*

The "Interpreters of Judaism" in the Letter to the Philadelphians

Ignatius of Antioch talks of judaizing in two of his epistles. The first of these is the letter to the *Philadelphians*, in which he warns his readers not to listen to those who "interpret Judaism" to them (VI.1). P.J. Donahue suggests that the heretics Ignatius is castigating are Jewish-Christians who are forcing Ignatius to justify his rejection of the Mosaic law (Donahue 1978). Ignatius' polemic might appear, then, to fit in very neatly with the "conflict theory", showing evidence of a church on the defensive against Jewish influences. However, there is reason to doubt both the identity of the heretics and the source of the controversy as defined by Donahue, thus putting into question the conflict setting of these passages. The full warning against the "interpreters of Judaism" in *Philadelphians* VI runs as follows:

> But if any one interpret Judaism to you do not listen to him; for it is better to hear Christianity from a man having circumcision than Judaism from an uncircumcised man. But both of them, unless they speak of Jesus Christ, are to me tombstones and sepulchers of the dead...(VI.1).

The first point to be made is that it seems to be preaching some kind of "Judaism", not Christians of Jewish origins who attract Ignatius' ire (Meeks & Wilken 1978: 20). As Lloyd Gaston rightly suggests, while the first man may refer generally to someone like Paul, it is clearly the second man who represents Ignatius' opponent—that is, the gentile Christian who misinterprets Judaism (Gaston 1986a: 37; cf. Trebilco 1991: 28). Indeed, Ignatius' opponents are Christians, not Jews, and the danger that he warns against comes from within the Christian community, rather than from without (Kraabel 1968: 184). In fact, Ignatius' statement portrays *Jews* preaching Christianity in a relatively positive light, for they are deemed preferable to the opponents targeted in the letter. This passage lends confirmation, in other words, to the generally accepted theory that judaizing was a gentile Christian, internal phenomenon. Secondly where Ignatius touches on the subject of controversy, refers to the practices or interpretations that he so strongly objects to, we discover that to "interpret Judaism" can have a much more diffuse meaning than is envisaged by scholars ever-quick to see in all the statements of the fathers, the all-pervasive influence of a powerful Judaism.

John Gager mentions in passing that the absence of exegetical arguments in Ignatius' polemic is curious (Gager 1983: 129). This is indeed unusual because, as we have seen, the interpretation of the Scriptures seems to have been at the very centre of the anti-Jewish polemic. Some suggest that Ignatius knew little of Old Testament models (Laeuchli 1974: 89), or that he was simply a bad exegete, but it seems as though his avoidance of scriptural

arguments was more deliberate and rooted in principle than could be
attributed to lack of education or ability. Ignatius himself clarifies the issue
when he reports his confrontation with the Philadelphian heretics:

> For I heard some saying, "If I do not find it in the archives, I do not believe in the
> gospel" And when I said to them, "it is written", they replied, "That is just the
> issue." But for me "the archives" are Jesus Christ; the inviolable archives are his
> cross and death and his resurrection and the faith which comes through him
> (VIII.2).

Ignatius is here stating his "own hermeneutical principle" (Meeks & Wilken
1978: 20), against those who seem to have made the acceptance of beliefs and
practices conditional on their documentation in the Hebrew Scriptures (cf
Gager 1983: 129). It seems that "the "Judaism" of Ignatius' uncircumcised,
Gentile opponents consists *only* in their ability to argue their...case from the
LXX in a way that he cannot refute" (Gaston 1986a: 37).[17] It is entirely possible that the heretics Ignatius is combatting were simply "conservative"
Christians, anxious that the church's doctrines and practices should be properly and thoroughly backed by proof from the Scriptures, the repository of the
church's traditions. Perhaps, as Gager suggests, they were simply sceptical of
"unbridled christological exegesis of the Old Testament" (Gager 1983: 129).
To "interpret Judaism" could well mean in this context, to be more literally
tied to the Scriptures than Ignatius saw as appropriate, or even to interpret the
Bible in a way which went counter to Ignatius' own concept of orthodoxy. If
we assume, as some scholars have done, that Ignatius is here combatting the
same opponents as in the letter to the *Magnesians*, the Docetist heretics, then
to "interpret Judaism" could well mean misreading the Scriptures in the manner of the heretics.[18]

The main point here is that the judaizing heretics need not have been any
closer to or more influenced by Judaism than Ignatius and the rest of his
church were. That Ignatius labelled these Philadelphians as "interpreters of
Judaism" need not tell us anything about their connection to the neighbouring
synagogue. It is possible that not even the heretics themselves accepted this
designation. Perhaps it was even intended as an insult to provoke them.

Life "according to Judaism" in Magnesians

It is generally assumed that Ignatius was also combatting judaizing practices
in his letter to the church in Magnesia. Here he seems to condemn

---

[17] The LXX or Septuagint is the most influential of the Greek versions of the Hebrew Bible.

[18] Several scholars argue that the judaizers condemned in *Philadelphians* and *Magnesians*
are one and the same group. See Gaston 1986a; Barnard 1966: 19-30; Barrett 1976; Molland
1954. On Docetic Christians and Ignatius' opposition to them see the following discussion of
the letter to the *Magnesians*.

those living "according to Judaism" (VIII.1-2); he appears to berate the practice of "Sabbatizing" (IX.1); and he refers to the monstrosity of those who "talk of Jesus Christ" and "judaize" (X.3). Yet if we examine these passages in the context of the letter as a whole, and if we read them without assuming a priori that they are combative vis-à-vis Judaism, then they appear in quite a different light.

Ignatius' main opponents in this letter are Docetic heretical Christians.[19] "I wish to warn you, though I am less than you, not to fall into the snare of vain doctrine, but to be convinced of the birth and passion and resurrection which took place at the time of the procuratorship of Pontius Pilate" (XI.1). Ignatius' aim is to convert these heretics from their erroneous ways, and to reestablish an obviously badly strained unity in the Magnesian church, where a young bishop was having difficulty asserting his authority (III; IV.1). These dissenters were meeting separately (IV.1), and were perhaps even holding their own Eucharist apart from the bishop (VII.2; cf. also Gaston 1986a: 38). Ignatius no doubt hopes, that in his exhortations to harmony, he can bring them around: "Do all things in harmony with God, with the bishop..." (VI.1) and "Do not attempt to make anything appear right for you by yourselves, but let there be in common one prayer, one supplication, one mind, one hope in love..." (VII.1).

If we keep the main thrust of the letter in mind, and if we do not simply assume that any reference to Judaism must by definition be polemical in intent, then it becomes evident that Ignatius' anti-Jewish passages are not injunctions against judaizing, but rather illustrative arguments directed at the dissenters to whom Ignatius addresses his main appeal. Chapter VIII begins as follows: "Be not led astray by strange doctrines or by old fables which are profitless. For if we are living even at this time according to Judaism, we confess that we have not received grace" (VIII.1). Ignatius is here drawing an illustrative parallel between the "vain doctrines" of the Docetists, and the way of "Judaism". All Magnesian Christians would no doubt be familiar with the church's anti-Jewish tradition which held that the "Jewish" way was abrogated, outdated, and constituted an admission that one was not inspired by the "grace" of Christ. Ignatius seems to be warning the dissenters in the Magnesian church, not against Judaism or judaizing, but against that which the "Jewish" way has come to represent. He is warning them, in other words, that if they continue with their unorthodox ideas, they will, like the Jews did, forfeit their claim to "live according to Jesus Christ" in harmony with the church.

---

[19] The Docetists considered the humanity of Christ as apparent rather than real.

In the same vein, the reference to worship on the Sabbath is not a warning against "Sabbatizing", but once again, an illustrative comment describing the transformative power of Christ's advent:

> If then they who walked in ancient customs came to a new hope, no longer living for the Sabbath, but for the Lord's Day, on which also our life sprang up through him and his death...and by this mystery we received faith, and for this reason also we suffer, that we may be found disciples of Jesus Christ our only teacher...how then shall we be able to live without him...? And for this reason he whom they waited for in righteousness, when he came raised them from the dead (X.1-2).

The focus here is clearly not on the Sabbath worship itself. Ignatius places this reference within an "if" clause, implying that his audience would surely agree with this initial statement. He is describing through a series of rich images the revolutionary nature of the new life with Christ, and he is calling on the heretics within the Magnesian church not to endanger or forsake that which they gain as true disciples of Christ. The same applies to the mention in the next chapter of "judaizing". Chapter X begins with a warning to the Docetists to put aside the "evil leaven, which has grown old and sour, and turn to the new leaven, which is Jesus Christ." Once again, Ignatius turns to the anti-Judaic corpus for use in an analogy, the better to drive home his point about the dangers of heresy. Just as it is "monstrous to talk of Jesus Christ and to practise Judaism (judaize)", because, as everyone knows, "Christianity did not base its faith on Judaism, but Judaism on Christianity", so you too should avoid being "corrupted" by false doctrines, "since by your savour you shall be tested" (X.1-3).

It appears, then, that scholars have been too hasty in their assumptions about the judaizing phenomenon in the church. The term "to judaize" was obviously used in a variety of ways in the writings of Ignatius, none of which had any connection with Judaism, or with a supposed Jewish-Christian conflict. Sometimes, as in the letter to the *Philadelphians*, the allusion to "Jewish" ways was employed to castigate practices which were thought to deviate in some respect from orthodoxy (cf. also Typology IV.3). At other times, when Ignatius talks of judaizing, he is simply borrowing familiar imagery from the anti-Judaic tradition for purposes of illustration, the better to drive home a point of intra-mural significance. It seems that "(n)ot all Judaisms are Jewish" (Gaston 1986a: 44).

Though he firmly believes that all references to judaizing are a reflection of the proselytizing efforts of the Jews, even Marcel Simon recognizes, in his discussion of the church's view of itself as the new Israel, that Christians used the Jewish label quite loosely and not always accurately. The "terms Jew and

Judaizer are often linked together and treated as synonyms", he points out. And the charge of Judaism also includes:

> all those who deviate from officially accepted teaching and profess erroneous opinions. Thus, those who are in error concerning the person of Christ, who deny his divinity or insist more strongly than is proper on his humanity are accused of being Jews. So are those who hold unorthodox views about grace and freewill (Simon 1986: 96).

Contrast as Means of Illustration in the Didascalia Apostolorum

The next text to be considered is the *Didascalia Apostolorum*, a compendium of ecclesiastical teachings on a variety of subjects, dated to between 200 and 250 (cf. Gager 1983: 125). It is generally assumed that the authors of the *Didascalia* were preoccupied with the problem of judaizing. This is partly because, in their prescriptions on the celebration of Passover, the Sabbath, and the fixing of fast days, these authors seem intent on altering the character of the festivals so as to make them distinct from the Jewish feasts. Secondly, in their discussion of the "deuterosis", or "Second Legislation" of Deuteronomy, the writers of this text distinguish sharply between the first and second redactions of the Sinaitic convenants as a means of pronouncing on the invalidity of the ritual commandments. It is suggested that this argument must have been intended to dissuade those members of the community who continued to observe these very commandments (Simon 1986: 325). Let us consider each of these aspects in turn.

(1) The Spirit of Christian versus Jewish Feasts

First, with regard to the celebration of the feasts, it is important to note that the *Didascalia* does not undertake a simple and straightforward rejection of everything Jewish. While the church often changed the dates of ceremonies to distinguish them from the corresponding Jewish feasts, the *Didascalia* preserves the Jewish calendar for Christian practice. The traditional date of 14 Nisan, according to Jewish calculations marks the beginning of the paschal feast for the Christians in this community. The authors of the *Didascalia* do not seem concerned with the coincidence of dates. It is rather the spirit of observance of the Christian as against the Jewish feasts that is their focus. Where the Jewish passover is a joyful festival, celebrating the escape from Egypt, the *Didascalia* portrays the Christian pascha as a solemn occasion, marking the blindness of the Jews vis-à-vis Christ (5.14.22). Holy Week thus becomes a sorrowful time of rigid fasting, and the Sabbath in particular is marked as a day of penitence (5.19.9).

Marcel Simon suggests that the document is seeking to prevent the assimilation of Jewish and Christian rites by transforming the spirit of the Christian festivals in order to eradicate the "contaminating influence of Jewish ritual"

(Simon 1986: 312-13). But given that the crucifixion and resurrection of Christ were at the very centre of the Easter celebration, making it, by definition, into a peculiarly Christian feast, I wonder what kind of assimilation our authors are supposed to have been fearing. It makes much more sense to see their prescriptions as intending to establish guidelines for the proper and fitting way of marking the Christian paschal feast. In this context, the contrast with Judaism would have served to illuminate the real meaning of the feast for Christians and to set the tone for its celebration.

It is possible, for instance, that the congregations being addressed by the authors had shied away from taking on the full obligations of Holy Week, or that the authors of the *Didascalia* were particularly rigourous in their expectations. In order to restore what they viewed as a proper solemnity to the occasion, these authors placed a renewed or heightened emphasis on the sorrow and penance that should accompany the marking of Christ's passion. Judaism and Jewish ways provided a useful argumentative foil in the authors' appeal. The association of Judaism with that which had been abrogated and surpassed was no doubt a familiar one to all in the community. In this context, reference to the joyfulness experienced by the "blind" Jews in the celebration of their Passover, served to highlight, by contrast, just how intrinsic to the genuinely Christian way of marking Easter, were the practices of fasting and penitence. It was intrinsic to the Christian message that the coming of Christ brought about a radical transformation, and what better way to illustrate this transformation than by way of contrast between the old and new ways of celebrating the paschal feast?

(2) Insistence on the Abrogation of the Cult as Theological Motif

We turn now to the discussion of the deuterosis. In the *Didascalia*, the "deuterosis" refers to those precepts of the old covenant which have been abrogated by the coming of Christ. Though it is contained in the Holy Scriptures, the second redaction of the Sinaitic covenant is considered to be devoid of spiritual validity, and is said to have been imposed on Israel as a form of punishment.

> Yet when thou readest the law beware of the Second Legislation, that thou do but read it merely; but the commandments and warnings that are therein much avoid, lest thou lead thyself astray and bind thyself with the bonds which may not be loosed of heavy burdens. For this cause therefore, if thou read the Second Legislation, that thou know and glorify God who delivered us from all these bonds (1.7)

We might well wonder why our authors felt the need to issue warnings against this second legislation, to place it so firmly in the category of that which is intended to be read and not observed. Simon and Gager argue that these words were written as a response to judaizers who sought to reinstate some of the Jewish laws in the church (Simon 325-27: Gager 1983: 127). Yet this interpretation is certainly not warranted by the overall tenor of the work as a whole. One would expect that if they were seeking to guard against Jewish influence, the authors of the Didascalia would have been ever vigilant and consistent in their warnings against Jews and Judaism. Yet if we consider the tone of the work, it appears that its authors are well disposed to, rather than wary of, Judaism. The text acknowledges and shows respect for Jewish influences and standards. Even in the discussion of the Jewish rejection of Christ, the Jews are referred to compassionately as brethren:

> Know therefore, our brethren, that the fast which we fast in the Pascha, it is on account of the disobedience of our brethren that you are to fast. For even though they hate you, yet ought we to call them brethren; for we have it written in Isaiah thus, "Call them brethren that hate and reject you (5.14.23; Isaiah 66.57)

Does the *Didascalia* exhibit contradictory attitudes to Judaism, or should we perhaps reevaluate the intentions of our authors in their warnings against the second legislation. I would suggest that this contrast between the old and the new dispensations should be understood in theoretical rather than practical terms. Simon himself acknowledges that discussions in the church fathers relating to matters of the law had an important theoretical dimension (Simon 1986: 325). He is also willing to concede that on some level, judaizing and anti-judaizing stemmed from internal theological discussions, relating to the church's self-definition. The judaizing tendency was derived partly from the "church's commerce with the holy book, and from its own idea of itself as the new Israel" (Simon 1986: 269). Simon attributes this to the "position of Christianity" (Simon 1986: 369) as a movement that had simultaneously appropriated and rejected selective elements of the Jewish tradition.

The need to explain how and why Christians, who proclaimed the Scriptures as the sacred word of God, no longer adhered to the law that these Scriptures proclaimed as everlasting, was one of the most central theological problems faced by the early church. As will be shown in the consideration of "theological" anti-Judaism (Typology IV.1), theoretical dissertations on the Mosaic law make up one of the central themes of the anti-Jewish literature as a whole, explaining why this law was promulgated, why and how it was later abrogated, and demonstrating that the one, just and omniscient God had intended both its promulgation and its abrogation from the very beginning. It is in this context, I believe, that we should understand the *Didascalia*'s firm declaration concerning the invalidity of the cultic commandments.

Indeed, this illustrative contrast between the old and the new precepts seems to be operative in another passage in the *Didascalia*. The question un der discussion here relates to that which constitutes genuine as against ritual purity. Let men and women...

> assemble without restraint, without bathing, for they are clean. But if a man should corrupt and defile another's wife after baptism, or be polluted with a harlot, and rising up from her should bathe in all the seas and oceans and be baptized in all the rivers, he cannot be made clean (6.22.8).

Though Simon suggests that instructions such as these imply that "some people did observe the precepts referred to", and that this creeping Jewish influence had to be kept within the proper confines (Simon 1986: 326),[20] I do not agree. The passage above is much more concerned with that which makes a man genuinely unclean, and with stressing the severity of sexual sins of this kind, than it is with the revocation of ritual purity requirements. The reference to the ritual laws is made, not to guard against them, but rather, for purposes of contrast, in order to lend rhetorical flourish to the argument. No amount of conventional washing, no matter on how grand a scale (all the seas and oceans), say the authors, can rinse away the stain of moral transgressions. Let every man therefore take stock of his life.

To sum up: the presuppositions of the conflict theory have led modern scholars to see judaizing and the reaction against it in the early church as by-products of the Jewish-Christian conflict. Basing themselves primarily on post-Constantinian evidence, these scholars describe the judaizing phenomenon as one of the main problems posed for the church by a vital and aggressive Judaism. Yet if the pre-Constantinian evidence for judaizing is examined more closely, free of presuppositions, and in its proper context, then its connection to Judaism, to external Jewish pressures and influences, becomes remote. Interestingly, the very same scholars who seem so convinced that judaizing was an extension of the Jewish-Christian conflict are also prepared to identify the early judaizers as gentile Christians, in other words as full-fledged members of the church. Again, these same scholars also recognize both the complexity and variety that characterized judaizing.

It seems that the term to "judaize" had no fixed meaning within the early church, but was used rather in a variety of circumstances. It might on occasion have been used against fellow Christians who were thought to be too attached to some aspect or other of Jewish ritual or tradition (cf. Gaston 1986a:44; Gager 1983:18), but it also had a purely theoretical dimension, which served in the definition of theological issues and in the illustration of a peculiarly Christian way of life. In neither its practical nor its theoretical manifestations does it appear to have had any meaningful or substantial connection with Judaism itself. There is absolutely no evidence to suggest that it was ever actively welcomed or encouraged by the people of the neighboring synagogue.

---

[20] On Jewish influence in the Didascalia see also Strecker 1971: 245-51.

TYPOLOGY I.3
EMBITTERED ANTI-JUDAISM

The last type of anti-Judaism that falls under the category of competitive anti-Judaisms is what I call "embittered" anti-Judaism. Just as scholars see the phenomenon of judaizing as an indication that Jews came fishing for conquests in the Christian camp, so it is assumed that the Christians, on their side, had an interest in winning over their rivals the Jews, as well as in making new gentile converts. Indeed, "embittered" anti-Judaism characterizes what is generally thought to be the church's reaction to its failure to convert the Jews, its inability to convince the people to whom the Messiah was first sent, that He had come at last. The idea behind "embittered" anti-Judaism is that the early Christians were haunted by the fact that the Messiah of the Jews was not recognized by the Jews, and they feared this paradox would undermine the credibility and legitimacy of the church, both within the movement, and vis-à-vis the non-Christian world. According to this view, the Jews came to represent a constant reminder of the church's inability to win over the first chosen people of God, and they became, as a result, the brunt of the church's disillusionment.

In his effort to define Christian anti-Semitism, Simon describes it as "in the first instance an expression of the resentment aroused by Israel's resistance to the gospel". Christianity's "essential contribution" to anti-Semitism is that it "expressed the opposition that the church felt toward the Jews as obdurate dissidents. It expressed the condemnation uttered by Christian teaching of those who crucified Christ and *rebuffed* his call" (Simon 1986: 207 & 208). David Flusser also sees the "failure of Christianity to convert the Jewish people to the new message" as "precisely the reason for the strong anti-Jewish trend in Christianity" (Flusser 1983-84: 39). Fred Bratton also concludes that "many of the anti-Judaic utterances of the Fathers arose from the Jewish refusal to acknowledge the divine character of Jesus' person" (Bratton 1969: 80; cf. also Lovsky 1955: 161; Meagher 1979: 19).

Indeed, the Christian writers frequently berate the Jews for their unbelief. Justin bemoans the fact that the Jews who possess the writings of the prophets did not understand them. "Not only did they not recognize Christ when He came, but they even hate us who declare that He has come, and who show that He was crucified by them, as it was foretold" (*First Apology* 36). The church father shows signs of regret that the Jews are not to be won over. Addressing them in the Dialogue, he says to those who "curse Him and all who believe in Him": "While we do not hate you, neither you nor those who have taken these things up after you, we pray that even now you may have a change of heart and find mercy with God the benign and compassionate Father of the Universe" (Dial. 108.3; cf. 16.4; 93.4).

The accusation that the Jews rejected Jesus goes hand in hand with the charge that they were responsible for the crucifixion of Christ, the "essential charge" against Judaism throughout the patristic period (cf. Oesterreicher 1970: 190-203; Flannery 1985: 288; Efroymson: 1976: 14 & 22). Tertullian refers to the Jewish rejection of, and responsibility for, the crucifixion of Christ in twenty passages in ten separate works.[21] In *On Spectacles (De spectaculis)*, the church father looks forward with exultation to the Second Coming of the Lord and to the Day of Judgement when at last the Jews will be forced to recognize the disastrous error of their ways. Commentators interpret Tertullian's expressed eagerness to witness the punishment of the Jews as a blood-thirsty desire for revenge (cf Efroymson 1976: 125). On the Day of Judgement, he intends to pay little attention to the fire that will consume "monarchs", "governors", "tragedians" and "charioteers", in his "eager wish rather to fix a gaze insatiable on those whose fury vented itself against the Lord".

But it appears in the following lines that Tertullian is much more concerned with the vindication of Christianity, than he is with the chastisement of the Jews. The Day of Judgement is the occasion when the rejecters of the Lord will be forced to recognize and worship Him in all His undeniable Glory. Tertullian is more interested, in other words, in proving the Jews wrong, in "rubbing their noses in it", than he is in seeing them suffer.

> "This", I shall say, "this is that carpenter's or harlot's son, that Sabbath-breaker, that Samaritan and devil-possessed! This is He whom you purchased from Judas! This is He whom you struck with reed and fist, whom you contemptuously spat upon, to whom you gave gall and vinegar to drink! This is He whom His disciples secretly stole away, that it might be said He had risen again. (*On Spectacles* 30).

Origen also expresses hostility against the Jews on account of their unbelief, and he portrays this as the cause of their present and future downfall.

> On account of their unbelief and other insults which they heaped upon Jesus, the Jews will not only suffer more than others in that judgment which is believed to impend over the world, but have even already endured such sufferings. For what nation is in exile from their own metropolis, and from the place sacred to the worship of their fathers, save the Jews alone? And these calamities they have suffered because they were a most wicked nation, which, although guilty of many other sins, yet has been punished so severely for none as for those that were committed against our Jesus (*Against Celsus (Contra Celsum)* IV).

---

[21] *Against the Jews* 8.18; *Apology* 21.18; *On Prayer (De oratione)* 14; *On Patience (De patientia)* 5.22-25; *On the Resurrection (De resurrectione)* 26.13; *Against Marcion (Adversus Marcionem)* III.6 & 18.3 & 19.3-6 & 23; IV. 42.2 & 8; V. 15.1-2; *On Idolatry (De idololatria)* 7.3; *On the Rites of Women (De cultu feminarum)* I.3.3; *On Spectacles* 3.4-8; 30.

The notion of "embittered" or "disillusioned" anti-Judaism raises some interesting points about the nature of Christian anti-Judaism. "Embittered" anti-Judaism seeks to account for the radical language used by the Christians, in their diatribe against the Jews, in terms of feelings, on the level of emotions. This is fair enough, but psychological categories must be used with caution in historical explanation. In this instance, disappointment, disillusionment and bitterness are attributed to the Christians as emotions that are thought to be experienced collectively, and over several generations. Indeed, it is considered that these feelings were magnified over time, as the hope of converting the Jews waned. Where Paul lived with "hope tempered by disappointment", "Augustine lived with the reality of 400 years of Christian history. What hope there was, was rapidly disappearing as the disappointment gradually grew into bitterness" (Wilken 1967: 322). Gager also explains the intolerant and hardened language used by the later Christian writers in terms of disappointed hopes. The Christians, he argues, entered the debate with the Jews in all good faith, but "when neither exegetical discourse nor textual criticism proved capable of settling any of the major issues, Christians resorted to the assertion that the Jews were blind to their own Scriptures". "At this point", Gager goes on, "debate ended and diatribe began" (Gager 1983: 159). It is possible, of course for an emotion such as "bitterness" to be experienced by a group as a whole. It is also conceivable that this kind of emotional response could have been passed down from generation to generation, and for it to have become radicalized rather than attenuated over time.

The hostility in Northern Ireland is the first example of this kind that comes readily to mind. Yet we must be clear what level of social reality is being described when we refer to such persistent collective emotions. The conflict in Northern Ireland is constantly being fueled by new acts of violence that succeed, periodically, in rekindling the fire of hatred. One might even want to say that these acts of violence are designed to keep the struggle alive, by renewing the cause of hatred, by giving to this hatred a concrete focus, making the motivation for it very real and present to each new generation. So, in Northern Ireland, the conflict has both an ideological and a practical dimension, and though religiously rooted, the bitterness is fueled by concrete acts of aggression. One would expect that, in the absence of such confrontation, the perceptions and attitudes of Protestants and Catholics towards one another would be markedly different.

In the case of the condemnation of Judaism by ancient Christian writers, modern scholars seem to assume that the "conflict theory" entitles them to describe this opposition in terms of collectively experienced and socially rooted emotions. Yet they make no attempt to clarify the level on which this Christian "bitterness" and "disillusionment" is thought to have operated. Scholars come to the texts with a presupposition and it is this presupposition that determines their reading of the texts. Where the texts are allowed to speak for themselves, the Christian response to Jewish disbelief appears in quite a different light. The animosity that is assumed by scholars to express an emotional reaction to rejection reveals itself rather to be part of a well developed, sophisticated aetiological myth. Psychological categories give way to theological ones.

Let us consider anew what the Christians have to say about the Jewish rejection of Christ. First of all, the only concrete criminal charge held against the Jews is their supposed original responsibility for the crucifixion, the rejection of Jesus and of his first followers. Were this "crime" viewed as no more than a simple act of violence, it wouldn't continue to carry such weight centuries after the fact.[22] The real import of this "crime" lies in what it reveals about the Jews as archetypical sinners in the Christian version of salvation history. In other words, the Christians are more focused on the symbolic significance of the Jewish rejection than they are on Jewish responsibility for the physical act of rejection. Second of all, it is not really accurate to refer to Christian charges against Judaism as a product of "disillusionment", because in some respects the notion of Jewish rejection was actually indispensable to the church. It came to play a central, even pivotal role in the Christian vision of salvation history, implying that it was a deliberately adopted theological concept, rather than a response to unfortunate circumstances. Jewish sin and rejection of the Christian God formed the backdrop for the claim that the church had displaced the synagogue as the chosen people, as heirs to the promise.

What does this imply about the attitudes of Christians to living Jews, to their Jewish contemporaries? If the real "crime" of the Jews is portrayed in the Christian writings as an ongoing crime, this is because the occasion for recognizing and turning to Christ is ever-present, and the Jews represent that people who continue, in *virtue* of their continued existence as Jews, to hold out against the Messiah. So what the Christians hold against the Jews is not so much their persistence in concrete acts of aggression, but, in the most simple of terms, that they are not Christians. True, if there were no Jews, then there would be no cause for continuing condemnation, but this condemnation in no way implies contact with living Jews. The real objection against Judaism, in other words, is an objection against their whole religious position, their stubbornness in clinging to Judaism, their refusal to abandon their old allegiances in order to turn to Christ as Messiah. The objection holds on a theological rather than on a practical level, and there is no evidence to suggest that it was rooted in concrete actions that might have produced an emotional reaction.

It is of course possible that the Christian opposition to the Jews as the archetypal rejecters of Christ and Christianity had some spill-over effect, and

---

[22] On attributing responsibility to the Jews for the crucifixion, see Typologies II.1; III.1; IV.1.

influenced the way ancient Christians viewed and reacted to their Jewish contemporaries. But it is important to remember that we have no direct evidence of this. Secondly, even if this were the case, we must not lose from view the fact that this would have been a secondary effect of the so-called "bitterness" expressed in the writings, and not a *cause* of it, which is what we are trying to determine here. The most significant point to be made, then, about the passages that are thought to reveal elements of an "embittered" or "disillusioned" anti-Judaism is that they portray anti-Judaism as rooted, not in a conflict between Christians and Jews, but in the church's theological vision which condemned Judaism in order to deny the legitimacy of its continued existence.

CHAPTER TWO

CONFLICTUAL ANTI-JUDAISM

The "conflict theory" in its most simple form evokes the image of two equal groups struggling for the same prize. In the chapter titled "Competitive Anti-Judaism", we saw Christians and Jews depicted as two parallel groups vying for new adherents from the gentile world. But scholars have also stressed the importance of seeing the Jewish-Christian conflict in its larger context, and suppositions about the socio-political context of this rivalry add a further dimension to the "conflict" model. Marcel Simon insists that seeing the two religions in their setting within the Roman empire is essential to obtaining a satisfactory picture of relations between the two groups (Simon 1986: 98). Meeks and Wilken also warn against the danger of examining the relationship between Christians and Jews in isolation, and argue that it must be understood as "intertwined with the complex attachments and reactions of each group to the Greco-Roman culture and government" (Meeks & Wilken 1978: 2). In the following consideration of "conflictual" anti-Judaism, we will focus on social and political factors, and on the sense in which the unequal power relationship between the two groups is generally thought to have generated anti-Jewish feelings among the early Christians. It shall be demonstrated that while these efforts at contextualization appear on the surface to be progressive and plausible, they serve, in the study of the patristic anti-Jewish texts, only to compound the erroneous preconceptions of the "conflict theory".

As has already been stated, if the "conflict theory" has gained such widespread acceptance, and has come to form the basis of a general consensus in the study of relations between Christians and Jews, it is in part because it fits in with general trends in recent biblical and post-biblical hermeneutics. Scholars have sought to adopt a deconfessionalized, less theoretical approach in their reconstruction of early Christian history.[1] In their study of the ancient Christian texts, modern interpreters have sought to broaden their focus, no longer restricting themselves only to the study of the religious aspects of early Christian existence, but endeavouring also to uncover the social and political dimensions of reality revealed in the writings. The sixties saw the development of new interpretive techniques, and the adoption of tools and methods

---

[1] For clear and explicit statements of these aims see Kee 1989: 22; Elliott 1981: 1; Scroggs 1980: 165-6; Holmberg 1978: 2; Esler 1987: 3; Smith 1975: 19.

from the social sciences in the name of gaining a firmer understanding of the "life situations" behind the texts under study.[2]

In their effort to uncover the social and political underpinning of Jewish-Christian interaction, historians studying the early Christian texts on Judaism have sought to situate church and synagogue within Roman society. The aim has been to determine, on the basis of the little that is known about the social and legal status of the two minority groups, what the balance of power between the two groups might have been, and how this might have had a bearing on the supposed conflict between them. In effect, scholars have gathered the historical evidence, scarce as it is, in an attempt to develop a schematic model depicting the relative social and political positions that are believed to have been held by church and synagogue in the early centuries of the Common Era. This model which, as we shall see, emphasizes the inequalities between the two groups, has served as a hermeneutical tool in the interpretation of the Christian anti-Jewish passages, and has formed the basis of several hypotheses which claim to account for the social and political motivations of anti-Judaism within the church. I will look first at the historical evidence, and at the way in which the conflict theorists have made use of it in their efforts to emphasize the contrasting social and political positions of church and synagogue. Then I will focus on the theories that have been generated by this exercise in contrast. My aim will be to show how these hypotheses fail both historically and hermeneutically.

The contrast operates both on (1) the political, and (2) the socio-economic levels.

(1) Roman Policy: the Privileged and the Persecuted

Those scholars who contrast the political situations of church and synagogue, make much of the legal status enjoyed by the Jews, while at the same time highlighting the persecutions experienced by the early church. Indeed, while Hadrian (117-138 C.E.) had made himself an enemy of the synagogue, in particular with his prohibition of circumcision,[3] the reign of Antoninus (138-161 C.E.) marked the beginning of a period characterized by a generally benevolent Roman policy towards the Jews. We learn from the *Digest Justianini* (48.8.11) that Antoninus reversed his predecessor's edict and exempted the Jews from the ban on circumcision, allowing them to practice their rite again (cf. Smallwood 1976: 167-8; Simon 1986: 100). The privileges of the Jews, so

---

[2] For methodological overviews justifying the approach, examining its aims, reviewing its techniques, and evaluating its strengths and weaknesses see Smith 1975; Scroggs 1980; Harrington 1980; Gager 1982; Malina 1982; Remus 1982; Best 1983; Edwards 1983; Elliott 1986; Esler 1987; Kee 1989.

[3] *Historia Augusta, Hadrian*, 14; *Dio Cassius* 69,12,1; cf. Juster 1914: I:267, II:191; Simon 1986: 99.

long as circumcision was restricted to the sons of Jews, were not to be seriously threatened again before the victory of Christianity (Simon 1986: 100; cf. also Juster 1914: I.245-6). The Christians, by contrast, are known to have suffered periodic persecutions during this period, and the conflict theorists make much of this contrast in their portrayal of the respective positions of church and synagogue. At a time when the Christians were ordered to conform to imperial religious practice and to offer sacrifices to the Emperor, the Jews appear to have been exempt from this general rule, and to have enjoyed the status of a *religio licita* in the empire (Smallwood 1976: 540).

Marcel Simon characterizes the period between Hadrian and Constantine (138-312 C.E.) as a time of transition in Roman policy in which relations between the Roman state and the two religious minorities changed in "completely opposite directions". The gradual crystallization of imperial hostility towards Christianity coincided with a period in which the Jews slowly climbed back into favour. While in Hadrian's time, Judaism had been identified as the enemy of Rome, after Decius (250 C.E.) the empire was at war with the Christians, and Simon suggests that this development was "no accident" (Simon 1986: 103). In fact, he links the fate of the two groups taking into account in his explanation the sense in which imperial policy was both reflected in and generated by popular sentiment.

Throughout the early centuries, the Christians were viewed as an upstart religious group. Their relative youth was a mark against them in a society that revered antiquity. In addition, their religious practices, which were seen as strange and mysterious, aroused suspicion in certain circles. Simon links the destiny of the two groups in his assumption that this concentration of hatred on Christianity actually benefited the Jews, by supposedly shifting onto the church the hostility to which the Jews had once been exposed (Simon 1986: 104; 117). The Christians are portrayed as taking the place of the Jews as popular scapegoats in times of uncertainty, and in the wake of natural or economic disasters. Simon suggests, then, that the Jews derived advantage not only from their own good fortune, but also from the persecutions suffered by the Christians. John Gager also describes the period after Bar Kochba as one in which the fortunes of church and synagogue were reversed, and he too sees the political fate of the two groups as being connected: "the rise of Christianity provided Rome with a source of concern that soon became a fixation. Judaism seemed to grow in favour as Christianity grew in prominence" (Gager 1983: 112).

(2) Living in the Shadow of the Jewish Community

The contrast of political favours enjoyed by Jews and Christians is assumed by the conflict theorists to extend also to the social and economic realm. The so-called "vitality" of Judaism, so central to the whole construct of

the conflict theorists, is thought to refer not just to the supposed religious
expansionism of the Jews but also to their social dynamism. There is certainly
no doubt that the Jews not only enjoyed the status of a *religio licita*, but that in
certain parts of the Mediterranean, they also prospered in wealth and
influence. Judaism is described by Meeks and Wilken as a vital social as well
as a vital religious force in the first centuries of the Common Era (Meeks &
Wilken 1978: vii). "A fresh consideration of the place of Jews in the later
Empire will show that the Jewish communities continued to be a major factor
after Bar Kochba, during the third, fourth, and fifth centuries, and that this
period was a time of new life and vitality for the Jews, of material prosperity
and economic growth, of spiritual and intellectual creativity" (Wilken 1980:
461). Evidence of this social and economic strength comes largely from
archaeological and epigraphical findings from the cities of the eastern
Mediterranean. The most striking of these findings, which will be discussed
shortly, is the recently excavated synagogue in the ancient city of Sardis in
Asia Minor.

Three New Hypotheses about Christian Anti-Judaism

The social and political contrast of the positions held by church and synagogue pits a rapidly expanding church with low social status and a precarious
legal position, against a well-established synagogue enjoying relative stability
and security. If the conflict theorists emphasize this contrast, it is because they
hope thereby to add greater depth and substance to their understanding of
Jewish-Christian relations, and to extend their list of those factors that are
thought to have generated anti-Jewish sentiments in the church. Given the
premise that the two religious groups came into collision with one another, the
portrayal of a power imbalance between church and synagogue creates a
whole new set of possible motivations for Christian anti-Judaism. In this context, scholars have hypothesized about three kinds of anti-Judaism:

(1) The first hypothesis focuses on the psycho-social dimension of Christian reality and of Christian identity. The Christians are portrayed as a group
with an inferiority complex, struggling to establish their identity in the face of
the powerful and secure synagogue. It is presumed that the privileges enjoyed
by the Jews generated feelings of "resentment", "irritation", "bitterness", and
"envy" within the church (Efroymson 1976: 58, 61-2; Wilken 1976: 56),
feelings which are said to account for the emotionally charged, intense tone of
the fathers' anti-Jewish passages. I refer to this as "reactive" anti-Judaism.

(2) Though the Christians are thought to have suffered from a sense of
their own disadvantage in relation to the Jews, scholars have suggested that
they were determined to alter their fortunes. The Christians were a group on
the rise, and it is assumed that their strategy for expansion included an attempt
to appropriate for themselves some of the political privileges enjoyed by the

synagogue. The anti-Judaism that is thought to form an integral part of this strategy will be examined under the heading of "strategic" anti-Judaism.

(3) In their reconstruction of the social and political underpinning of the Jewish-Christian conflict, scholars have also made suppositions about the Jewish role in the struggle. Assumptions are made, in particular, about the Jewish response to the church's rapid expansion and impressive successes. In the context of a presumed rivalry, Christian advances are inevitably viewed as having posed a direct threat to the synagogue, and the notion that the Jews were hostile towards the Christians, and even ready in some instances to take action against them, has become an integral part of the "conflict theory". The anti-Judaism that is thought to have been generated as a reaction to this supposed Jewish antagonism shall be considered in the section on "recriminatory" anti-Judaism.

Each of these kinds of anti-Judaism shall be examined in turn in order to show that these hypotheses are not only dubious in their own right as theories of historical explanation, but that they are also without foundation in the very texts which they claim to illuminate. Rooted in the faulty premises of the "conflict theory", these hypotheses seek to reconstruct the patterns of Jewish-Christian interaction, not through a careful and discerning reading of the early Christian writings, but on the basis of probabilities with little historical or hermeneutical foundation.

TYPOLOGY II.1
REACTIVE ANTI-JUDAISM

"Reactive" anti-Judaism touches on the sense in which the inequality of power, and the relative social inferiority of the church vis-à-vis the synagogue, is thought to have fueled Christian hostilities against the Jews. The Christians, it is generally believed, were awed and intimidated by the Jews as adversaries. Nicholas De Lange talks of the conflict as an uphill battle for the church, struggling with the "more favoured synagogue" to win the hearts and minds of the Roman world (De Lange 1976: 135). Elsewhere the synagogue is characterized as a "formidable adversary" (Shukster & Richardson 1986: 23).[4]

But scholars also propose that the sources of anti-Judaism go beyond Christian resentment of the more powerful position enjoyed by the synagogue. Judaism, it is assumed, also posed an implicit threat to Christian identity. Many scholars emphasize the sense in which Christians are thought to have lived in the shadow of the synagogue. Robert Wilken describes the situation in the following terms: "the Christian movement was a newcomer not tied to a land or a people. Judaism was well established and respected…it possessed a venerable and ancient tradition; it cherished a sacred book which even some pagans read and cited to support their philosophical views" (Wilken 1976: 68). Gaston uses similar imagery: "Second century Christian writers all wrote in the shadow of the synagogue, of whose existence they were much aware, but with whom they did not dare enter into debate" (Gaston 1986b: 165). For Gager this sense of inferiority gives us an angle, a lens through which to interpret what Christians had to say about Jews. The Christian pronouncements about Jews were shaped by their relative "cultural and social inferiority", and it was from this inferior vantage point that they "encountered a well-established, self-confident, widely appreciated Judaism" (Gager 1983: 114; cf. Freyne 1985: 118). In sum, "reactive" anti-Judaism is thought to stem from the church's need to affirm and assert itself over against a "venerable", "respected", and "self-confident" synagogue, a group whose power and influence the young church allegedly sought to counter and appropriate.

The Christian text most frequently appealed to in efforts to illustrate this kind of "reactive" anti-Judaism is Melito of Sardis' *Paschal Homily* (*Peri Pascha*). Melito's homily, it is assumed, represents a text-book case of the anti-Jewish sentiments generated by the encounter of a tiny, insecure, oppressed Christian minority and a powerful, prestigious Jewish community.

---

[4] The sense in which the powerful and influential position of the Jews is thought to have contributed to the phenomenon of judaizing and to have provoked an anti-Jewish reaction among ecclesiastical leaders has already been discussed (cf. Typology I.2; Gager 1983: 133; Efroymson 1976: 58-59; Shukster & Richardson 1986: 30-1).

Melito's accusations against the Jews are among the most vitriolic to be found in this period of Christian history. In addition, he lived and ministered to the Christian community in Sardis, the city where we have the most striking evidence of Jewish wealth and influence. These two factors form the basis of the now generally accepted theory that Melito's homily was directed against those very Jews whose power and prominence appear to have been so remarkable.

It is interesting that the scholar who is credited with breaking ground in the characterization of Melito's "reactive" anti-Judaism, A. T. Kraabel[5], came to his study of Melito through his involvement in the analysis of evidence from the Sardis synagogue excavation. Not surprisingly, then, the starting point of Kraabel's study is a description of the Sardis synagogue in all its grandeur. The Sardis edifice is by far the largest synagogue anywhere in the ancient world (Kraabel 1971: 77). In addition, it enjoys one of the "more prominent sites in the city". It is located at what seems to have been the "civic centre of the Roman and early Byzantine periods", and actually "forms part of the monumental Roman bath and gymnasium complex". Its size and visibility, Kraabel estimates, would have ensured that it made an impression on the people of the city. "The upper walls and roof of the Synagogue would have been clearly visible rising above the shops and road colonnades, and citizens walking past would have been able to look directly inside, when the doors were open, through the entire length of both rooms" (Seager and Kraabel 1983: 168). The Forecourt may even have contained a "municipally licensed fountain" that could have been accessible to the population at large (Kraabel 1983: 184).

So the Jews of Sardis did not live an isolated and confined existence in a Jewish ghetto. Far from it. Their place of worship was a "huge and lavishly decorated structure on 'Main Street'", and they were able to retain control of this structure as long as the city existed (Kraabel 1979: 488). Paul Trebilco's review of the Sardis evidence corroborates Kraabel's conclusions. "The overall effect of the colours, shapes, the great space, the luxurious furnishings illuminated with many lamps, must have been magnificent and very impressive. Clearly members of the community had considerable wealth which they were prepared to use for the splendid decoration of the building" (Trebilco 1991: 42; cf. 41-51).

The inscriptions from the floor of the synagogue are chiefly donors' records, and seem to confirm what we learn from the archaeological evidence. Many of the donors referred to themselves as *Sardianoi*, that is as citizens of the city of Sardis. Nine used the title of *bouleutes*, which identifies them as members of the city council, composed of citizens from the wealthier and

---

[5] Krabbel is one of the only conflict theorists who questions assumptions about Jews as proselytizers. See beginning of Chapter One.

better educated classes. In addition, three of the donors to the synagogue
counted themselves as members of the Roman provincial administration: a
comes (or count), a procurator, and an imperial agent, assistant in the state archives. In sum, these were clearly "men of substance, economic and social
power, as well as political leaders" (Kraabel 1971: 83-84; Kraabel 1983: 184).

The most striking factor about the Sardis inscriptions, and that which distinguishes them from other known epigraphical evidence from the Roman
world, is that they tell us about the status of Jews, not simply within their own
community, but in society at large. They stress "the status of Jews outside the
Jewish community, in the city and its government, and even beyond" (Kraabel
1983: 184). These were not "ghettoized" Jews, but Jews who, by all appearance, were very much "at home" in their pagan environment in the Diaspora.
Without abandoning their ancestral heritage, the Jews of Sardis, seem to have
"flourished" and prospered among their gentile neighbours (Kraabel 1983:
178).

For Kraabel, the main impact of the Sardis discovery is its challenge to
what was long the consensus view of "Jews under Rome".[6] "The importance
of the discovery of the Sardis synagogue", Kraabel states, "is simply that it
reveals a Jewish community of far greater wealth, power, and self-confidence
than the usual views of ancient Judaism would give us any right to expect"
(Kraabel 1983: 178). The important work of Kraabel, among others, has
helped bring about a reconsideration of the traditional and by now outdated
view of post-biblical Jewry as a "debased", "paganized" religious group
whose members lived as low status aliens in the Roman world (Kraabel 1982:
449-450; cf. also Trebilco 1991: 57). Indeed, the Sardis evidence is
impressive, convincing, and illuminating in what it tells us about Judaism.

Unfortunately, however, its very confirmation of Jewish strength and
vitality, has made it a useful tool in the attempt to validate and corroborate the
mistaken assumptions of the "conflict theory". Indeed the insight gained from
the archaeological and epigraphical discoveries about the wealth and
prominence of the Jewish community in Sardis, has been used in the creation
of suppositions about the Christian contemporaries of these Jews, and more
specifically in the generation of assumptions about the Christian response to
Jews. It is this connection that I shall challenge in the following discussion.

After expounding on the Sardis evidence, Kraabel asks how what we have
learnt from the remains of the synagogue might influence our vision of the
church. "Does it only supplement, or does it contradict and revise what had

---

[6] See Kraabel 1983, the "Impact of the Discovery of the Sardis Synagogue" and also Kraabel 1982, "The Roman Diaspora: Six Questionable Assumptions". Kraabel refers in particular
to the "ancient Christian bias" (which we identified earlier as the "Harnackian position" refuted
by Simon) that as Christianity grew and expanded in the Roman empire, Judaism "all but
passed from the scene", fell into the background, became "unimportant", "impotent".

been said about Sardis Christianity?" (Kraabel 1971: 78). This is a key question, and Kraabel, along with most modern scholars, argues that the evidence of Jewish wealth and prominence is key to our understanding of Christian attitudes to Judaism. The knowledge gained about Judaism in the Sardis excavation is thought to provide a "context", a "social location" for the interpretation of the Christian texts. It goes without saying that Kraabel believes this to be true in a particularly direct and obvious way in the case of the writings of Melito, who, he claims here, acted as bishop of Sardis when "the Jews were first putting their fine building into use" (Kraabel 1971: 78).[7]

Melito's *Paschal Homily* contains the most prolonged, vitriolic, even violent, attack on Israel known in pre-Constantinian Christian writings. His denunciation of the Jews is sharper and more radical than that of other Christian authors writing in the "Adversus Judaeos" tradition in his time (Wilson 1986c: 101). His style is "caustic" and "satirical", his language is "excessive" (Wilken 1976: 57) and "sinister" (Werner 1966: 210). The degree of animosity in his polemic has even led some scholars to suggest that he should be seen as a "rabid anti-semite" (Manis 1987: 398).

> What strange crime, Israel, have you committed?
>   You dishonoured him that honoured you;
>   you disgraced him that gloried you;
>   you denied him that acknowledged you;
>   you disclaimed him that proclaimed you;
>   you killed him that made you live.(73)
>
> You prepared for him sharp nails and false witnesses
>   and ropes and scourges
>   and vinegar and gall
>   and sword and forceful restraint as against a murderous robber.
> For you brought both scourges for his body
>   and thorn for his head;
>   and you bound his good hands,
>   which formed you from earth;
>   and that good mouth of his which fed you with life
>   you fed with gall.
> And you killed your Lord at the great feast.
> And you were making merry,
>   while he was starving;
>   you had wine to drink and bread to eat,
>   he had vinegar and gall;
>   your face was bright,
>   his was downcast;
>   you were triumphant,
>   he was afflicted; (79-80)

---

[7] See page 59 (under "The Applicability of the Archaeological Findings") and Kraabel 1983 where Kraabel proposes a much later date for the synagogue.

This language is shocking and disturbing and it is of course important to make some attempt to determine what underlies this vehement attack. Kraabel quite rightly criticizes that generation of scholars who first read the *Paschal Homily* and remained apparently oblivious to Melito's polemic against Israel. L. Goppelt in his book *Christentum und Judentum im ersten und zweiten Jahrhundert* devotes no more than one sentence to Melito (1954: 267). Campbell Bonner's (1940) and O. Perler's (1966) editions of the work ignore the attack on Israel altogether (Kraabel 1971: 81, n. 25).

However, for those Christian scholars who *do* try to come to grips with what lies behind the harsh words of this bishop of Sardis, the evidence from the Sardis excavations seems to provide a welcome solution to an historical, but also to a moral dilemma. The Sardis evidence seems, on the surface, to fit in neatly with efforts to contrast the relative social and political positions of church and synagogue. In as far as this contrast is thought to provide the underlying motivation for Christian hostility towards the Jews, scholars are exempt from looking further and searching deeper to try and explain or justify Melito's shocking words.[8] Not surprisingly, then, most modern scholars of Melito make much of this contrast. K. W. Noakes contrasts the "well established" and privileged Jewish communities in Asia Minor with the Christians whom he describes as "an unpopular minority group, subject to sporadic persecution" (Noakes 1975: 245). Adolf Hansen characterizes the Christian community as an "oppressed minority—religiously, economically, politically, and socially", and he describes this community as lacking "the outward strength of the Jewish community" (Hansen 1968: 176). Robert Wilken's characterization of the contrast is even more evocative.

> Presumably in Sardis the Christians lived in the shadow of the large and influential Jewish community. The Jewish community had deep roots in the city; the Christians were newcomers. Jews held prominent positions, as attested by inscriptions; what we know of Christians comes through their own literature and the evidence is meager. The Jews had their own building; the Christians had none. The Jews were granted toleration to practice their religion; the Christians had no such right. Christianity was a new and relatively unknown sect with little

---

[8] Frederick W. Norris is the one scholar who, to my knowledge, has raised doubts about the current approach in the interpretation of Melito's anti-Judaism, and of the motivations that lay behind it. Norris appeals to scholars not to ignore the "complexity" of the phenomenon of "Christian anti-Semitism" in their efforts to understand why Melito "made such harsh statements about Jews" (Norris 1986: 23-24). In his concluding statement, he calls for a broader perspective in the attempt to come to grips with the issue of Melito's motivations. We cannot take as given, Norris claims, that Melito's antagonism towards the Jews was rooted in sociopolitical factors. For it is also equally possible that "deeper motives" were involved, whether they were "embedded in an orientation towards the world, or in a type of personality", or in theological factors. "Unless we search through all such areas", including the theological dimension, Norris warns, "we shall have little success in combatting the problem" (Norris 1986: 24).

tradition, no sacred book, no claim to antiquity, and it had to make its way in the face of an established and imposing Jewish community (Wilken 1976: 56).

That the situation described above might have bred hostility and resentment on the part of the Christians towards the Jews sounds both plausible and comprehensible. It also has the added attraction of accounting for the intensity of Melito's intoxicated rhetoric. Kraabel, who is quoted with approval in most subsequent studies on Melito (Manis 1987: 388; Wilson 1986c: 97, 99; Wilken 1976: 56; Trebilco 1991: 31, 54), has the following to say about the implications of the Sardis discoveries. "Thanks to the Sardis excavations", he states, "the background of Melito's work has become much clearer". The "resulting picture is of a tangled set of relationships between him and second century Judaism (Kraabel 1983: 186). It seems "likely", according to Kraabel, "that there is a socio-political motivation, rather than a theological one behind Melito's attack" (Kraabel 1971: 84; cf. also Hansen 1968: 180)). In his article "Melito the Bishop and the Synagogue at Sardis: Text and Context", published in 1971, Kraabel puts forward two hypotheses to explain Melito's bitter polemic against Israel. The first, which falls under the category of "reactive anti-Judaism", is concerned with what are interpreted as the church's efforts to establish and preserve its own identity in the face of an influential and daunting Jewish community. The second hypothesis, which will be considered under the heading "strategic" anti-Judaism, claims that the early Christians used anti-Judaism as a political strategy in their attempt to improve their position with Rome.

Establishing Christian Identity in the Face of the Jewish Challenge

Kraabel's first hypothesis holds that, in an effort to "establish and preserve the identity of his religion against the Jews", Melito was driven to his attack on the synagogue by the "size and power" of the Jewish community (Kraabel 1971: 83-84; cf. Hansen 1968: 175-6). This was partly an issue for Melito, according to Kraabel, because of the somewhat fluid boundaries between the two groups. In Melito's time, he surmises, some of the Sardian Christians were no doubt "converted Jews or descendants of converted Jews", and Kraabel deems it likely that the "relationship of Christianity and Judaism was a perennial issue" for these members of the early Church (Kraabel 1971: 84). Stephen Wilson echoes Kraabel's theory. The Jews in Sardis were visible and prominent. They were a "force to be reckoned with, and it would have been virtually impossible for Christians to ignore them when attempting to establish their own identity", and when seeking to make their claim to the traditions of Israel (Wilson 1986c: 97-98).

Aside from the assumption that Melito expressed hostility against Judaism in an effort to establish Christian identity vis-à-vis the outside world, Kraabel and Wilson also see an internal reason for Melito's attack on Israel. Melito

was a Quatrodeciman. He celebrated the paschal feast on 14 Nisan, according
to the Jewish reckoning. Although this practice was not uncommon among
Christians in this part of the Roman world in Melito's day, the orthodox
church was becoming less and less comfortable with the idea that a major
Christian festival should be dependent on the Jewish calendar (Kraabel 1971:
81,n. 22), and the practice was eventually to be condemned at the council of
Nicaea (325 C.E.).

The question arises then, as to whether Melito might have been liable to
the charge from other Christians that his Christianity was too closely associated with Judaism (Kraabel 1971: 84). Perhaps he sought to meet potential
charges of "judaizing" by preaching sermons attacking Israel which made a
sharp division between church and synagogue (Kraabel 1983: 187). Melito
might have had to prove that he was "Christianizing" Judaism rather than judaizing Christianity. His association with "Jewish" ways in the celebration of
the paschal feast may have led him to be all the more firm in his rejection of
the Jews. This rejection might then be seen as part of a "paradoxical determination" to distance the church from the old Israel (Wilson 1986c: 97).

Part of the attraction of the hypothesis that Melito's denunciation of Israel
was rooted in his attempt to defend and establish the church's identity, stems
from its plausibility as a description of socially motivated antagonism. Indeed,
this theory reflects some of the principles of group interaction and conflict
established by sociologists. Erik Erikson's psychosocial theory, for example,
is echoed in some of the assumptions made here about Melito's response to
the Jews of Sardis. Erikson describes the way in which groups with "emerging
identities" can be threatened by old entities whose identity appears to be more
secure, leading to feelings of resentment and envy on the part of the groups or
classes suffering from low self-esteem or low social status (Erikson 1963:
353-57).[9] I propose to show, however, that despite its plausibility, this hypothesis fails to shed light on the motivations behind Melito's denunciation of
the Jews. It fails chiefly because it is based in probabilities with no foundation. Though initially persuasive, these probabilities reveal themselves, on
closer examination, to be historically dubious. By pointing to some of the discrepancies and lacunae in the argumentation of modern scholars, I will expose
the ease with which one can slide unwittingly from tentative suppositions to
absolute statements. I will examine dubious assumptions and hasty conclusions in three key areas. I will then proceed to a hermeneutical critique, in an

---

[9] Efroymson, in his attempt to account for the antagonism against Judaism expressed in
Tertullian's works, appeals to this theory, suggesting that the "not quite complete identity" of
the Christians in Carthage might have made them resentful of the Jews, who, he claims, were
perceived as a group that were successful in maintaining a secure and stable identity of their
own (Efroymson 1976: 59-61).

effort to show how and why current theories about Melito's motivations fail to find support in Melito's text itself.

(1) The Applicability of the Archaeological Findings

In his article on Melito published in 1971, Kraabel assumed a chronological coincidence between Melito's tenure as bishop of Sardis, and the time "when the Jews were first putting their fine building into use". Kraabel identified this time as the latter part of the second century (Kraabel 1971: 78). But when he published his article on the impact of the Sardis discovery in 1983, he was no longer convinced of the contemporaneity of bishop and synagogue. Basing himself on the stages of construction of the bath-gymnasium complex, Kraabel (along with Andrew Seager, co-author of the article), concluded that the building would probably not have been given over to the Jews and made into a synagogue before the late third century, around 270 C.E.(Seager 1983: 173).[10] In surmising about the impression made by the powerful, ominous Jewish community on the Christian bishop of Sardis, Kraabel is forced to fudge the issue by talking loosely of Melito's reaction to the "present synagogue or its *immediate predecessor*, and the people who controlled it" (Kraabel 1983: 187, my emphasis).

If, as is assumed, Melito delivered his *Paschal Homily* homily around 166 C.E., then he could hardly have had a synagogue in mind that was only to be occupied a century later. Indeed, "most historians find it inappropriate to use socio-political information one hundred years later than the event under investigation to explain its significance" (Norris 1986: 19-20). It is of course possible that the Jews who took possession of the synagogue in the third century belonged to a community that had also enjoyed prominence a century earlier. But it is one thing to surmise that this is the case, and quite another to base one's understanding of Melito's vituperations solely on the conviction that the second century Sardian Jews were as powerful and well established as their great-great-great grandchildren in the third century.

(2) Assumptions about Melito's Social Status

The second area where hasty conclusions are often made by scholars is in assumptions about Melito's socio-political background. Let us assume for a moment that the Jewish community was as impressive and prominent in Melito's day as it was later to become. Is the stark contrast portraying the church as an

---

[10] Although Trebilco considers the possibility that the building may have become a synagogue sometime between the late second century and 270 CE (between phases 2 and 3 of construction) (Trebilco 1991: 40), he also sees the end of the third century (phase 3) as the most likely time for the Jewish occupation of the site (Trebilco 1991: 52). Helga Botermann raises the possibility of an even later date for the transfer of the building into Jewish hands, namely phase 4 in the middle of the fourth century (Botermann 1990: 119).

unpopular, oppressed minority really warranted? We know that converts to Christianity came from different walks of life and different social classes in the early centuries. As early as the period of the New Testament Pastoral epistles (circa 85-95 C.E.), we find exhortations to the wealthy to fulfill their responsibility to the poor, as well as strong condemnations of the excessive accumulation of wealth and the love of money. It is in 1 Timothy that we find the proverbial statement "The love of money is the root of all evils" (6.9-10), and the author clearly has wealthy householders and masters in mind in his exhortations (MacDonald 1987: 197-200). If Christians at the end of the first century were dealing with ethical issues connected with the presence of wealth and power within their community, how can we simply take as given that Melito's Christians in the late second century were so downtrodden and underprivileged?

We know very little about Melito himself, but Jerome tells us that his rhetorical skills were praised by Tertullian, who described him as a man whose speech was characterized by "elegance" and "ingenuity" (*De viris illustribus* 24). He was probably a man of some education. This means he may well have come from a good family, and have occupied a position of prominence himself for "good families sent their sons to rhetorical schools so that they could be fitted for the life of the polis, the political decisions of the city" (Norris 1986: 18-19). On the other hand it is equally possible that he was a "bright slave" who had been given opportunities by his master, or even a "successful freedman". The main point is that while we can speculate at will, we can enjoy no certainty. "The point is distressing but clear. The one individual Christian from second-century Sardis about whom we know much at all, and the one social feature about him that is evident—his excellent education in Asiatic rhetoric, cannot be employed without question to place him within any stratum of his society. Each description of Melito's socio-political position, which is based on what we know of his life, remains speculative" (Norris 1986: 18-19). The social and political contrast that forms the very basis of hypotheses about Melito's motivations in denouncing the Jews is, therefore, in itself questionable.

When it comes down to it, the basis for the theory of "reactive" anti-Judaism is little more than evidence of Jewish wealth and prominence in Sardis, coupled with a heated denunciation of Israel in Melito's homily. How many conceptual leaps can any interpretive, reconstructive hypothesis demand of us and still retain its credibility? Not only is the dating of the Sardis excavations somewhat late to be applied with certainty to Melito's day, but we are then asked to assume outright that Melito was intimidated by the power and influence of the neighbouring synagogue without so much as an attempt to establish Melito's own social standing or that of his church. And that is not all.

(3) The Many Dimensions of Identity

The third point is the most important and it has to do with the tendency to assume a direct correlation of socio-political factors and psycho-social motivations. Let us imagine, once more for the sake of argument, that the Jewish community in second century Sardis was wealthy and powerful, and that Melito's Christians were insignificant and underprivileged by comparison. Does this mean that we now automatically possess the key to understanding Christian attitudes towards Judaism in this city and at this time? To assume that socio-political conditions inevitably and unquestioningly determine social perceptions and attitudes strikes me not only as historically irresponsible but as frightening in its sociological implications. Melito is thought to have reacted against a formidable Jewish community in an effort to secure and define the identity of his church, but this interpretation of the church's subjective reality rests on very flimsy ground. Identity is a complex phenomenon with many dimensions.

The scenario describing the church's reaction to the synagogue, as it is laid out for us here by Kraabel and others, sounds plausible, as has already been said. The emotions evoked are believable, understandable, and we can easily identify with the early Christians as their insecurities are described for us. And yet the plausibility of this reconstruction of Christian attitudes and feelings, and the coherence of the theory as a whole is problematic in itself. Suppositions about how Christians might have reacted to the Jews can be no more than speculations and we should not lose from view the fact that these hypotheses are based on very little actual evidence. Our knowledge of the social reality is in itself very fragmentary. Presumptions about the way in which this reality would have been experienced subjectively by the parties involved must be made even more tentatively. They sound credible if we accept the point of departure. The theories of Christian identity seem to extend logically from the social and political portrait drawn for us initially by Kraabel, Wilken and Gager. But even if we suppose for a moment that the model used is both valid and applicable in this case, we cannot assume that the subjective experience of this social reality would be reflective of it.

Modern sociologists interested in questions of identity, refer to just such discrepancies in their studies. Frederik Barth distinguishes between what he calls "etic" and "emic" aspects of a group's ethnicity. The objective features that distinguish a group, including language, religion, economic status and cultural traits, cannot be assimilated to the way in which the group itself defines and maintains its own ethnic boundaries with respect to the outside world (Barth 1970: 10-15; cf. also De Vos & Ross 1975). Mary Douglas establishes that the external manifestations of identity in a group may not directly reflect the values held by that group. Alan Dundas demonstrates that we cannot rely on labels and stereotypes to diagnose the way in which groups experience their own identity or that of other groups (both from Jacobson-Widding 1983: 23).

We cannot presume, then, that the social status of the Christians in relation to Judaism, even if we had a clear picture of it, would necessarily reveal to us their view of, and response to, the people of the synagogue. Even if the Jews occupied a prominent and well-established position in Roman society, their status need not have posed a practical threat to the Christians. The members of the church may well have found other more symbolic ways of affirming the identity of their movement,[11] and have lived in complete indifference to the privileges enjoyed by their Jewish contemporaries.

That Christians could respond in varied ways to wealthy and prominent Jews is illustrated in the following example. At about the same time as Melito led his flock in Asia Minor, Theophilus served as bishop of Antioch in Syria. The Jews in Antioch held an important place in the city's life (Meeks & Wilken 1978: 6). Scholars estimate that 14 to 15% of the population of the city was Jewish, a substantial minority (Meeks & Wilken 1978: 8). There is even evidence of a Jewish magistrate in Theophilus' day. John Malalas, a Byzantine historian, makes reference to a Jew named Asabinos whom he identifies as a landowner and *curialis* (a member of the Roman administration). The property of Asabinos is said to have been purchased in 193 C.E. to build a new plethrion or public stadium, and one of the city's synagogues may even have been named for him (Meeks & Wilken 1978: 6,9; Norris 1986: 21). Archaeological evidence from the city of Antioch is unfortunately quite slim, and none of the city's synagogues have been uncovered, but literary sources suggest that there were several in existence, including one large synagogue in the southern quarter (Meeks & Wilken 1978: 8-9).

All in all, the evidence that has come down to us suggests that, as in Sardis, the Jewish community in Antioch enjoyed considerable prestige and influence. As we have no reason to believe that Antiochene Christians were any more privileged than those of Sardis, we might well imagine that, on the basis of socio-political factors, the relations between the two communities were comparable in both cities. Yet the contrast between Theophilus' attitude to the Jews, as expressed in his apology composed about a decade after Melito's homily, and Melito's vitriolic attack against Israel could not be more marked. The most striking feature about Theophilus' attitude to the Jews is perhaps the way in which he feels free to ignore them.[12] In describing the story of Christian origins, he freely appropriates the Jewish past, without so much as a reference to the possibility of conflicting claims to this tradition. Moses is

---

[11] This avenue will be explored further in Typology IV.1.

[12] This aspect of Theophilus' writings has already been touched on in relation to the judaizing question. See Typology I.2.

"our prophet" (*To Autolycus (ad Autolycum)* III, 18), and David is "our forefa-
ther" (III.25). The sacred writings, "more ancient than those of the Greeks and
Egyptians" are also claimed for the Christians and the Christians alone, without comment or justification (III.26). Theophilus also shows himself to be free
of any need to distance himself or his tradition from its Jewish roots, as even
the "Hebrews...from whom we have these sacred books" are taken over as
"our ancestors" (III.20). Nor does he attempt to obscure the connection between Hebrews and Jews. Where he does make reference to Jews he does so
in the most glowing of terms. Talking of the ten commandments, he says:

> Of this divine law, then, Moses, who also was God's servant, was made the min-
> ister both to all the world, and chiefly to the Hebrews, who were also called Jews,
> whom an Egyptian king had in ancient times enslaved, and who were the right-
> eous seed of godly and holy men...God led them through the desert to Ca-
> naan....and gave them a law, and taught them these things. Of this great and
> wonderful law, which tends to all righteousness, the ten heads are such as we
> have already rehearsed (III,9).

The contrast between Theophilus and Melito is indeed striking. "Theophilus
and Melito both faced powerful, influential Jewish communities. Melito
preached with scathing rebuke; Theophilus wrote with great respect" (Norris
1986: 220). This contrast should give us pause. Unfortunate as it may be, our
understanding of Melito's psycho-social response to his Jewish neighbours
must remain in the realm of speculation. We cannot assume that the characterization of Judaism in his writings was in any way connected with his
church's perceptions of Jews in day to day life. So while it is commendable to
try to situate Melito's work in its socio-political setting, it is also incumbent
on the historian to start out the reconstructive process with a full recognition
of the limitations imposed by the fragmentary nature of the evidence at hand.
Surely we do more justice to our understanding of Melito, by any standards, if
we remain agnostic where the evidence will not allow us to proceed further,
rather than launching into highly speculative theories built upon escalating
presuppositions, all in the name of a supposed sensitivity to the social setting
of the ancient texts.

Returning from the Realm of Socio-Political Speculation to the Text

So far, in our discussion of the "context" of Melito's homily on the Paschal
feast, very little has actually been said about the text itself. It has been noted
that a large section of the work is devoted to the denunciation of Israel, and
one quote has been offered as illustration, not of the content of Melito's accusations, but of the tone, and of the intensity of his rhetoric. Indeed scholars
seek out the social location of Melito's *Paschal Homily* not in the words of
Melito, but in the evidence confirming the strength and power of the Sardian
Jewish community, and in the vehemence of the bishop of Sardis. This em-

phasis on external evidence and on the tone of Melito's anti-Judaism is interesting in light of the fact that attention to the content of Melito's harsh accusations does not encourage us to view these accusations as directed at his Jewish contemporaries. The Jews who Melito so vigorously castigates, and the crime that he so urgently denounces, belong not to second century Asia Minor but to first century Palestine. K.H. Rengstorf points this out in his discussion of Melito: "The Jews he has in mind and the Jews he accuses, are not the Jews of his time, and certainly not the Jews of his diocese, but rather the Jews of old, the Jews of the first Good Friday in Jerusalem" (Rengstorf and Kortzfleisch 1968: I.73). So the substance of Melito's condemnation of the Jews does not immediately lend support to current hypotheses about Melito's motivations.

Unfortunately, however, most scholars continue to emphasize tone over substance in their interpretation of Melito's accusations. Stephen Wilson makes reference to Rengstorf's observation, but promptly dismisses it as an attempt to "take the sting out of Melito's language" (Wilson 1986c: 93). The reasons Wilson gives to back his claim that, despite the content of Melito's words, the bishop of Sardis was denouncing contemporary Jews, illustrate the confusion that reigns in this area of study. First of all, Wilson argues, the wealth and prominence of the Jewish community would presumably have made the Jews impossible to ignore. In making reference to the Jews of the bible, Wilson assumes, Melito must also have been thinking of the influential community in his own city. Secondly, Wilson believes in the likelihood of a spill-over effect. It seems improbable, Wilson argues, that such an impassioned tirade vilifying the Jews of old for deicide would "lead Melito or his community entirely to ignore the existence of contemporary Jewish communities, not least in their own city, who were in some senses successors to those who 'murdered God'" (Wilson 1986c: 93). Ultimately then, Wilson is not defending the claim here that Jews are being *directly* addressed in the homily. It is rather that he sees it as unlikely that Melito's audience would, on hearing his words, "have thought solely of the Jews of the first century who killed Jesus and not of their Jewish contemporaries" (Wilson 1986c: 94).

The pernicious effects of hate literature, whether it be directed against a group's past or present activities, is well documented. Nevertheless, as was discussed above, the extent to which the condemnation of historical Jews would have manifested itself in the attitudes of Sardian Christians towards their Jewish contemporaries is not a given. In this instance, therefore, we cannot simply take for granted that such a spill-over effect took place. In addition, though this is a valid question for consideration in its own right, it remains a secondary issue concerned with effect rather than cause, and is thus not directly relevant to our discussion here. For even if we accept, for a moment, Wilson's argument that Melito's flock could not have heard their bishop's words of denunciation without applying them somehow to the people of the synagogue in their city, this does not really further our efforts at textual interpretation. The aim is to uncover what *Melito* had in mind when he composed his text, and not to determine what influence his words would have had once spoken. A vitriolic tone is simply not in itself justification enough for the transformation of biblical Jews into formidable contemporaries. Melito may well have had other reasons for using such intense language in his homily, as we shall see shortly.

Exploring the Theological Dimension

While the main focus for most scholars remains the determining role played by local circumstances in explaining Melito's vituperative attack on Israel, a number of scholars seem willing to recognize some kind of theological dimension in Melito's homily against the Jews.[13] Stephen Wilson's long list of the "influences on Melito" begins with a recognition of the sense in which anti-Jewish ideas emerge out of the church's need to define Christianity as independent of Judaism, while adopting certain Jewish "beliefs and structures". "However obvious, it is worth noting that a number of the implicitly anti-Jewish themes in Melito are the reverse side of his attempt to articulate his definition of Christianity". The important point to note here is that, unlike "reactive anti-Judaism" which is linked directly and specifically to the peculiar social conditions of Melito's community, this theological anti-Judaism is recognized as an inevitable part of being Christian, "not only for Melito but for all Christian writers" (Wilson 1986c: 95). In other words, Wilson is recognizing here that Melito's anti-Judaism might not be unique to Sardis, and that Melito is dependent to some extent on Christian tradition in general. Indeed, "the implications of the Christian appropriation of Jewish scriptures and traditions for the fate of empirical Israel had to be faced from the earliest days

---

13 Kraabel however, seems to deny any role to theological conventions in shaping Melito's ideas. He judges attempts to understand the *Paschal Homily* in theological terms as having been unsatisfactory, though he doesn't really explain why this is so (Kraabel 1971: 85). He raises the issue of how Melito might fit into the "Adversus Judaeos" tradition, but dismisses this question in a few sentences. The Christian authors over against whom Melito is compared by Kraabel, are Justin and Tertullian, and once again it is the question of tone not substance that is deemed to be the deciding factor. "Justin's *Dialogue with Trypho* contains nothing of the frontal attack on the Jews", and Tertullian's *Adversus Judaeos* is less a personal attack than a battle over the Old Testament in which Tertullian sees Jesus everywhere prefigured". The fact that Melito, like Tertullian, sets out to demonstrate how Jesus was prefigured in the Old Testament, seems to escape Kraabel in his determination to contrast the two authors. Despite the similarities of theme in the anti-Jewish writings of both Melito and Tertullian, what Kraabel describes as the "bitterness of Melito's attack" enables him to conclude that "Melito appears to be thinking of flesh-and-blood Jews, Tertullian of shadow-figures, theological abstractions" (Kraabel 1971: 83).

of the Christian movement" (Wilson 1986c: 101). In another article on Melito, Wilson makes this point even more clearly and forcefully:

> For Melito, as for Justin, Origen, Chrysostom and Aphrahat, affirmation of Christian belief and ritual meant denial of the Jewish equivalent. Melito's exposition of Old and New Pascha may be more sharply defined than many, but it merely makes explicit a tacit strain in Christianity which appeared in its earliest days (Wilson 1985: 354).

Andrew M. Manis also recognizes the sense in which Melito's hermeneutic allows the bishop to "keep part of his Jewishness", while enabling him at the same time "to relativize severely the claims of Judaism" (Manis 1987: 398). Although Manis traces this theological need back to the competition between Christians and Jews, he also concedes in his concluding statement that the "rich fund of Christian tradition may have held the precedent for...the bishop's thought" (Manis 1987: 401). Robert Wilken also acknowledges that there were theological issues at stake in Melito's works. The christological interpretation of the Old Testament was a significant question for Melito, both in his homily and in the fragments interpreting the sacrifice of Isaac, which Wilken studies in detail. Melito's theological argument was a supersessionary one, and in this respect it is recognized by Wilken as "characteristic of the early Christian writings against the Jews" (Wilken 1976: 57).

Despite their acknowledgement of a theological dimension, it is unfortunate that none of these scholars really takes the theological motivation seriously in their attempts to account for the real causes of Melito's anti-Judaism. They concede that Melito was partially motivated by theological considerations because they cannot do otherwise. But they are ultimately swayed by Kraabel's main hypothesis. The real underlying cause of Melito's hostility against the Jews must, in their eyes, inevitably stem from the church father's reaction to the prominent Jewish community. We have discussed some of the reasons that the socio-political explanation lacks credibility. I would like now to demonstrate why the theological motivation not only makes sense as a possibility, but is the most convincing way of accounting for Melito's anti-Judaism.

My point of departure is the content and theme of Melito's argument. Proving that Melito's attack is directed against first-century Jews should in no way "take the sting out of" his anti-Judaism.[14] Indeed it should encourage us to take his anti-Jewish ideas more seriously. If Melito's harsh language represented an isolated instance of hostility attributable to specific and unrepeated historical circumstances, then his attitude to the Jews would be of no more than historical interest to us. But if Melito's accusations against the Jews fit in with a whole tradition of Christian theological thinking then we have to rec-

---

[14] As Wilson suggests above. See Wilson 1986c: 93.

ognize the continued significance of his anti-Judaism. It becomes more than just as an historical example of Christian hostility to the Jews, because it presents us with a moral and theological dilemma that must be addressed by modern Christians today.[15]

The Paschal Homily and the Christian Anti-Jewish Tradition

Let us examine Melito's argument in the Paschal Homily in an attempt to situate him in the Christian anti-Jewish tradition. The Paschal Homily is divided into two main sections. The first deals with the typological exposition of the Exodus story. The second is taken up chiefly with a denunciation of the Jews on account of their responsibility for the crucifixion. It is this second section that has received the most attention from scholars and it is on the basis of the accusations in this section that Melito has been dubbed as the "first poet of deicide" (Werner 1966: 191-210). As we saw in the discussion of "embittered" anti-Judaism (Typology I.3), attributing responsibility to the Jews, or to Jewish leaders for the crucifixion of Jesus, the Christ, the Messiah, had crept into Christian lore from the days of the early gospel accounts of the passion. However, Melito was the first Christian writer to make this into "an unambiguous accusation of deicide" (Wilken 1986c: 91). He was the first in other words to equate the passion of Christ with the murder of God.

This is "the one horrendous novelty introduced by Melito" (Wilson 1986c: 101) in the tradition of Christian anti-Judaism. It is rooted, I would argue, not in Melito's greater hatred for the Jews, but in the bishop's christological ideas. Melito's thought has been characterized as a kind of "Christocentric monotheism". He addresses doxologies to Christ, he rarely distinguishes the Son from the Father, and Justin's Middle Platonist ideas of the Logos as a kind of secondary God would have been quite foreign to him. Indeed, Melito attributes "to Christ all the acts of God without exception" (Hall 1979: xliii), and christology is at the very heart of the Paschal Homily. It is central of course to the final section where we find the charges against Israel (72-99) that have so troubled scholars, but it gives meaning also to the typological exposition of Exodus in the first section (1-45), and finally it is the central theme that connects the two sections and makes sense of the whole. Let us examine each section in turn in an effort to reveal the link that exists between them.

(1) Typology and Supersession

The first section of the Paschal Homily consists in a typological exposition of a traditional passover text, Exodus 12, the story of the first passover and of the liberation of the people of Israel from the Egyptians. Melito's aim in interpreting this text is to show that the real meaning of Passover is christological.

---

[15] See Conclusion.

Christ is the true Paschal Lamb, and Israel's deliverance is a "type" of the redemption in Christ. The bondage and subsequent liberation of Israel by the
sacrifice of the sheep prefigures the spiritual liberation of believers in Jesus by
the sacrifice of the true Paschal lamb.

> O strange and inexpressible mystery!
>   The slaughter of the sheep was found to be Israel's salvation,
>   and the death of the sheep became the people's life,
>   and the blood won the angel's respect.
> Tell me, angel, what did you respect?
>   The slaughter of the sheep or the life of the Lord?
>   The death of the sheep or the model of the Lord?
>   The blood of the sheep or the Spirit of the Lord?
> It is clear that your respect was won
>   when you saw the mystery of the Lord occurring in the sheep,
>   the life of the Lord in the slaughter of the lamb,
>   the model of the Lord in the death of the sheep,
>   that is why you did not strike Israel,
>   but made only Egypt childless. (31-33)

In the sections which follow this passage (35-45 and 57-58), Melito goes on to
outline, in very explicit terms, the key to his hermeneutic of the Scriptures.
Prefigurations are essential for all important events because "What is said and
done is nothing, beloved, without a comparison with a preliminary sketch"
(35). And it is through the prefiguration that the new and great realization of
this prefiguration gains its credibility:

> But first the Lord made prior arrangements for his own
>   sufferings in patriarchs and in prophets and in the whole people,
>   setting his seal to them through both law and prophets.
> For the thing which is to be new and great in its
>   realization is arranged well in advance,
> so that when it comes about it may be believed in,
>   having been foreseen well in advance. (57)

So the prefiguration is essential to the reality, but the coming of the reality
also has implications for the status of that which is prefigured. The "type" establishes the worth of that which is realized, but, in this realization, the "type"
also loses its worth. To clarify this point, Melito sets forth his analogy of the
sculptor's model. A sculptor uses a model to outline a future work of art. But
once the more powerful, more beautiful finished work arises out of the perish-
able model, then the model has outlived its usefulness.

> But when that of which it is the model arises,
>   that which once bore the image of the future thing
>   is itself destroyed as growing useless
>   having yielded to what is truly real the image of it;
>   and what once was precious becomes worthless
>   when what is truly precious has been revealed. (37)

In this instance, of course, the "model" is the people of Israel and that which is "truly real" is the salvation wrought through the Lord for his church; the type is the law, and its fulfillment the gospel. We find in Melito, therefore, a clear and uncompromising statement of the supersessionary argument which is so central to all of Christian theology.

> For the salvation and reality of the Lord were
> prefigured in the people, and the decrees of the
> gospel were proclaimed in advance by the law.
> The people then was a model by way of preliminary
> sketch, and the law was the writing of a parable;
> the gospel is the recounting and fulfillment of the law,
>   and the church is the repository of the reality.
> The model then was precious before the reality,
>   and the parable marvelous before the church arose,
>   and the law was marvelous before the gospel was elucidated.
> But when the church arose,
> and the gospel took precedence,
> the model was made void, conceding its power to the
> reality, and the law was fulfilled, conceding its power to
> the gospel.(39-42)

Both in his christological interpretation of the Old Testament, and in his exposition of the supersession of Judaism by Christianity, Melito fits right in to the tradition of Christian anti-Jewish literature.[16] So far in our discussion, there is no evidence to suggest that Melito had any special or peculiar reasons for holding a grudge against the Jews. Let us now turn to the charges levelled directly against the Jews.

(2) Murder of God and Supersession

The bulk of the final section of the homily consists in an impassioned denunciation of Israel for the crime of deicide, of which some passages were quoted in our initial discussion of Melito. As we have seen, this is the part of the homily that has received the most attention. It is here that Melito's vehemence makes him stand apart from other anti-Jewish writers, contributing to the theory that his antagonism toward the Jews was socially rooted. Yet if we follow the progression of Melito's argument closely, then it becomes apparent that in important respects the deicide section actually follows directly from the typological discussion. In the first half of his homily, Melito told the story of the first passover which was to be the type of the real passover that occurs in Christ's passion and resurrection. It is the passion that then becomes the focus of the second portion of the *Paschal Homily*. Melito never loses sight of the

---

[16] The sculptor's model itself, for instance, is also found in Origen's *Homilies On Leviticus* (*Homiliae in Leviticum*) 10.1. A typological interpretation of the Exodus story is also found in Irenaeus *Against Heresies (Adversus Haereses)* 4.28.3.

connection between the two stories recounted in his homily, and, in his rendition of the story of the crucifixion, he appears to remind his parishioners of the link in interesting ways.

The Jews figure in both stories, but their role in the second event is a reversal of the part they played in the first, and the irony of this reversal is not lost on Melito. The story of the first passover tells of Israel's liberation from Egypt. In the real passover, however, the Jews, who once *prefigured* the church, come to be identified as the *enemies* of Christ. Those who were once saved, have now become the enemies of salvation (cf. Wilson 1986c: 88). The irony, for Melito, is that while the Jews celebrate their own salvation, they commit the ultimate crime in bringing about the death of the true paschal lamb. In rejecting Jesus, they show themselves to be oblivious to the true meaning of their own salvation, and through their own actions, those who were once saved are now damned. Just as they prefigured the church, so their ultimate fate was in turn prefigured by that of the Egyptians in the Exodus story. In the following two passages, one taken from the first section describing the exclusion of Egypt, the other from the second section referring to the rejection of the Jews, Melito's language suggests that he sees a parallel between the fate of the foes in both stories:

> But while the sheep is being slain
>   and the Pascha is being eaten
>   and the mystery is being performed
>   and the people is making merry
>   and Israel is being marked,
> then came the angel to strike Egypt,
>   the uninitiated in the mystery,
>   the non-participating in the Pascha,
>   the unmarked with the blood,
>   the unguarded by the Spirit,
>   the hostile, the faithless. (16)

> So you quaked at the assault of foes;
> you were not terrified in the presence of the Lord,
> you did not lament over the Lord,
> so you lamented over your firstborn; (99)

Though the first passage refers ostensibly to the Egyptians, who were struck by the angel because they were unmarked by the blood (sign of protection), Melito seems to have the Jews in mind when he talks of those who "make merry" while the "mystery" is being performed, and when he refers to the "faithless" who remain "uninitiated" in that mystery, and who therefore do not participate in the true paschal feast. Though the second passage bemoans Israel's failure to recognize her Lord, the reference to the "assault of foes" and the "lament" over the "firstborn" is clearly reminiscent of that which befell the first enemies of the Lord, the Egyptians.

But aside from this continuity between enemies of the past and enemies of the present, there is also a more vital connection between the two sections, vital because it is crucial to the development of Melito's theological argument. Melito's first section talked of the christological meaning of the Jewish Passover, and the sense in which Israel was displaced by the church, once the real significance of the paschal celebration was revealed. The Hebrews, Melito argues, had once fulfilled a necessary and precious function, but that function was made void in the coming of Christ. The main purpose of the second section is to continue the christological exposition embarked on in the first section.

In the second half of his homily, Melito tells the story of Christ's triumph through the ordeal of the passion. Ultimately, this story should be interpreted as a doxology to Christ which illustrates the correct response to the Lord by contrasting it with a vivid description of the rejection of Jesus, and of the terrifying consequences of that rejection. In this contrast between the faithful and the faithless Melito also continues his treatment of the supersessionary argument, already addressed in the first section. While in the first section Israel was superseded as a matter of course, as part of the inevitable progression of God's plan for salvation, in the second part of the homily, Melito gives a much more forceful and powerful reason for the substitution of Israel: supposed Jewish responsibility for the murder of Christ.

It is in this context that both Melito's christological ideas and his anti-Jewish accusations should be understood.[17] The Jews, who are displaced, are not just guilty of rejecting a Christian Messiah, but are responsible for the murder of their very own God, to whom they owe their life, their name, and their salvation. Melito recounts here what he sees as the terrible paradox of Israel's brutal rejection of the very God who brought His chosen people out of Egypt. It is perhaps to drive this point home that Melito juxtaposes his two stories. The very horror of the crime stems from the fact that Israel's rejection of Christ is not just a rejection of the "King", the "captain", the "Lord", the one who "rose from the dead", and who is "glorious in his own right", but that it consists in the most brutal act against the very God who the Jews claim to worship. To illustrate this, Melito proceeds to retell the story, from the very beginning, of the great deeds performed by the God of Israel on behalf of his now ungrateful people. More significantly, Melito describes how, in turning against their God, the people of Israel lose their right to the title that He bestowed upon them:

> O Lawless Israel, what is this unprecedented crime
> you committed, thrusting your Lord among unprecedented

---

[17] Though Stephen Wilson recognizes this connection, he unfortunately gives relatively little importance to it in his account of Melito's motivations cf. Wilson 1986c: 99.

sufferings,
   your Sovereign, who formed you, who made you, who
honoured you, who called you "Israel"?
But you did not turn out to be "Israel;
   you did not "see God",
   you did not recognize the Lord.
You did not know, Israel,
   that he is the firstborn of God,...
It was he who chose you and guided you,
   from Adam to Noah,
   from Noah to Abraham,
   from Abraham to Isaac
   and Jacob and the twelve patriarchs.
It was he who guided you into Egypt,
   and watched over you and there sustained you.
It was he who lit your way with a pillar
   and sheltered you with a cloud,
   who cut the Red Sea and led you through
   and destroyed your enemy.
It is he who gave you manna from heaven,
   who gave you drink from a rock,
   who legislated for you at Horeb,
   who gave you inheritance in the land,
   who sent you the prophets,
   who raised up your kings (81, 83-85)

Ungrateful Israel, come and take issue with me about
your ingratitude.
How much did you value being formed by him?
How much did you value the seeking out of your fathers?
How much did you value the descent into Egypt?...(87)

Melito's argument is logical and consistent throughout. Though much of his homily is descriptive, recounting the ignominious fall of the Egyptians, relating in graphic detail the agonies of the crucifixion, it remains clear that these illustrations serve a theological purpose. The Sardian Christians who came to hear their bishop's paschal homily, were made to understand that the christological significance of this feast extended beyond the mere commemoration of Christ's passion and resurrection. In the Pascha, Christians celebrated the mystery of that turning point around which all of history revolved. This was the key historical event that earned for Christians their status as the new chosen people, and sealed the fate of those who failed to recognize in Christ's passion their own God's ultimate act of salvation. In the Pascha, then, Christians celebrated the justification of the faithful and the corresponding condemnation of the faithless.

    Though Melito is unyielding in his historical, and therefore in his theological, judgement of the Jews, he does not give any indication, as far as I can detect, that his castigation of Israel might be rooted in personal or social frustrations vis-à-vis his Jewish contemporaries. In fact he seems to take little pleasure in the denunciation, portrayed here almost as a necessary burden.

> And who has been murdered? Who is the murderer?
> I am ashamed to say and I am obliged to tell.
> For if the murder had occurred at night,
> or if he had been slain in a desert place,
> one might have had recourse to silence.
> But now in the middle of the street and in the middle of
> the city, at the middle of the day, for all to see,
> has occurred a just man's unjust murder. (94)

Elsewhere, he seems to struggle against the inevitability of the horrifying fact that God's first chosen people should turn against Him, almost as though Melito wished for a moment that he could rewrite history:

> He had to suffer, but not by you;
> he had to be dishonoured, but not by you;
> he had to be judged, but not by you;
> he had to be hung up, but not by you and your right hand.
> This is the cry, Israel, which you should have made to God:
> "Sovereign, if indeed your Son had to suffer,
> and this is your will,
> then let him suffer, but not by me;
> let him suffer by foreigners,
> let him be judged by uncircumcised men,
> let him be nailed up by tyrannical right hand,
> but not by me". (75-76).

As for the intensity of Melito's language, I see it as an indication that he took the subject of his homily with the greatest of seriousness. The assumption that such vehemence could only be addressed to flesh and blood Jews, and could only relate to issues of social and political relevance, shows a misunderstanding of the mind-set of the early Christians, and of the issues that concerned them. For the authors of the early church, the passion of Christ, and the positive and negative responses that He elicited could never be a matter to be related with calm indifference. There can be no doubt that Melito attached great importance to the christological question, and that, as a bishop, he saw it as part of his ministry to instil in the members of his congregation, a sense of the momentous significance of the Easter event. The charges against the Jews in the *Paschal Homily* form an integral part of this endeavour and have little to do with the Sardian Jews of Melito's day, however prominent or influential.

In this consideration of "reactive" anti-Judaism, we have examined the sense in which anti-Judaism is thought to have been rooted in the psycho-social dimension of reality. I have considered and sought to refute the assumption that the early Christians were resentful of the synagogue's privileged civil status in Roman society, and were threatened by the secure identity of the Jews. I will now turn to a discussion of what we identified earlier as Kraabel's second theory of socio-political motivation. This second hypothesis holds that in some instances, the church's anti-Judaism formed part of a deliberate strategy on the part of the Christians to displace the Jews in their favoured position with Rome.

This "strategic" anti-Judaism, along with "recriminatory" anti-Judaism, which will be considered next, are both based on the extension of the notion of *conflict* itself to the socio-political dimension. So far we have examined notions of conflict as founded in a rivalry for religious converts, and in socio-politically rooted jealousies. We now turn to suppositions about a supposed struggle for political power in the empire. Under the heading "strategic" anti-Judaism we will consider this struggle from the Christian point of view. We will examine the theory that Christians used anti-Judaism as part of a deliberate attempt to out-manoeuvre the Jews. In the next section entitled "recriminatory" anti-Judaism, and based in suppositions about the motivations and actions of Jews, we will explore the theory that anti-Jewish feelings also stemmed from Christian resentment of Jews who sought to prevent the rise of the church.

TYPOLOGY II.2
STRATEGIC ANTI-JUDAISM

In his second hypothesis about the sources of anti-Judaism, Kraabel suggests that church leaders such as Melito were not content simply to express their resentment toward the Jews, but actively sought to enhance their own position with the Roman authorities at the expense of the synagogue. Kraabel seeks confirmation of this hypothesis in Melito's *Apology*, addressed to the emperor Marcus Aurelius (fragments of which survive in Eusebius' *History of the Church (Historia ecclesiastica)*). Melito is believed to have composed this work in the wake of a bout of persecution in Asia Minor. In it, he seeks to demonstrate that supporting the church is in the interest of the empire. To back his claim, he argues that both church and empire trace their origins back to the same period, and that the era of Christian development has coincided with the general prosperity of the state.

> Our philosophy first grew up among the barbarians, but its full flower came among your nations during the glorious reign of your ancestor Augustus; it became a good omen for your empire, since from that time the power of the Romans has grown mighty and magnificent (*History of the Church* 4.26.7).

Kraabel sees a connection between this attempt to gain favour with Rome and Melito's attack on the Jews in the *Paschal Homily*. In effect, Kraabel interprets Melito's condemnation of Judaism in the light of the bishop of Sardis' efforts to rehabilitate the church in the eyes of the imperial authorities. The assumption here is that Melito was motivated, in his attack on the Jews, not only by envy of their civil status, but by an active desire to displace them, and to acquire their privileged position in Roman society. This hypothesis is presented, in some form or other, by most scholars studying Melito. Indeed the assumption that Melito's attack on Judaism forms part of an active conflict between church and synagogue with religious as well as social and political dimensions is firmly entrenched (Hansen 1968: 180; Noakes 1975: 246; Wilson 1986c: 95-100; Manis 1987: 399).[18]

The question arises then: is it possible to say that the Christians were politically motivated to some extent in their denigration of Judaism? More

---

[18] Interestingly enough, in his 1983 article on the impact of the Sardis discoveries, Kraabel seems to have modified his position slightly. Though he still interprets Melito's denunciation of Israel as an attack on contemporary Jews, Kraabel affirms that it is doubtful whether Melito's vituperations formed part of an active Jewish-Christian conflict. He acknowledges that there is no evidence of this from the Jewish side, and "Jewish wealth and influence are such as to suggest Christian envy of the Jews from afar rather than actual confrontation with them" (Kraabel 1983: 179). Though he talks of competition between Jews and Christians, Stephen Wilson also admits that the lack of evidence forces us to remain agnostic on certain key questions: "We have no explicit evidence to show how Jews and Christians in Sardis viewed each other" (Wilson 1986c: 98).

particularly in this instance, did Melito condemn the Jews partly in order to gain favour with Rome? This question must be answered in the negative, and w shall see that the notion of a "strategic" anti-Judaism is historically dubious. Kraabel's theory is built on three historical assumptions which he claims account for the circumstances surrounding the composition of Melito's *Apology*. While Kraabel's case only holds true if all three assumptions can be proven to hold true, I propose to show that each of these suppositions is problematic in its own right.

The assumptions which form the basis of Kraabel's hypothesis are as follows:

(1) Some scholars have suggested that Melito may have presented his *Apology* to Lucius Verus, co-emperor of Marcus Aurelius (161-9 CE), who is believed to have passed through Asia in 166 CE (Mitten 1966: 62; Johnson 1961: 87; Kraabel 1971: 79).

(2) A Hebrew inscription may have been put up in Verus' honour in the Sardis synagogue.[19]

(3) The reference in the *Apology* to the "barbarians" among whom the church's philosophy is said to have first grown up (see the passage quoted above), is thought by Kraabel to be an allusion to the Jews. Kraabel assumes that Melito sought, through this allusion, to give the Jews a bad name, the better to undermine and appropriate the synagogue's privileged position with the state.

If the conjunction of events, as described by Kraabel, did indeed take place, then, according to Kraabel, "the elements of a vigorous Jewish-Christian conflict are all present". Both religious groups would have been trying to outdo each other in vying for the attentions and goodwill of the emperor. The conflict that Kraabel assumes flared up in the wake of Verus' visit is proposed as the occasion for the *Paschal Homily*. The harsh and vehement language of Melito's homily would thus be accounted for in terms of acute tensions that are presumed to have escalated between Christians and Jews at a politically sensitive time (Kraabel 1971: 84).

Kraabel's reconstruction of a supposed competition between Christians and Jews for the attentions of the emperor stands on very shaky ground. Indeed Kraabel builds his theory on the supposed convergence of uncertain events whose exact dating is almost impossible to confirm. Let us reexamine each of his assumptions in turn:

(1) There is no solid evidence to suggest that Melito presented his *Apology* to Verus. The chronology would *allow* for it, but this makes it no more than a possibility. Kraabel himself admits that there are conflicting views on this

---

[19] Transliterated as "beros"—from the annual reports of the Sardis excavations, GMA Hanfmann, *Bulletin of the American Schools of Oriental Research* 187 (1967) 25.

question. M. Sordi, for example, suggests that the *Apology* was composed a decade later, when Marcus Aurelius himself was in the East (Sordi 1961: 365-368).[20]

(2) The inscription, of which only a fragment remains, has been read as "beros", and, on this basis, it has been suggested that it represents a transliteration of Verus. But, again, this is only a suggestion, part of an attempt to put some kind of interpretation on a puzzling and somewhat obscure inscription that might have had other meanings.[21] Even if we assume that the inscription was dedicated to Verus, this proves nothing about Melito's Christian community, let alone about a conflict between Christians and Jews.

(3) Finally, what of the suggestion that "barbarians" refers to Jews? This proposal too seems highly doubtful. It fits in neither with the usual meaning of the term nor with the general character of other Christian references to Jews. Firstly, there is no reason to believe that the term "barbarians" was meant as a denigration. It was not an abusive term, but simply the way Greeks referred to non-Greeks. In addition, it is doubtful that Melito even had the Jews in mind when he made this affirmation. The Christians tended to use biblical terminology when they referred to the Jews. The Jews were generally castigated and occasionally praised in the Christian writings, but it was always in terms of their relationship to God that they were spoken of.[22]

Aside from the questionable nature of Kraabel's specific hypothesis about the motivations of Melito, there are also more general reasons to doubt the existence of a politically motivated competition between Christians and Jews. These shall be considered in the next section on "recriminatory" anti-Judaism.

---

[20] On Lucius' journey to Asia Minor see Barnes 1967: 7-72. There is only direct proof of a visit to Ephesus.

[21] Trebilco emphasizes the tentative nature of this suggestion, and points out that the "wall from which the fragment probably fell was built a century and a half after Verus' death" (Trebilco 1991: 44).

[22] Stephen Wilson suggests that "barbarians" refers to the empires that preceded Rome, under whom the Jews lived (Wilson 1986c: 100).

TYPOLOGY II.3
RECRIMINATORY ANTI-JUDAISM

We turn now to a third kind of anti-Judaism with political ramifications. As in the case of "strategic" anti-Judaism, the notion of "recriminatory" anti-Judaism is based on the assumption that the rivalry between Christians and Jews extended to the political realm. Where "strategic" anti-Judaism was concerned with Christian strategy, "recriminatory" anti-Judaism starts from the Jewish perspective. Through a complex series of assumptions, which will be exposed and criticized shortly, scholars have made presumptions about the Jewish response to the rise of Christianity. The idea that the Jews were hostile towards the church, even willing on occasion to condone and participate in the Roman persecution of the Christians, is now widely held. "Recriminatory" anti-Judaism is thought to be born of Christian feelings of resentment and "recrimination" against a group that they numbered among their oppressors.

Melito and his homily will not be the focus of this section, but we cannot leave him behind quite yet. Despite the fact that Melito refers solely to the Jews of Jesus' time, and makes no reference to the attitudes, let alone to the actions, of contemporary Jews, it is both telling and disturbing that scholars have assumed the existence of this kind of "recriminatory" anti-Judaism in the works of the bishop of Sardis. Telling, because it provides further confirmation of the tendency among modern scholars to impose preconceived notions on the Christian writings. Disturbing, because of the way in which it so freely attributes negative motivations to Jews who do not even make an appearance in the texts.

The argument runs as follows. In their attempt to appropriate the special relationship that the Jews enjoyed with the Romans, the Christians threatened the people of the powerful synagogue, put them on the defensive, and forced them to retaliate in order to safeguard their interests. K.W. Noakes proposes, for instance, that the "well established" Jewish communities in Asia Minor were "jealous of their privileges", and were "no doubt...very active in stirring up popular feelings against the Christians" (Noakes 1975: 245). Andrew Manis refers to the inevitably "negative affect" on the "Jews' privileged position with the state", of Christian efforts to gain imperial support. He seeks to explain the degree of animosity towards the Jews in the *Paschal Homily* by suggesting that some of the "powerful Jews" might have been "using their influence with the State against the Christians" (Manis 1987: 399). In his conclusion he moves from tentative suggestion to bold statement of fact, and, in this shift, the role of the Jews grows in importance: "Melito's church was ex-

periencing some type of persecution which he believed to have been insti-
gated by the powerful Jewish community" (Manis 1987: 400).[23]

Despite the authoritative fashion in which these suppositions are presented,
they are based purely in speculation. They have no foundation either in historical fact or in the anti-Jewish references in Melito. There is no evidence
that Melito's community was suffering from persecution at the time he delivered his homily, and even if such a persecution were taking place, there is no
reason to believe that the Jews would have had any part in it. But it is quite
clear that the cavalier judgements of scholars about Jews as persecutors have
little to do with what can be learnt from the text of Melito itself. In the following, I examine what lies behind the notion of Jews as persecutors. I will show
that the presuppositions about Jewish actions and motivations on which this
notion is based, emerge, not from evidence in the Christian texts, but from the
conflict model of Christian-Jewish interaction, and from the distorted interpretation that this model imposes on the texts.

The idea of a "recriminatory" anti-Judaism, that is, an anti-Judaism rooted
in the Christian response to Jewish hostility, is held quite widely by the
"conflict" theorists: "Christian opposition was no little nourished by the re-
bound and hatred of the Synagogue in the first days of Christianity, nor any
less by the cooperation of the Jews with Roman persecutors" (Alvarez 1975:
76). "From its inception, the Christian movement provoked criticism and polemic from its Jewish opponents. Christian responses constitute one of the
principal spawning grounds for anti-Jewish arguments...In the background
are always clear echoes of... persistent criticism" (Gager 1983: 153-4).

The first thing to be noted about this type of anti-Judaism is that, in our examination of it, we enter into new territory. The underlying assumption of the
"conflict theory", as we have seen, is that Judaism was a proselytizing movement, and a rival to the church. But so far, in our discussion of various "types"
of anti-Judaism, our main concern has quite naturally been with Christian perceptions and motivations. "Recriminatory" anti-Judaism, on the other hand, is
founded on assumptions about the *attitudes and actions of Jews*. Indeed, an
elaborate hypothesis is constructed to explain and account for these attitudes
and actions, and it is to this hypothesis that we now turn. I will then show how
this hypothesis fails to stand up as a theory of historical explanation, and how
it fails miserably as a hermeneutical theory as well.

---

[23] Kraabel makes allusion to the threatened position of the Jews in his thesis completed in
1968, but he seems to abandon this avenue in later publications (1968: 216-17). In an article
published in 1983 he acknowledges that Melito's hostility need not be mirrored by similar
feelings in the Jewish camp. Melito certainly identified the Jews as the enemy, but "there is no
firm evidence that the Sardis Jews were even aware of Melito, or that a direct hostility provoked his attacks" (Kraabel 1983: 187).

(1) The Struggle for Supremacy

As we have seen, the rivalry between Christians and Jews is portrayed by modern scholars as much more than a simple competition for pagan souls and for the rights to guardianship of the Holy Writings. We saw, in the discussions of "reactive" and "strategic" anti-Judaism, the attempt to give the conflict model a social and political dimension, and the subsequent characterization of the conflict between church and synagogue as a struggle for political recognition (Typology II.1 & 2). In this struggle, church and synagogue are said to identify each other as chief foes, each constituting the main obstacle for the other—the success of one group only being attainable at the expense of the other.

Indeed the contest is seen to take on an annihilatory character, in which the very survival of the religious cults is thought to lie in the balance. This was an all-out struggle to the finish, the theory goes, in which all the privileges of Roman society were at stake. "Each religion contested the right of the other to exist at all" (Simon 1986: 135). Both claimed to bear an ultimate truth, and each supported its own claims by appeal to the same books. Both groups are thought to have recognized, then, that the fate of one was dependent on the other, and that the "spoils" of the "internecine feud" could be "nothing less than life itself" (Wilken 1967: 318). The controversies, it is believed, were seen as a "matter of life and death" (Gager 1983: 134). The stakes in this struggle are portrayed as being very high indeed. If we assume that Jews and Christians were competing for political privileges, then it seems that, in its accession to the imperial throne, the church won the ultimate prize in this contest. The conflict between church and synagogue is somehow seen, then, as paving the way for the conversion of the empire. And the struggle between church and synagogue inevitably becomes nothing less than a struggle for ultimate political supremacy.

(2) Winners and Losers

This understanding of the Jewish-Christian conflict, has major implications for the way in which the participants involved in this conflict are described. If Christians and Jews were really involved in a battle for supremacy, then we are forced to view this battle as one taking place between "winners" and "losers". The conversion of Constantine becomes the endpoint in the light of which the prior history of Jewish-Christian relations is interpreted. In as far as this conversion represents the "triumph" of the church, it comes, by extension, to be seen as a corresponding defeat for the church's rival, the synagogue. We have here a paradigm of pre-Constantinian history which pits an expanding Christian community, fighting against the odds but full of promise for the future, against an influential and established Jewish community, enjoying temporary favour with the Roman authorities, but in a gradually weakening position. Judaism after Constantine is described by Simon as the "defeated party" that "withdrew" from the conflict and faded from the scene (Simon 1986: xii).[24] "Our discussion has made clear what was at stake for each group in this struggle...Judaism was defeated in the battlefield; it did not withdraw in surrender" (Donahue 1973: 254). "Christians and Jews were competitors for power and influence in the new society of the eastern Empire, and the advantage of the Christians brought the direct decline of the Jews" (Meeks & Wilken 1978: 27). This characterization of the Jewish-Christian conflict as leading towards, and ending in, Christian "triumph" is also very clearly expressed in the concluding remarks made by Nicholas De Lange in his book on Origen. In the days when "political power was in the hands of the pagans", the church "vied with the more favoured Synagogue by polemical means to win the minds, hearts and souls of the entire world." This "great and strenuous contest" was to be "convincingly won", and the Christian faith was to "reign supreme" in a world in which "Paganism had been vanquished, and Judaism humiliated" (De Lange 1976:135).

(3) The Synagogue on the Defensive

The imposition of the winner-loser paradigm on pre-Constantinian history adds a new and very important dimension to the consensus model of Christian-Jewish interaction. Though they have the advantage of relative strength, the Jews are shown, according to this view, to be in an incredibly precarious position. Thought to have established a relatively comfortable modus vivendi with the Roman authorities at a time when the Christians lived under threat of persecution, the Jews nevertheless remain dependent for their favours on Rome. In addition, and more importantly, we are told that the Jews are the ultimate losers in the contest as it has been defined for us here. The synagogue must fight for its life in this struggle. In these circumstances, the expansion and success of Christianity inevitably comes to be viewed as a direct attack on the legitimacy of the Jews, and as a direct threat to their position in Roman society. The Jews "more than anyone else stood to lose by the spread of Christianity" (Frend 1970: 294).

(4) Suppositions About the Jewish Response to the Christian Threat

Once it is established that Judaism was the party on the defensive, it becomes all too tempting to speculate about what the perceptions and attitudes of the Jews towards the church might have been. Indeed, in this context, suppositions about the response that Christian successes are likely to have elicited among the people of the synagogue become almost unavoidable, and the sug-

---

[24] On the notion of Jewish "defeat" and the implications of this idea see concluding chapter.

gestion that the Jews were hostile towards and envious of the Christians seems plausible, even inevitable. John Gager explains the Jewish interest in disputations with the church in the following terms: The Jews feared that Christianity would "upset the delicate balance which governed relations between the Jewish communities and the local authorities." In the second and third centuries, "Christians who claimed to be the true Israel must have been seen as a direct threat to the political and social standing of Judaism" (Gager 1983: 156).

References to Jewish resentment and jealousy of the expanding church abound in the literature. Meeks' and Wilken's attempt to account for Christianity's emergence as a powerful movement in the midst of a pagan society, progresses almost immediately to a statement affirming the *inevitability* that the "Christians would complicate life for the Jews, and *threaten* the delicate balance" of their position in pagan society. Indeed the Christians would "finally" become "the synagogue's *most dangerous enemy*"!!! (my emphasis; Meeks & Wilken 1978: 2). Edward Flannery affirms that the "Synagogue resented Christianity's claims" (Flannery 1985: 30), and that it would be unrealistic to attempt "to explain away all of the Jewish hatred of Christianity" (Flannery 1985: 36). Paul Monceaux, in his study of the literary history of African Christianity, also assumes that the Jews were jealous of the rapidly expanding church, and that they sought to secure their own position by encouraging fear and suspicion of the church in the Roman populace (Monceaux 1966: 39, 294). G.N. Stanton refers to the "opposition" and "overt hostility" which the church had to face from Judaism (Stanton 1985: 377; cf. also Bratton 1969: 79; Grayzel 1946: 84).

(5) The Jews as Aggressors

It is but an easy step from the assumption that the Jews were threatened by Christian successes to the belief that the Jews would also willingly have taken steps to prevent Christian advances. Some scholars take this step with certain reservations, and we will examine the nuances in scholarly opinions shortly. For now, it is important to see how the tendency to cast the Jews in the role of aggressors is a direct extension of the conflict model. The Jews, the theory goes, were so threatened by the rise and rapid success of Christianity that in some instances they actually joined the Romans against a common enemy, and assisted in the imperial persecutions of the Christians. On the grounds that sharing the same enemy makes fast friends, it is suggested that the Jews would have been prepared even to ally themselves with the representatives of the idolatrous "nations" in their supposed determination to suppress the growing Christian movement. When we find references hinting at an association between Jews and gentiles against the Christians in the early writings of the church, the "conflict theory" interprets this association in terms of a political alliance. "Jews and pagans united in common action" (Frend 1967: 241;

cf. Monceaux 1966: 39). "The Jews, aroused by Christian claims and successes, indulged in occasional violence and slander, and participated to some
extent in the imperial persecutions of Christians" (Flannery 1985: 35).[25]

That which is known about the political and social status of the synagogue
is also appealed to in order to lend credence to the idea of a Jewish-pagan alliance. Firstly, as an influential community, the Jews are assumed to have been
in a powerful enough position to have made life difficult for the Christians.
W.H.C. Frend describes the connection between Jewish wealth, power, rivalry
and persecution as an inevitable one. He characterizes the Jews as "the
wealthy, powerful, long-established religion with a traditional place in society
using every means to drive its upstart rival from the field" (Frend 1970:293).
The Jews "had the means of making their enmity felt" (Frend 1967: 252), because "the Jews were but the Christians were not a *religio licita*" (Frend
1970:296).

Secondly, and more importantly, the notion of the Jews as a privileged
community links the synagogue to the Roman authorities in a relationship of
dependence, in which the Jews are shown to be indebted to the established
powers for the benefits they enjoy. The idea of cooperation with Rome is thus
made to seem all the more credible. For the Jews, who are portrayed as having
reason to fear the success of Christianity, and who are said to live freely and
without tensions in Roman society, assisting the Roman authorities in the persecution of the young sect becomes an act of sound strategy, a comprehensible move, in the circumstances, even a natural one. Simon certainly makes
this sort of connection between the social position of the synagogue and collaboration when he says that Jews and pagans united the empire's
"conservative forces" in an "endeavour to stem the overwhelming and disrup-
tive flood of Christianity" (Simon 1986: 114-15). Frend dates the "strange alliance" between pagans and Jews to the defeat of 135 C.E., and describes it as
the means by which "Israel saved itself from destruction". He assumes that
"pagans and Jews were threatened by the same enemy, and for the first time
for many generations united against him". "From now on, the domestic
struggle between the Old Israel and the New becomes merged in the general
conflict between Church and Empire" (Frend 1967: 194).

Review of Scholarly Opinion

Let us now turn to a review of scholarly opinion on the question of Jews as
persecutors. The belief that the Jews were involved in the persecution of
Christians is to be found in many traditional histories of the early church

---

[25] cf. Wilde 1949: 30, 130, 141-47. On persecution of Melito's community see Noakes
1975: 245; Manis 1987:399-400, both quoted above. On credibility accorded to the Smyrnaean
persecutions see page 102 under "Persecution by the Jews as Measure of the True Christian".

written in the late 19th and early 20th centuries.[26] Writing in 1934, James
Parkes referred to this view as a "commonplace". These traditional scholars
adopt the view that Jewish antagonism toward the church was
"characteristic", as a direct extension of their own theologically-determined
view of the early church as sole defender of the truth in a world where all non-
Christians were by definition hostile. Marcel Simon sees his "conflict theory"
as an advance over this traditional outlook, because he bases his supposition
about Jewish hostility on a theory of social interaction, and dresses it up to
sound like an objective observation of historical fact. My aim is to show that,
in its modern version, the notion of Jews as persecutors remains just as rooted
in Christianizing presuppositions as it was in its traditional form. All scholars
who opt for the "conflict theory" remain prisoners, in some form or other, to
faulty preconceptions about Jewish hostility towards Christianity. Of course,
there are variations in the way in which the question of Jewish aggression is
approached in the scholarly literature.

Some scholars take a maximalist view of Jewish participation in aggression
against the Christians. W.H.C. Frend falls into this category, and some of his
views have already been referred to. Frend outlines what he sees as the progressive stages in the development of Jewish antagonism towards the church.
What began as expulsion from the synagogues progressed to bitter literary
warfare. From here, "it was both natural and fatally easy to pass to outright
persecution" (Frend 1970: 296). In fact, Frend so takes the hostility and men-
ace of the Jews for granted, that they occasionally overshadow the pagan officials in his descriptions of the persecutions. In Frend's *Martyrdom and
Persecution*, the Jew is "often in the background" of persecutions, and he is
determined "to stir up trouble wherever" he can (Frend 1967: 194, cf. also
179, 239, 241, 252). Jewish "malevolence" is emphasized (178); the Jews are
assumed to have taken "an active part" in local outbreaks against the church
(215); and to have "exploited" the situation wherever they could (305).

A slightly less extreme and more nuanced view of the Jewish role in the
persecutions is defended by Marcel Simon. He makes some efforts to moderate the charges against the Jews found in the traditional histories of the
church. He tries to distance himself from "those scholars, making scarcely any
examination of the matter, who have taken it for granted that the Jews were
heavily implicated". But the logic of the "conflict theory", which pits Jew and
Christian against one another in a duel to the finish, demands that he see the
Jews as fundamentally hostile towards the church. Simon's Jews don't figure
as largely as do Frend's in the role of oppressors of the church, but this is not

---

[26] For example, Allard 1894: 395-96; Aubé 1885: 140; Cadoux 1938: 378; Gregg 1897: 57;
Lightfoot 1889: 469-70; Harnack 1908: 66, 116. Ironically Harnack, who relegates the Jews to
insignificance in his history of Christianity, still lends credence to the idea that they had a role
in Roman persecutions.

due to a more subtle understanding of Jewish attitudes. Indeed Simon rejects any attempt to raise doubts about the negative disposition of the Jews, dismissing it as a well-meaning but naive refusal to face up to an unpleasant reality. Those who "lean over backwards" to absolve the Jews, have "given way too much" to "pro-Semitism" (Simon 1986: 115-16, 120). Simon includes James Parkes in this latter category.[27] Simon is here responding to Parkes' attempt to challenge the traditional tendency among scholars of early Christianity to place moral blame on the Jews in depictions of early Jewish-Christian interaction.[28] In Simon's view, Parkes is "a little too ready to exculpate the Jews" of all responsibility in the persecutions (Simon 1986: 116).

If Simon has reason to doubt the maximalist version of Jewish participation in the persecutions, it is not because he tempers his view of Jewish hostility, but because he imposes artificial limits on Jewish actions from without. If the Jews weren't always in the front lines of battle, it is because they lacked power, or influence, or authority. "They did in fact persecute when in a position to do so" (Simon 1986: 120). The Jews are portrayed by Simon as acting against the Christians whenever they are given the opportunity to do so, the limits being set by the Romans. As long as "the Roman authorities weren't interested in exploiting Jewish hostility to the Christians", the Jews, "had to fall back on ineffectual maledictions, or else cast themselves in the role of informers" (Simon 1986: 116). Reduced to "active and spiteful" associates of the pagans in the persecutions of Christianity, lacking sufficient influence to "set the blaze going in the first place", they "did what they could to stir the fire" (121,119).

Simon is thus able to limit the damage inflicted by the Jews, making the charges seem somewhat less objectionable, without moderating his dramatic portrayal of the rivalry between the two monotheistic groups. Ultimately, then, the Jews who emerge from Simon's analysis are as guilty vis-à-vis the Christians as those represented by Frend. They commit the crime in their hearts if not in their deeds. Even where they are not directly responsible for Christian persecution, their maliciousness makes them guilty by intention.

There is a third category of scholars who take an even more measured and critical approach to the question of the Jewish role in persecutions, but who nevertheless remain tied to the idea of Jewish hostility and antagonism. They temper the charges against the Jews without dismissing them altogether. Parkes, who, as we saw, was accused of "pro-Semitism" by Simon, is one of these. Parkes challenged the traditional presumption that Jewish hatred of the church was "universal", and argued that this assumption had "no existence in historical fact". "Of a steady, deliberate, and unsleeping hostility there is no

[27] For other similar critiques of Parkes cf. Abel 1975: 150; Flannery 1985: 303, n.18.

[28] For Parkes' views see below, this section.

trace" (Parkes 1969: 150). However, even Parkes was not prepared to assume an absence of hostility between the two groups. In an effort to get away from the tendency to lay entire blame on the Jews for this hostility, he portrayed the Christians as the instigators of the conflict. If the Jews expressed antagonism towards the church, it was because they were provoked, Parkes maintained, and "no organised group could be expected to pass over in silence such perpetual libel on their history as were being produced by Gentile theologians" (Parkes 1969: 107). Parkes does not escape from the notion of Jewish-Christian conflict, then, but simply provides a justification for Jewish antagonism. Douglas Hare also argues that the Jewish "persecution was by no means as severe as frequently alleged by Christian authors". He remains convinced, however, of the hostility felt by the Jews toward the church. "It need not be doubted that intense hostility was aroused in Jewish communities by Jewish Christian evangelists" (Hare 1967b: 446; cf. also Hare 1967a). Hare traces his assumptions about this hostility directly to the "conflict theory". "On account of religious rivalry they had more cause for hostility towards Christians than the general population, and it is therefore not surprising that they should assist in the persecution of Christians" (Hare 1967b: 451).

Finally, two Jewish scholars have categorically denied the veracity of Christian charges against the Jews as aggressors. David Rokeah finds the theory that the Jews collaborated with the Roman authorities against the Christians to be completely without basis (Rokeah 1982: 49), and he characterizes the tensions between church and synagogue as no more than "empty bickering" (Rokeah 1983: 55).[29] Y. F. Baer sees the notion of Jewish collaborationism as being rooted in a theologically-biased depiction of the church as "standing singlehanded in its holy struggle against paganism and the kingdom of evil" (Baer 1961: 80). In an effort to counter this view, Baer emphasizes the forgotten part played by the Jewish community in the struggle against idolatry. The Christians were not alone to suffer at the hands of the Roman authorities, Baer argues. The Roman rulers meted out penalties to Jews as well, and these measures should not be "considered as political repression only, but had a marked religious emphasis" (Baer 1961: 81). Baer's argument that the Jews were subject to religious persecutions is controversial,[30] but his study makes an important contribution in that it exposes the theological preconceptions that underlie assumptions about the alleged common alliance of Jews and pagans against Christians. The status of the Jews in the empire was certainly more complex than many scholars of early Christianity seem to assume.

---

[29] Rokeah also challenges the notion of Jews as proselytizers so central to the "conflict" theory. See Typology I.

[30] For a critique see Rokeah 1982: 49-50.

It is unfortunate, however, that, in his efforts to defend the integrity of the Jews, Baer limits himself to proving that they suffered in equal measure to the Christians. Surely the suffering of oppression is not a necessary credential for religious integrity, and, indeed, the assumption that most needs to be challenged in the current literature is the presumed connection between Jewish privileges and moral laxity. In other words, even if it could be proved that the legal status enjoyed by the Jews entitled them to complete exemption from all oppressive measures by the Romans, and even if we believed that the Jews lived fully integrated lives in Roman society, these facts need not necessarily reveal anything at all about the patterns of Jewish-Christian-pagan interaction, let alone about Jewish attitudes to the Christians, or actions against them. Hence, though Baer's insights are useful, they do not address the root of the problem being tackled here, in that they fail to challenge the premises and assumptions of the conflict model itself. I would like now to turn to such a critique.

As I have already stated, the suppositions made by scholars about Jewish hostility towards the church, and about Jewish involvement in Christian persecutions, are groundless both from a straightforward historical point of view, and because they lack confirmation in the Christian texts themselves. First, historically this view is without foundation because it is based on assumptions about Jewish motives and aspirations that are coloured by Christianizing preconceptions. Second, the inaccuracy of the view is further confirmed by the fact that its depiction of the supposed competition between church and synagogue for Roman attentions is incompatible with Roman religious policy. Third, hermeneutically, the notion of Jews as persecutors is based in an uncritical reading of the "charges" against the Jews in the early Christian writings. This has resulted in a misinterpretation of the theologically rooted principles enunciated in the Christian writings, and in the mistaken assumption that these theological statements reflect current reality.

(1) Faulty Assumptions About Jewish Aspirations

Underlying the view that Jews were antagonistic to the Christians, and supplying the motive for this antagonism, is the belief that Jews and Christians were in competition for the same prize, that they were rivals in their active missions for pagan converts. As I have argued in Typology I, the notion of Jews as proselytizers stems from the imposition of a Christian model of development on Judaism. In my view, the notion of Jews as persecutors stems from an extension of this erroneous approach. Scholars have assumed not only that Jews and Christians shared the same aspirations, and that these aspirations brought the two groups into conflict, but that this conflict conditioned, even determined their perceptions and motives in relation to one another. The assumption seems to be that the roles played by the two parties were clearly defined

and delineated, and that the patterns of Jewish-Christian interaction and perception emerged directly from these roles. It is this unidimensional view
which has led scholars to presume that the Christian writings can give us direct access to reliable evidence about Jewish actions and motivations. When
stating his goals in the introduction to his book on Origen, Nicholas De Lange
simply assumes that, as a matter of course, his study of Origen's works will
allow him simultaneously to "shed light on the Judaism of the third century",
and to get "some idea" of how Jews "saw themselves at this time" (De Lange
1976: 13).

Broad-ranging goals of this kind are not only overly-ambitious in my view,
but are bound to produce biased results. As we have seen, even the attempt to
make judgements about Christian attitudes and motivations, as they are
revealed in the sources produced by the church itself, is a tricky business (see
"reactive" anti-Judaism, Typology II.1). Since we cannot assume that the
perceptions of Christians, whose writings we possess, confirm what we know
of their social reality, how can we possibly expect to make presumptions
about something as elusive as the motives and aspirations of Jews, on the
basis of vague references in the writings of another group?

Central to the argument about Jews as aggressors is the belief that the Jews
saw the church's theological attack against them as a direct and dangerous
threat that needed to be countered at all costs. The Jews who emerge from the
Christian texts allow their hostility towards, and battle with the church, to play
the primary defining role in their relationship with the gentile world. Not only
does the church appear to be the main preoccupation for these Jews, but this
preoccupation is said to determine their relationship with the Roman authorities. Scholars do not stop to inquire, however, whether the image of the Jews
which this hypothesis leaves us with, is a credible one. I would suggest that
the balance of forces as it is portrayed in the Christian texts reveals more
about Christian perceptions than it does about the habits of Jews. No matter
what intentions the Christian authors may have had in their negation of Judaism, it seems highly unlikely that these writings can provide us with an objective assessment of the importance accorded by the Jews to the church.[31] The
Christians naturally operated with the presumption that their movement was of
central importance not only to themselves but to the world. There is no reason
to believe that this perspective was born out in the actions and concerns of
their non-Christian contemporaries, whether Jewish or pagan.

Due to a lack of authentically Jewish testimony in the Roman Diaspora
after Philo, we cannot be certain how the people of the synagogue defined
themselves vis-à-vis gentiles, both pagan and Christian. But the Jews shared

---

[31] Such objectivity is even less likely if the writings are assumed to be polemical, and
therefore, by definition, distortive.

with the Christians a strict monotheism, and the adherence to rigorous moral standards. Like the Christians, they lived in what they saw as an idolatrous environment, into which they refused to be amalgamated. They were reproached often enough by pagan writers for their stubborn adherence to commandments that kept them apart, that divided them from the Roman world (cf. Schürer III.1.152). Even if we accept, then, that they enjoyed certain legal rights in Roman society, and that they were exempt from the requirement to sacrifice, on what basis should we assume that they would have been willing to compromise their beliefs, to take on the role of adjutants to the leaders of the idolatrous nations in a supposed struggle against the church?

The situation of any minority religious group, no matter how well-established, no matter how well integrated, involves ambiguities. Scholars seem much more willing to allow for these ambiguities in their assessment of the circumstances experienced by the church, where there is a wealth of first hand testimony, than in their evaluation of the role of the synagogue. The Christians made frequent overtures to the pagan authorities in their apologetic literature, they freely adapted Greek philosophical ideas in their theological argumentation—yet this is not seen as cause to question their religious integrity. Several early Christian writers emphasize the sense in which Christian practices are compatible with the customs generally observed in the wider environment. "Christians are not distinguished from the rest of mankind by either country, speech or customs. The fact is, they nowhere settle in cities of their own; they use no particular language; they cultivate no eccentric mode of life" (*Diognetus* 5). In his *Apology (Apologeticum)* to the rulers of the Roman empire, Tertullian states: "We live with you, we have the same food, the same clothes, the same way of life" (Tertullian, *Apology* 42.1). Justin's Jewish disputant Trypho addresses him in the following manner in the opening chapters of the *Dialogue*:

> You claim to be pious, and believe yourselves to be different from others but do not segregate yourselves from them, nor do you observe a manner of life different from the Gentiles (Justin, *Dialogue* 10).

These statements are not taken as admissions of moral laxity or compromise. We can imagine, then, that the balance between integration and separation maintained by Jewish communities in Roman society also varied to some extent. If they succeeded in securing certain privileges for themselves, it was presumably in order to be better able to practice their faith and keep their laws, and not to abandon or compromise them (cf. Kraabel 1982: 450; Trebilco 1991: 34, 57).

In addition, the notion of an all-out political rivalry is not born out historically. Judaism continued to flourish after the rise of Christianity, and even after the so-called "triumph" of the church. There is no concrete historical evidence suggesting that the advance of the church, in the period when church and synagogue lived as minority groups in a pagan empire, detracted in any way from the strength or vitality of the synagogue. Of course, some time after the Christianization of the empire, the Christian state did institute legislation restricting Jewish practice, but if this is what scholars have in mind when they speak of the threat posed to the synagogue by the church, then they are forced into the absurd position of arguing that second and third century Jews formed their political alliances, and identified their chief foes in the light of events that were to occur more than a century later.

(2) A Faulty Conception of Roman Religious Policy

Apart from the fact that the hypothesis about Jewish hostility and Christian re-crimination is based on unfounded assumptions about the motivations and atti-tudes of both Christians and Jews, it also lacks credibility in the suggestions it makes about Roman religious policy. As we have seen, the credibility of the idea of Jewish hostility rests not only on the assumption that the Jews were ri-vals of the Christians as active proselytizers, but on the further belief that church and synagogue vied for political supremacy in the empire. Scholars seem to take as given that Christian claims involved an implicit threat to the political position of the Jews, that the church threatened somehow to displace the synagogue, and to rob it of its privileges. "Imperial support of Christianity would have negatively affected the Jews' privileged position with the State" (Manis 1987: 399). Certainly, for the early Christians, there could only be one genuine Israel, and the supersessionary argument provided a justification for the church's claim to sole inheritance of the ancestral traditions of the Jews, and to their status as God's chosen people. It is also true that these claims in-volved a negation of the continued legitimacy of Judaism. Yet even if we as-sume, for the sake of argument, that the synagogue responded to these affirmations, and that the two groups denied legitimacy to one another in their conflicting claims to a common religious inheritance, it makes little sense to propose that a religious conflict of this sort would have extended into the po-litical realm. Firstly, it seems highly unlikely that either the Christians or the Jews would have looked to the Roman authorities to pronounce judgement on questions of this nature. Secondly, there is no reason to believe that the Ro-man authorities would have been influenced, in the formulation of their relig-ious policy, by how convincingly the Christians denigrated the Jews.

One of the more striking features of Roman religious policy was its ability to show a measure of tolerance to a wide variety of religious groups. "They were willing at almost all stages of their history to accept foreign cults and practices" (North 1979: 86). The Roman authorities proved capable of toler-ance towards foreign religions in so far as these posed no threat to the pros-perity and cohesion of the empire. It was exclusivism that the Romans objected to. The official recognition of two religious groups, both of whom claimed inheritance of the same religious tradition, need not have posed a problem for them. Celsus characterized the dispute between Jews and Christians as "a fight about the shadow of an ass" (*Against Celsus (Contra Celsum)* III.1). His assessment may well have reflected a general indifference to the outcome of the polemic between church and synagogue.

(3) Hermeneutical Critique

For confirmation of the notion that Jews assisted in the persecution of the church, scholars turn to the "charges" against the Jews found in the writings of the early church. Based on a prior judgement about the inevitability of Jewish hostility and aggression, the "conflict" model of Jewish-Christian relations lends credence indiscriminately to all passages which appear to refer to the "opposition" of the Jews in some form or other. The hermeneutical approach adopted by these scholars is overly literal and uncritical, and fails to understand the real meaning and intention of these Christian charges against Judaism. I will undertake a critique of this approach, and suggest an alternative reading of the references to Jewish opposition and hostility. There are two main features of the writings that cast doubt on the historicity of the "charges" against the Jews: the paucity of references and their "retrospective" character. Let us consider each in turn.[32]

The Paucity of References.

There are two sorts of evidence referring to Jewish hostility. There is the testimony of the ecclesiastical writers, and there are the accounts in the acts of the Christian martyrs. If Jewish persecution of the Christians had indeed been a common occurrence, one would expect this fact to be reflected, not just in the general statements of Christian authors, but also in the stories of Christian persecution, which recount in some detail the circumstances surrounding the martyrdom of celebrated members of the church. Yet, as Parkes points out, "from the second century onwards, there is almost complete silence as to any Jewish responsibility for, and even interest in, the fate of the heroes of the church" (Parkes 1969: 132, 150). Simon also notes the fact that between Hadrian and Constantine, the period of "the great flowering of this kind of hagiographical literature, the evidence for Jewish involvement becomes very

---

[32] Aside from the paucity of references, and their "retrospective" character, to be considered below, some scholars have also questioned the accuracy of the Christian charges against Jews on the grounds that polemical tracts cannot be relied upon for information about the actions and motivations of an antagonistic group (Millar 1966: 233; Parkes 1969: 148; Baer 1961: 80, 103; Simon 1986: 116). Since I do not accept the premises of the "conflict theory", "polemical" is not, in my view, the best characterization of the Christian references to Judaism. Christian references to Jewish hostility are unhistorical not because they distort the truth but because they are concerned with truth on a different plane of reality (see Typology IV.1).

thin" (Simon 1986: 120-21; cf. also Schreckenberg 1982: 269; Millar 1966: 233).[33] Though many of the *acta martyrum* are recognized as fabricated stories, it is nevertheless telling that the Christians did not choose to exploit what would have been a golden opportunity to lay blame on the Jews for inflicting suffering on the church's martyrs.

David Rokeah points to another area where the paucity of corroborative evidence raises doubts about the applicability of Christian references to Jewish hostility. In *Against Celsus*, Origen refers to a "malicious rumour" to the effect that Christians practice ritual murder and incest, and he seems to trace this rumour back to libels spread by the Jews in earlier times (*Against Celsus* VI.27). This passage is generally quoted as evidence that the Jews were responsible for slander against the Christians (Simon 1986: 116; De Lange 1976: 76). Yet as Rokeah points out, it is odd that the calumnies referred to here are typically pagan accusations. Origen refers to the same charges only a few paragraphs later, but this time makes no allusion to the Jews whatsoever (*Against Celsus* VI.40). Indeed, though we may find allusions among many other Christian authors defending the church against the very same accusations, none of them associate these slanderous charges with the Jews in any way (Aristides 17; Tatian 25; Justin, *First Apology* 26; Theophilus *To Autolycus* III.4; Tertullian, *Apology* IV.11). If indeed the Jews had been responsible for spreading these rumours, one would expect that apologists "who busily defended the Christians against such widespread popular accusations, would not have refrained from emphasizing their Jewish origin" (Rokeah 1982: 67 n. 74). In fact, as De Lange points out, Origen himself makes remarkably few references to Jewish hostility and persecution, "considering the many opportunities he had of mentioning them" (De Lange 1976: 85).

The "Retrospective" Character of the References.

Apart from the argument from silence, the contemporaneity of the allusions to Jewish hostility in the early Christian texts must also be put into question. As Parkes notes, charges against the Jews are often justified by "relating events of a previous millennium…bearing no relation to Jewish conduct at the time" of the author (Parkes 1969: 148). In their accusations against the Jews, the Christians "are forced to seek witnesses from the sacred writings and from the distant past alone" affirms Baer (Baer 1961: 102). De Lange also expresses doubts as to whether the few references to Jews as oppressors of the church in Origen's writings refer to "events occurring in Origen's own lifetime" (De Lange 1976: 85). Efroymson too points out that Tertullian's writings on Judaism are backward looking. By far most of the church father's

---

[33] See below on the acts of *Polycarp* and *Pionius*.

accusations against the Jews, "roughly ninety per cent", refer to biblical Jews, to the "Israelites of the Old Testament, to Jewish contemporaries of Jesus, or to contemporaries of Paul and the apostles. The few that remain are either general references to Jewish antagonism toward Christianity or to the inadequacy of the Jewish cult, or only slightly less general allusions to biblical disagreements" (Efroymson 1976: 62).

Indeed the charges against the Jews made by the ecclesiastical writers refer either to biblical crimes denounced by the prophets and ascribed by the church fathers to the Jews, or to the Jewish rejection of Jesus and of his apostles. Where they make allusions to Jewish acts of aggression against the church, it is to the measures taken against the very early church (as evidenced in *Acts of the Apostles* 13.50; 17.5ff; 28.13).[34] Justin, for example, accuses the Jews in chapter 17 of his *Dialogue* of sending out emissaries who spread lies about the Christians. He characterizes the Jews as "authors of the wicked prejudice against the Just One", and several scholars have presumed that this passage provides evidence that the Jews conducted a propaganda campaign, drawing upon the church "suspicion and then active repression" (Simon 1986: 117). Yet as Hare points out, these scholars seem to have overlooked the fact that Justin's accusation is clearly directed at past actions which no longer hold true in the present in a literal sense. He holds the Jews responsible for the crucifixion of the Messiah, and then continues:

> You not only did not repent of the wickedness which you had committed, but *at that time* (*tote*) you selected and sent out from Jerusalem chosen men through all the land to tell that the godless heresy of the Christians had sprung up, and to publish those things which all they who knew us did not speak against us. So that you are the cause not only of your own unrighteousness, but in fact of that of all other men" (*Dialogue* 17, my emphasis).

The Jews Justin had in mind here were the emissaries dispatched soon after the death and resurrection of Jesus, as is made clear by his use of the word *tote* (Hare 1967b: 447). If these crimes appear from Justin's description to have a present relevance, I would suggest that this is because of the seriousness of their nature, and because of the theological significance attached to them.[35] In the previous chapter Justin states categorically that Jewish aggres-

---

[34] Such incidents, if indeed they took place, cannot properly be called acts of persecution. They would more accurately be viewed as disciplinary measures imposed by the synagogue authorities at a time when the division between church and synagogue was as yet unclear.

[35] Justin makes frequent allusions to Jewish curses against the Christians (*Dialogue*. 9.1; 16.44; 26.4; 32.5; 47.5; 93.4; 95.4; 97; 108.3; 117.3; 123.6; 133.6). Modern scholars have commonly taken Justin's complaints to refer to the twelfth benediction of the *Tefillah*, the benediction against the heretics, *Birkath ha-Minim*. There is some controversy over who this benediction referred to, and the discussion is complicated by the existence of many variants (Finkelstein 1925-26: 156-7). I agree with the view that the benediction was aimed at Jewish sectarians, and, in as far as it touched on Christians at all, castigated Jewish-Christians as here-

sion against the church belongs to a past time. Though he words his affirmation provocatively, there is no mistaking its practical implications. Addressing himself to Trypho, Justin says: "You cannot assault us now, but as often as you could you did" (*Dialogue* 16).

The "retrospective" character of the Christian charges against the Jews calls into question the usefulness of these passages in the task of historical reconstruction. Parkes, for instance, warns that "to take these texts out of their context and use them to justify generalisations in the modern sense, is to ignore the actual evidence...and to produce a distorted picture" (Parkes 1969: 149). In other words, if the passages really are inspired by biblical themes, or refer to events from apostolic times, then they cannot be expected to shed light for us on the attitudes of Jews and Christians living at the time the writings were composed.

Most conflict theorists naturally refuse to accept this negative assessment of the contemporaneity of the Jewish passages. They argue that if the Christian anti-Jewish passages were purely backward-looking, fossilized caricatures with no contemporary relevance to the Christian communities who produced these writings, then both the persistence and vehemence of the anti-Jewish tradition would be very difficult to account for. It is certainly true that the early Christian authors did not write about the Jews in an indifferent manner, as though they were alluding to a matter of little concern to them. On the contrary, anti-Judaism is revealed in the writings of the church as an issue of vital and present importance, and the conflict theorists make much of this fact. For the conflict theorists, the vivid and intense tone of the Jewish references provides a sure indication that they are based on "deep felt experience at the hands of the Jews" (Frend 1970: 294). These scholars thus dismiss the retrospective character of the passages as a question of form, style and language, which, they claim, has little to do with the actual objections of the Christians vis-à-vis Judaism.

The challenge, and it is one the conflict theorists fail to live up to, is to take account of the contemporary quality of the anti-Jewish references, without thereby denying their retrospective character. The allusions to Jewish aggression against the church in the early Christian texts are not pure literary reminiscences, but neither are they responses to actual contact with living Jews. They are best interpreted, rather, as statements of theological principle that draw on the past to describe the Christian vision of the present. This explains both the heavy reliance of the church writings on biblical material and on bib-

---

tics. It is thus not directly relevant to our discussion (Kimelman 1981: 226-244; Flusser 1983-4: 36-38; Katz 1984: 43-76; Thornton 1987: 429-30). See also Simon 1986: 183-186, 406-409; Horbury 1982: 19-61.

lical themes, without detracting from their immediate relevancy to the readers for whom they were composed.

As will be explored in greater depth in the discussion of "theological" anti-Judaism (Typology IV.1), the fathers of the church were preoccupied in their exegetical endeavors with defining the role of the church in salvation history. The church fathers were concerned, in other words with the church's self-conception. In making the charges against the Jews, the early authors of the church drew upon Christian tradition, and told the story of Christian experience, though not in the way that has often been assumed. It is my belief that the Jewish oppressors portrayed in the church's literature represent an intellectual and not a literal reality. When the fathers spoke of Jewish hostility toward the church, they were neither simply referring to events of the past, nor alluding to concrete circumstances in the present, but to a theological reality whose truth transcended time. This aspect of the texts makes the "charges" against the Jews completely unusable as historical evidence for Jewish attitudes to Christianity. I propose to demonstrate this by examining a passage that provides an interesting test case for the historicity of the references to Jewish aggression in the early Christian texts.

Tertullian's famous "Synagogas Judaeorum fontes persecutionum" in *Antidote to the Scorpion's Bite (Scorpiace)* 10 is perhaps the most well-known and widely quoted charge against the Jews in the early Christian writings. This short phrase is one of the key references quoted in support of the belief that the Jews of the empire played a role in the Roman persecution of the Christians. The definitive and all encompassing nature of Tertullian's pronouncement, distinguishing it from some of the more cryptic, vague or limited allusions to supposed Jewish antagonism, has contributed to what is thought to be its credibility. Tertullian would not have spoken with such force and in such a straightforward manner, it is argued, if he had not been referring to events of present significance, if he had not been identifying the group who his Christian contemporaries in Carthage saw as the main source of their woes.

Yet this passage, like most of the references to Jewish hostility, relates not to the present but to the Christian past. The sentence as a whole reads as follows: "Synagogues of the Jews, founts of persecution—before which the apostles endured the scourge". Tertullian is not complaining, in other words, about Jewish violence against the Christians of his day, but about the disciplinary measures taken against the apostles in the early years of the church. The fact that Tertullian's charge against the Jews clearly refers primarily to apostolic times has indeed led some scholars to question the contemporary relevance of Tertullian's allegations.[36] On the other hand, for scholars convinced of Jewish antagonism toward the Christians, the "fontes persecutionem" passage provides corroborative evidence for their theory, and is too useful to be dismissed lightly. Frend, for instance, one of the more noted defenders of the contemporaneity of the charges against the Jews, will not be deterred by the "retrospective" character of Tertullian's passage. He protests that Tertullian was not an "antiquary", a mere preserver of relics, but should be seen rather as a "journalist", who made mention of the suffering endured by the apostles for the sake of emphasis (Frend 1970: 295). That Tertullian considered his words to have present relevance emerges from the very tone of his argument. But to describe him as a reporter, a mere recounter of current events is to misunderstand both the nature of Tertullian's discourse and his purpose in characterizing the Jews as the source of the persecution of the church. I would suggest that if Tertullian's statement about the Jews is set in its proper context, then the meaning of his statement emerges quite clearly, a meaning which makes sense both of his reference to the past and of his contemporary perspective.

Antidote to the Scorpion's Bite, or *Scorpiace*, was written in the early 200s as a tract in praise of martyrdom against the Gnostics (here likened to scorpions) who attacked the spiritual value of the "confession of faith" before the world. Tertullian clearly feared that the spread of these kinds of ideas would weaken or undermine the resolution of Christians in the face of persecution. Tertullian was concerned that if the public proclamation of the faith even in the face of hostility was not seen as essential to salvation, then the steadfastness and courage of the martyrs would lose its glory, and became meaningless, foolhardy exhibitionism.

Chapter 10 of Tertullian's booklet, sets out to prove that the "supposition" of those who think that "not within this environment of earth, nor during this period of existence, nor before men possessing this nature shared by us all, has confession been appointed to be made" is "at variance with the whole order of things of which we have experience". Tertullian seeks to discredit the Gnostic idea that salvation depended on the nature of the soul once it freed itself of the body rather than on the moral quality of a man's present life. If the true test is to be passed in heaven and not on earth, argues our writer with a certain note of sarcasm, then logic demands that the circumstances which provide the occasion for confession or denial be present in heaven also. He then asks rhetorically of the "presumptuous heretic" how he can reconcile

---

[36] See Millar 1966:234; Barnes 1969: 132; Barnes 1971: 175; Hare 1967b: 455. For a middle position on this question see Efroymson 1976: 66 n.7, who accepts the retrospective character of the passage, but qualifies it by saying that Tertullian was "at least open to the possibility of a Jewish hand in current or recent persecution". Interestingly, though Simon accepts the general spirit of the passage, he claims it overestimates Jewish influence (Simon 1986: 119).

transporting the apparatus of persecution to a world where "Christ rules at the right hand of the Father"?

In order to highlight what he sees as the absurdity of the Gnostic position, Tertullian proceeds to characterize the "whole series of means" that have been "proper to the intimidation of Christians", which the Gnostic, should he wish to be consistent, would be forced to produce in the next life. First he mentions the synagogues, where the apostles were scourged. Next he refers to the cries against the "third race" heard when heathen crowds come together at assemblies. In these two short phrases Tertullian attempts to capture in archetypal form the "means of intimidation" experienced by the church in its short existence. The Jewish rejection of Christianity is characterized by the chastisement or disciplining, presumably as heretics, of Christianity's first emissaries. In other words, the synagogues are described as "founts of persecution" not because they are at the source of intimidation of Christians in Tertullian's day but because they were the first to deny the Name by disowning the Lord and casting out His followers. Pagan intolerance is then summed up in the cries that ostracize the "third race" at group celebrations designed to promote social cohesion. "How long shall we suffer them?"

In neither case, I would argue, is Tertullian attempting to describe literally or relate directly events of his time. He is merely proceeding, in a systematic fashion, to explore the logical implications of his opponent's position the better to refute it, and he draws on all aspects of his experience as a Christian in formulating his rebuttal. Tertullian's argument is not with the Jews, but with the Gnostic heretics who downplayed the importance of the confession of faith. His reference to the Jews is not intended to reflect Christian experience in Carthage in a literal sense, but nor should it be dismissed as nothing more than a distortion of the truth. It testifies to the sense in which a theological role was ascribed to Jews and Judaism in attempts by leaders of the church to define Christian identity and to bolster the courage of early Christian believers. He refers in a paradigmatic way to the opposition experienced by the church, but his main preoccupation is with a question of internal importance. His aim is to instil in his fellow Christians a sense of what is required of them in the face of opposition. He is much more concerned with the Christian response to persecution than he is with the persecutors who provoked the occasion for this response.

Internal Orientation of the Christian Writings

Because the church was an actively missionary movement, it has often been taken for granted that the early Christians were an outwardly directed group, concerned with the formulation of apologetic and polemical arguments against those who stood in the way of Christian expansion. Yet, it seems that in the writings of the church, internal preoccupations loom much larger than the identity of the movement's enemies. In the texts that have come down to us, many lines are devoted to the preservation and promotion of the unity and integrity of the growing community, and to guarding against the internal problems created for the orthodox church by the spread of various heretical views. In this respect, Tertullian's passage is not unusual in its focus on the *internal* moral crisis generated by the threat posed by persecution, rather than on the actual *source* of oppression. As we shall see, many of the passages alluding to Jewish antagonism are really exhortations to martyrdom or texts dealing with the question of lapsed Christians. The writings of the early church are "self-referential". That is to say that their primary reference point is the "self", and references to the "other" all relate back to this self. The outside world, external forces and other communities are introduced into the exegetical dissertations of the fathers only to the extent that they impinge in one way or other on the community, and it is the *way* that they touch the community that is of interest, that is of importance. The church fathers may have had very definite opinions about the Jews down the road, but it will become clear that these are not revealed in their writings.

The Theological Roles Ascribed to Hostile Jews

Tertullian's passage is characteristic in its "retrospectivity" but it is also illustrative of the general character of Christian charges against the Jews in its typification of the role of the Jews as persecutors. The accusations against Jewish aggression in the Christian writings after 150 C.E. typecast the Jews in roles that conform to certain recurring patterns. Two important theological themes, both of which are found in embryonic form in Tertullian's *Scorpiace* passage, can be distinguised here.

As has already been mentioned, Tertullian's reference to the scourge of the apostles testifies to the special role of the Jews as the first persecutors of the church. But, in his attempt to typify the sources of oppression, Tertullian also makes reference to the intolerance of the heathen crowds. If he considered these two forms of opposition to the church side by side, this is because together they conveyed the sense in which antagonism against the Christian movement was believed to be both continuous and widespread. In some passages, then, it is the primary responsibility of the Jews for Christian suffering that is emphasized. In other instances, however, the emphasis is on the universal and perpetual nature of opposition to Christianity in a non-Christian world (to be considered at a later stage in this chapter). I will examine some of the passages most often thought by scholars to provide proof of Jewish aggression against the Christians, and show that these passages reveal the theological roles ascribed to Jews as aggressors by the Christian authors, rather than the motivations of Jews in their interaction with the church.

The Jews as First Persecutors

Even in a gentile church that had long since broken with Jewish practices, the Jews and Jewish tradition formed a part of the church's global "experience", perhaps in a more deeply felt and fundamental way than could be said of day-to-day experiences. In the attempt by church thinkers to make sense of God's unfolding plans, the Jews naturally had an important role to play, and this was a role full of paradox. They were both the first chosen people of God, and the first guardians of the Holy Scriptures, but also the first to deny Christ and the truth of Christianity. They were the people to whom the Lord first came, but also the people who first rejected Him. The stories of what came to be known as their betrayal of Christ and of the actions that they took against the first disciples form an essential part of Christian teaching.

The attribution of a hostile role to the Jews forms part of a theological tradition within the church which sought to make sense of a paradox, to re-solve the contradictions inherent in the claim that Jesus was the Messiah long promised to a people who had rejected Him. This was an important theme at least partly because it was intrinsically tied to the issue of rightful election. The notion of Jewish guilt, of Jewish sinfulness, envy and hostility were fundamental to the supersessionary argument of the church.[37] If the church had inherited the right to take the place of the Jews as the true Israel, it was in virtue of its positive response to Christ, a response which was contrasted with the rejection of Christ by the Jews. The denial and betrayal of Christ by the Jews was portrayed in the Christian writings as the culmination of a long history of sin. It was the ultimate crime which ensured that the Old Israel permanently forfeited its privileged status, and ceded its place to the community of Christ (eg. Origen, *Against Celsus* 8.22; Lactantius, *Divine Institutes (Divinae institutiones)* 21). In the context of this argument, the continued hostility of the Jews toward the church made sense theologically, as shall be illustrated below.

In other words, then, even for those Christians who had little or nothing to do with living Jews, Jewish rejection was very much a part of the experience of faith. The fact that actual instances of Jewish aggression belonged to the history of the church's infancy did not detract from their relevance. When the fathers drew on biblical tradition in their deliberations, they affirmed their belief in the timeless significance of the revelations recorded in the Holy Books,

---

[37] See Typology IV.1, for more detail.

revelations which were thought to play a definitive role in the interpretation of the present.

Though several scholars have made allusion to this theological dimension of the early Christian references to Jewish hostility, unfortunately, not enough weight or significance has been attached to this aspect of the texts when it comes to the task of historical reconstruction. Parkes, for instance, acknowledges that the "statement of Jewish hostility in general terms is based on theological exegesis and not on historical memory", but he feels unable to dismiss Christian references to Jewish hostility entirely (Parkes 1969: 148). Gager also recognizes that the "theme of Jewish rejection of the Christian message is itself part and parcel of the ideology of Christian anti-Judaism", and though he calls for "restraint" in the emphasis placed on this phenomenon, the notion of Jewish antagonism continues to play an important role in his interpretation of Jewish-Christian interaction (Gager 1983: 26). Douglas Hare makes an even more sweeping statement: "it seems probable that from the time of Justin, if not from the time of Acts, the proposition that Jewish hostility was primarily responsible for the church's sufferings was a *theological convention* requiring little or no evidence in its support". Like Gager, however, Hare sees this as cause for "great caution" in the use of the data from Justin, Origen and Tertullian, but he remains unwilling to "entirely disregard" the possibility "that Jews did in fact have a role in Gentile persecution need not be denied" (Hare 1967b: 456).

I spoke above of the sense in which the notion of Jews as first persecutors was built into the theological argumentation of the church. It made sense theologically. Let us now turn to some examples that illustrate this. The conflict model presupposes that the Jews were threatened and irritated by the success of the church. It is my belief that passages from the early Christian writings which seem to suggest this are reflective, rather, of the presuppositions of the Christian theological argument. Let us examine three theological motifs:

(1) The Envy of Those Who Have Been Superseded

The claim that the Jews were jealous of the Christians is a common theme in the Christian writings. That this notion was theologically derived rather than based in observation is made evident by the fact that it invariably accompanies the church's supersessionary argument. Perhaps inevitably, the claim that the church had displaced the Jews led to the expectation that the people of the synagogue would respond with envy toward those who had been designated by God in their stead. But this jealousy and the hostility that was said to stem from it only make sense if one accepts the theological affirmations of the church.

Origen illustrates this connection between supersession, jealousy and hostility by drawing on a classical passage from the Scriptures. Quoting Deuteronomy 32.21, "I will stir them to jealousy with those who are not a people; I will provoke them with a foolish nation", he claims that this prophecy refers to the Jewish reaction to God's disinheritance of them. Jewish jealousy and hatred of the church is then described by Origen as being at the root of what he sees as the failure of the Jews to live up to their moral obligations. Though the Jews do not rage against the idolatrous and blaspheming pagans, claims Origen, they are "moved in insatiable hatred against the Christians, who have abandoned idols and turned to God" (Origen, *Homilies on the Psalms (Homiliae in Psalmos* xxxvii (xxxvi)). The Christocentrism of these lines rings out loud and clear. Jewish jealousy forms an integral part of Origen's theological perspective, and only holds true for those who accept and ascribe to the logic of the supersessionary argument.

Origen makes a very similar point in his *Commentary on Romans (Commentarii in Romanos)* 11.28. He interprets Paul's characterization of the people of Israel as "according to the Gospel, enemies because of you", directly in terms of the theologically rooted notion of Jewish envy: "When he (Paul) says 'because of you' he means the people whose salvation they envy, prohibiting the apostles from speaking to the Gentiles, and persecuting those who announce Christ" (*Commentary on Romans* VIII.12 (13)). Irenaeus also makes a reference to the "plots and persecutions" suffered by the church "from the Jews", but once again, it is in the context of the supersessionary argument, and the reaction that this is assumed to have provoked in the disinherited party. Using the imagery of Isaac's two sons, Irenaeus claims that just as Jacob received the rights of the first-born over his older brother, so too, "the later people has snatched away the blessings of the former from the Father". The reference to persecution that follows is a mere extension of the transfer of blessings, a continuation of the parallel between the two brothers and the two religious groups. "For which cause his brother suffered the plots and persecutions of a brother, just as the Church suffers this self-same from the Jews." (Irenaeus, *Against Heresies (Adversus haereses)* IV.xxi.3; cf. also Origen, *Homilies on Genesis (Homiliae in Genesim)* 13.3; Tertullian, *Apology* 7).

In each of these passages, the notion of Jews as persecutors is ascribed directly to God's supposed preference for the church over the synagogue. The theological foundation of these claims is further confirmed by the non-specific nature of the references to "plots", "persecutions" and "hatred". There is no reason to believe that the fathers are referring to actual incidents in their own day. Their charges against the Jews are either based in the general expectation that the disinherited brother would turn on the favoured son, or in the stories,

so central to Christian teaching, of the Jewish rejection of Christ and of his
first followers.

(2) Persecution by the Jews as Measure of the True Christian

As we have seen, the notion that Christ and the first Christians suffered at the
hands of the Jews became a central theme in Christian teaching, and formed
part of the no doubt often retold story of Christian beginnings. To the extent
that later Christian martyrs saw themselves as following in the way of Christ,
and as descendants of the first disciples, they laid claim to this early Christian
tradition, and aspired to be worthy of it in all respects. It is in this light that the
Martyrdom of Polycarp (Martyrium Polycarpi) should be interpreted. It is one
of the few *acta martyrum* from the period under study here that makes mention of Jewish involvement in the persecution of the Christians (cf. Schreckenberg 1982: 268-9). There are several reasons to doubt the historicity of the
references to the Jews in this text, but the most important is that they can be
explained as forming part of a story that clearly aims to glorify the tradition of
the "*imitatio Christi*". The author of the *martyrium* makes plain his purpose in
the opening passage of his tale:

> We are writing to you, dear brothers, the story of the martyrs and of the blessed
> Polycarp.... For practically everything that had gone before took place that the
> Lord might show us from heaven a witness in accordance with the Gospel. Just as
> the Lord did, he too waited, that he might be delivered up, that we might become
> his imitators, *not thinking of ourselves alone*, but of our neighbours as well.[38]
> For it is a mark of true and solid love to desire not only one's own salvation but
> also that of all the brothers (*Polycarp* 1).

The aim is to show how willingly Polycarp "delivered himself up" "in accordance with the Gospel", so that the readers of the act might be inspired by his
example to become "his imitators". "As the gospels aim to show that in the
sufferings of Christ the scriptures were fulfilled, so the *Martyrium Polycarpi*
makes the sufferings of Polycarp conform to the divine pattern afforded by
Christ" (Simon 1986: 122). The parallels are indeed striking, and it is possible
to trace the influence of the gospel accounts throughout the narrative of Polycarp's "passion". The officer who supervised the arrest, like the Lord's judge,
was called Herod. "Destiny had given him the same name, that Polycarp
might fulfil the lot that was appointed to him, becoming a sharer with Christ"
(*Polycarp* 6). Like Christ, Polycarp was also betrayed by one "of his own
household", so that "those who betrayed him might receive the punishment of
Judas" (*Polycarp* 6).

Polycarp, like Jesus had a premonition of his fate on the eve of his arrest,
and there are also striking similarities in the description of the arrest itself. The

---

[38] *Philadelphians* 2.4

author of the *martyrium* tells us that "the police and cavalry set out on Friday at the dinner hour with the usual arms as though against a brigand" (*Polycarp* 7). Jesus addressed his captors thus: "Have you come out as though against a brigand, with swords and clubs to capture me?" (*Matthew* 26.55). Polycarp is then led into the city "on a donkey" (*Polycarp* 8). As in the gospel accounts, the Roman official is portrayed as anxious to secure Polycarp's release, and it is the crowd that forces the issue, and shouts for his demise (*Polycarp* 12). Polycarp, like Christ before him, is pierced in his side (*Polycarp* 16), and the parallelism even continues after his death. The Jews attempt to convince the governor to refuse permission to the Christians to take the body, just as the Jerusalem authorities went before Pilate to try and prevent the followers of Christ from getting hold of his body (*Polycarp* 17).[39]

The historicity of the references to the Jews in this *martyrium* must be viewed with great scepticism. The influence of the gospel accounts is so all-pervasive that it seems highly probable that Jews were included in this account to make the parallels with Christ's death all the more complete. But there is also another reason to question the notion of Jewish persecutors in Polycarp's time. The words and actions ascribed to the Jews here involve them in behaviour that would have gone directly against their beliefs and their laws.

The Jews are numbered among the "mob" who cry out against Polycarp and call him "the destroyer of our gods—the one that teaches the multitude not to sacrifice or do reverence!" (*Polycarp* 12). If we are to accept this account as accurate, then we have to believe that the Jews of Smyrna spoke of their God in the plural, and viewed the sacrifice to the "idols" in a positive light. Jews are also mentioned as providing assistance to the "mob" who "swiftly collected logs and brushwood" to stoke the fire that was to consume Polycarp (*Polycarp* 13). Once again, if we are to accept this rendition of events, then we must believe that the Smyrnaean Jews willingly contravened their own Sabbath laws to participate in a pagan ritual. Doubting the plausibility of this, I. Abrahams concludes that "if any so called "Jews" acted in the manner described in the *Martyrdom of Polycarp*, they were altogether alien in mind and conduct from any actually known class to whom the name "Jews" might be accurately applied" (Abrahams 1924: 67-69).

In my view the Jewish participants refer neither to full-fledged Jews, nor to "Jewish followers of the baser sort" as Parkes suggests (Parkes 1969: 137). These references are clearly interpolations that form part of the attempt by the writer to bring out the resemblances between Polycarp's martyrdom and the passion of Christ. That Polycarp was martyred "in accordance with the Gospel" was what made him worthy of being imitated in his own right. His story

---

[39] On detailed parallels with the gospels see von Campenhausen 1957.

was intended to encourage other Christians to remain steadfast in their confession of faith, even in the face of persecution. If Polycarp's martyrdom inspired his Christian brethren, it is in part because he is thought to have faithfully followed in the way of Christ, even to the extent of suffering at the hands of the Jews.[40]

We have further evidence that persecution at the hands of the Jews was somehow thought to make the measure of the true Christian in a passing reference to Jewish persecutions made by Eusebius. The church historian impugns the legitimacy of the Montanists,[41] "not one of whom was persecuted by the Jews, crucified for the name, or scourged in the synagogues" (*History of the Church* V.xvi.12). This passage is usually thought (even by Parkes 1969:126) to be an unintentional reference to Jewish persecutions, all the more convincing because it is made in passing. Yet this literal interpretation of Eusebius' words is problematic, because a few verses later (22), the church historian makes explicit reference to Montanist martyrs, thus seemingly contradicting his earlier claim that they had escaped persecution. In addition, Daniélou tells us that Montanism was known as the "party of Martyrs" (Daniélou 1964: 137), making it even more puzzling that Eusebius should challenge them on this point. I would suggest that we can only make sense of Eusebius' reference to the Jewish persecutions if we search for an alternative meaning for it.

Eusebius' statement should be seen, I would argue, not as a reference to the actions of contemporary Jews, but as an allusion to the first persecutions suffered by the church. The church historian's language seems to corroborate this. He alludes to "crucifixion" and "scourging", words commonly associated with the passion of the Lord and the disciplining of the first apostles. When Eusebius charges the Montanists with not having suffered at the hands of the Jews, he is no doubt seeking to deny them any part in the story of Christian beginnings, and therefore any claim to the tradition established by Christ and his first disciples. You call us "killers of prophets", says Eusebius (clearly responding to a biblically derived accusation levelled by the Montanists against the Catholics), but you cannot claim as ancestors, the first martyrs for the name. You have no right to the inheritance earned for the church by Christ and His apostles through their steadfast endurance in the face of "Jewish" denial. The measure of a true Christian is one who can claim to trace his lineage back to the earliest tradition, and it is this claim that Eusebius is denying to the Montanist sect.

---

[40] Unfortunately, many scholars either ignore or gloss over the gospel parallels, and lend credence to the Jewish references. See Lightfoot 1889: 468-70; Cadoux 1938; 365; Frend 1967: 195; Trebilco 1991: 29, 32, 35. For slightly more nuanced views see Simon 1986: 121-3; Parkes 1969: 137.

[41] An apocalyptic sect within the church. Cf. Typology IV.3.2.

(3) Jewish Opposition as Foil for Christian Faithfulness

We turn now to an examination of the *Martyrdom of Pionius (Martyrium Pionii)*, a text commonly considered to provide evidence of Jewish participation in the Decian persecution (250 C.E.).[42] More specifically, this text is said to testify to Jewish participation in the public victimization of Christians detained by the Roman authorities. Not only are the Jews said to be visible in the crowd that assembled to watch and gloat over the spectacle of Pionius' arrest and trial, but they stand out for their mockery and jeering laughter (*Pionius* 4). Unlike the story of Polycarp which is dubious on account of its many gospel parallels; as distinct from the vague, backward-looking references in the exegetical and doctrinal writings of the church; and over against the fanciful accounts of the fictional martyria, the *Martyrdom of Pionius* is generally thought to refer unambiguously and directly to specific actions by the Jews of third century Smyrna. As such, the act has universally been accorded a high degree of authenticity by modern scholars.

I propose to show that the criteria generally used to determine the historicity of this text are inadequate when it comes to determining the accuracy of the allusions to Jewish behaviour. This is made clear by a close and careful reading of the Jewish material in the context in which it appears in the *martyrium* proper. The Jews who are referred to in the account of Pionius' heroic martyrdom are not the Symyrnaean Jews who lived in Pionius' time, but a symbolic creation that forms part of an attempt to address the problem created by the "lapsi" phenomenon within the church.

One of the more recent and more ardent defenders of the *martyrium*'s historicity is Robin Lane Fox in his *Pagans and Christians*. The description of Pionius' martyrdom should be taken seriously as a historical document, he argues, because of the plausibility of its description of events as they unfold. The arrest and preliminary interview by the temple verger, the description of the crowds, the trial before the proconsul, and the roles played by other minor officials are all credible accounts of events that might have taken place in Smyrna under the Decian persecution, Lane Fox argues. "The details of Pionius's trial light up the place of Christians and martyrs in a great third-century city" (Lane Fox 1986: 461; cf. Den Boeft & Bremmer 1985; Trebilco 1991: 30-31; Lightfoot 1889; 722). The wealth and vividness of the topographical details in the Greek manuscript have also strengthened the assumption of genuiness.

In addition, the final redactor's claim that he relied in the composition of his document on Pionius' own account of events (1.2), and on the official rec-

---

[42] On the dating of the martyrium see Barnes 1968: 528-31; Den Boeft & Bremmer 1985: 122.

ords of the interrogation and trial (9.1 and 19.1), have contributed to the belief that his evidence was both contemporary and faithful to events as they took place (Lane Fox 1986: 470-72; Cadoux 1938:400; Harnack 1958:468). The redactor's access to contemporary accounts would ensure, it is further assumed, that his references to the Jews were also reliable. The author's rendition of events must be accurate for he did not err out of ignorance, and "it would be too skeptical to ascribe it all to his own imagination". The audience for which he wrote, if not already acquainted with events themselves, would have been familiar with the circumstances in which they took place. Lane Fox assumes, therefore, that the redactor would not have jeopardized his credibility by inventing accusations of this nature or creating fanciful claims incriminating the Jews (Lane Fox 1986: 480).

As to the dating and placing of the principal events, I have no argument with Lane Fox and others who have defended the authenticity of the *martyrium*. Lane Fox convincingly defends the precision and accuracy of the descriptions that give the *martyrium* its local colour (Lane Fox 1986: 462-72).[43] The setting, occasion and details of Pionius' arrest seem to be eminently believable. The author of the Greek manuscript also appears to have been well acquainted with the layout of ancient Smyrna. All these factors encourage us to deduce that Pionius did in fact live as a presbyter in third-century Smyrna; that his arrest was prompted by the edict of Decius requiring sacrifice to the gods; and that after refusing to comply with the authorities, after confessing himself a Christian, he was condemned to death by the proconsul who had sole authority in such matters. Lane Fox brings our martyr to life in an expressive and intelligible way. His lively reconstruction of events in our text provides for us a window into the life of ancient Smyrna. However, the "plausibility", "topographical accuracy" and "contemporaneity" criteria that are used to establish the authority of the *martyrium* as a whole,[44] are sadly inappropriate when it comes to judging the Jewish materiel. The Acts of Mar-

---

[43] See also Den Boeft & Bremmer 1985: 124; Gregg 1897: 248-9; Lightfoot 1889; 639. Louis Robert was unable to complete his promised investigation of this aspect of the *martyrium* on the basis of epigraphical and archaeological material (Robert, *Revue des Etudes Anciennes* 1960:319 n. 1).

[44] Lane Fox's defence of the *Martyrdom of Pionius* forms part of an attempt to rehabilitate the trustworthiness of ancient documents. He is reacting against a tendency among modern scholars to take undue liberties with ancient evidence: chopping and changing letters, words and sentences of supposed questionable authenticity, and ultimately rendering the document unrecognizable and its evidence unusable. But Lane Fox is so focused on the question of technical accuracy that he does not stop to enquire whether the texts were actually intended to be read as literal accounts of events. In addition, I would argue that he makes far too much of the scepticism of the examiners of the Pionius text. Compare Lane Fox 1986: 460 and Musurillo 1972: xxix.

tyrdom were preserved as documents of Christian teaching, and it is in this context that the allusions to Judaism must be understood. The author/redactor of the *Martyrdom of Pionius* was more than a mere transcriber of events as they took place. Even if we could be absolutely certain that the references to Jews in the text were uttered by Pionius or recorded by an eye-witness of his death, this does not entitle us to assume that these passages provide us with a literal account of Jewish actions and motivations. Indeed, as we shall see, the references to Jews, when they are examined closely, make little sense unless they are interpreted in the light of the pastoral intentions of the author who had a clear message in mind as he sought to recount and transmit the story of Pionius' martyrdom.

The act of Pionius' martyrdom seeks not only to commemorate and pay tribute to the resolve and conviction of a courageous man, but to instil this sense of commitment in other Christians called on to pass the test of faith. Just as Pionius saw himself, in dying for his beliefs, as heeding the call of Christ in a final and complete way, and as living up to the example of the great Poly-carp, so it was undoubtedly anticipated that his death would serve as a model to those Christians called on to endure the same fate in the future. It was in this spirit also that the account of Pionius' death was transcribed and transmit-ted through the generations. This is plainly stated in the introduction. The re-membrance of the saints gives strength to those who are striving to imitate the "higher things", and Pionius "left us this writing for our instruction that we might have it even to this day as a memorial of his admonitions to us" (*Pionius* 1).

Under Decius, from what we know of the edict that he issued, all Roman citizens were obliged to reconfirm their loyalty to the gods by offering sacri-fice, at which time certificates were issued as proof of their compliance. For the first time, persecution emanated directly from imperial order (Lane Fox 1986: 450), and for the first time a majority of Christians faced the challenge all at once. It is not surprising that the number of Christians who "lapsed" was alarmingly high. Some went of their own accord and offered sacrifice without further bidding, others succumbed to pressure and threats. Others still, had certificates forged so that they might avoid the reprisals of the authorities without actually having to perform an act which went directly against their church's teachings. The temptation to comply with imperial demands was no doubt overwhelming. Judging from the narratives that have come down to us, Christians subjected to the challenge generally had repeated opportunities to retract their beliefs and save themselves. They had in some instances to utter but one word in order to escape execution (*Martyrdom of Conon* 4).

The Christian faithful must have been faced with a terrible dilemma under Decius. For the ideal of martyrdom had come to form an integral part of

Christian identity. The church viewed the courage of its members in the face
of martyrdom as providing evidence to the world of the conviction of its followers. The public confession of the name: "I am a Christian" plays a key role
in all the *acta martyrum*.[45] To die for the Name was not just to die for the sake
of Christ, but for the sake of the Christian name, that is for the sake of the
Christian reputation.[46] If they weren't seen as literally redeeming their fellow
Christians through their act of self-sacrifice, the martyrs were at the very least
"redeeming" the name by which they identified themselves. The impression
created on their pagan neighbours by the resolve of martyrs is a recurrent
theme in the *acta martyrum*. We can well understand, then, why the sudden
and massive retreat that spread through the church like an epidemic on the occasion of the Decian persecution would have caused a crisis for the leaders of
the flock. The church's very identity was at stake in this contest. The Roman
authorities, in pressing the Christians to offer sacrifice to the gods and show
reverence to the emperor, were vying for apostates not martyrs. The large
numbers of so-called *lapsi* were thought to undercut the credibility of the
whole movement and to undermine its missionary efforts.

This issue forms the background against which we should understand and
make sense of the *Martyrdom of Pionius*. If the martyrs were seen as representatives of the Name, then the reverse was also true. Those who succumbed to
fear of torture or death and denied their faith were thought to be letting the
side down. Cyprian wrote a whole treatise on this question alone (*On the
Lapsed (De lapsis)*), and it is the central preoccupation in Pionius' document
as well. Pionius, or at the very least those who wrote about his death shortly
after his passion, viewed his act of martyrdom as an act of rehabilitation for a
church that had gone soft; that could no longer take pride and comfort in its
tenacity in the face of opposition; that could no longer rely on the courage and
devotion that had amazed the sceptics and left the oppressors in awe. At a
time when even the Bishop of Smyrna had failed them, it was to be the con-
stancy of a few individuals that would save the Church from ruin (Frend
1967: 304). Pionius was one such individual. His words and deeds address
this situation directly, and his passion is portrayed as an act of leadership. Not
surprisingly, he appears in our text to be "carrying out a well-conceived sce-

---

[45] See the acts of *Perpetua and Felicitas* 18.2; *Carpus* 5; *Maximilian* 2.4; *Marcellus* 2.2. It
is absent in but a select few.

[46] See *Pionius* 7.1. The act of *Perpetua and Felicitas*, martyrs in Africa in this period, is
also full of references to the amazement, good-will, and even belief generated by the martyrs'
steadfastness. Whether events actually took place in this manner or not, the point is clear
enough. (*Perpetua* 9.1; 16.4; 17.1).See also Tertullian *Apology* 50.13; Origen, *Against Celsus*
IV.32.

nario". He "even seems to be directing the course of events" (Den Boeft & Bremmer 1985: 124).

Even before his arrest, he dons the chains that are by his own admission worn to create a certain impression in the public mind. At a time when too many have faltered and succumbed to the pressure and threats of torture and death, Pionius wears a visible sign of his refusal to cooperate with the authorities in their attempt to coax him into compromise. It is the sight of the procession of Christians in chains that initially attracts the crowds "as though to a strange sight", and it seems that this is exactly what Pionius intended. Our martyr did not shun publicity. When a lawyer inquires about the chains in an attempt to mock the presbyter, Pionius cites the reasons that lie behind what might appear at first as an odd gesture. First and foremost he is concerned with the impression he makes on the people of Smyrna. They should have no doubts about his determination: "so that though we are passing through your city we might not be suspected of having come to eat forbidden foods" (6.2). The characterization of the city as "yours" emphasizes, I believe, his interest in making an impression on the pagans of Smyrna, that is on that section of the population of which he does not count himself a part. Pionius wears his determination as a decoration for all to see:[47] "we have made our decision and are going not to the temple of Nemesis but to the public gaol".

While in his actions he shows by example how a good Christian should behave and makes a public point of his devotion to the Name, in his discourse he addresses directly the dilemma which the frequency of the lapses has created for the church. His first speech is said to take place in the agora before the crowds.[48] We are told that Pionius delivers this speech to an assembled crowd of curious "Greeks, Jews and women" who have come together on this Great Sabbath to witness for themselves what is to become of the Christians arrested for refusing to obey the emperor's edict. He begins by entreating gentiles and Jews in turn to deal with the Christians according to the principles of mercy and fair play found in their own respective traditions. He calls on them, in other words, to have sympathy for the plight of the Christians rather than deriving satisfaction from it.

Yet Pionius' argument makes little sense as a literal address to the Smyrnaean populace, as a literal appeal to his persecutors. The martyr makes no attempt to justify his refusal to sacrifice, nor is the plight concerning which he

---

[47] Not as a "gesture of passivity" as suggested by Lane Fox 1986: 461.

[48] Virtually all the Jewish material within the text is found in Pionius' two orations. Aside from a mention immediately prior to the first speech of "Greeks, Jews, and women" in the audience (Latin is a slight expansion but is clearly an interpolation), the rest of the descriptive text makes no references to the Jews. They played no role in Pionius' arrest, trial, interrogation or execution.

is so anxious to elicit the goodwill or sympathy of both Jews and pagans the oppression of Christians per se. He is thinking rather of the shame of the deserters, particularly of those who have voluntarily offered sacrifice. It is on their account that he appeals to his audience not to laugh or rejoice. The "mockery" of the Jews which Pionius laments, then, has nothing to do with their involvement in or encouragement of the Roman persecution. Pionius reproaches the Jews, rather, for openly proclaiming the failure of so many Christians to *remain true* to their faith, and to *resist* the pressure of the persecutors. It is difficult to imagine the circumstances in which Pionius would have made a speech of this kind. His words are obviously addressed to a public who shares his religious and ethical standards, at least to the extent of viewing the failure of Christians to stand firm in their beliefs as a sign of moral weakness. But however Pionius' appeal is interpreted, when read carefully, his words can in no way be made to imply that the Jews either took part in, or were in sympathy with the Roman persecution of the Christians.

Interestingly, Pionius' apology for the *lapsi* leads right into a denigration of Jewish righteousness. Pionius draws on some of the standard biblical texts used in the "Adversus Judaeos" literature, and dredges up references in the Scriptures to idol worship among the Israelites. Among the stories he includes a mention of the sacrifice to Baal Peor (*Numbers* 25.1-2), according to which Israel was drawn into the worship of idols after the people had exposed themselves to the foreign ways of an idolatrous nation. These past sins of the people of Judaea, argues Pionius, are more reprehensible than the present lapses of Christians, just as "voluntary sins" are judged more harshly than "indeliberate ones". While the Israelites were led astray through their own fault, Christians who sacrifice are victims of circumstance. In this contrast of Christian and Jewish failings, Pionius seems to be trying to discredit the Jews, so as to make the Christian lapses seem less reprehensible. The Jews lack sympathy for their fellow-men against the teachings of their own law maker, Moses. They have a long history of deliberate and shameless apostasy against God. Against this foil, the single-mindedness of faithful Christians appears all the more praiseworthy. "I, at any rate," exclaims Pionius with outstretched arm, "in obedience to *my* Master, have chosen to die rather than transgress His commands, and I make every effort (literally "struggle" or "fight") not to depart from the things that I first learned and later taught" (4.7). Again, there is no mention of Jewish involvement in persecution, but rather a comparison of Jewish versus Christian lapses, so as to reduce the demoralizing impact of the *lapsi* phenomenon on the beleaguered Christian community. The Jews who appear here are an illustrative foil in Christian argumentation.

(2) Universal Opposition

We have discussed a number of passages in which the Jews are identified as the first persecutors and original opponents of Christ and His followers. We now turn in our appraisal of the supposed role of Jews in persecution to a second group of passages which clearly emphasize the Christian/non-Christian split, rather than the special role of the Jews. Wherever the fathers discuss their vision of the church as the lone source of light in a dark and hostile world, Jew, gentile and even heretic are all given equal status as potential enemies of Christ. Where scholars have assumed that these passages provide evidence of Jewish collaboration and cooperation with the Romans, a careful examination reveals that these texts are revelatory rather of the sense in which the Christian authors tended at times to universalize conceptually their opposition, lump together all those who they saw as standing against them. This reading is confirmed by the fact that heretics are occasionally included in the list of enemies supposedly seeking to undermine the faith of the true followers of Christ. These texts are clearly designed to emphasize the sense in which the leaders of the orthodox church conceived of their movement as standing alone, as guardian of truth in the world.

Tertullian adopts this perspective in a widely quoted passage from his *Apology*. Christianity has "as many foes as there are strangers (*extranei*) to it" pronounces the church father (*Apology* 7). He then goes on to elaborate on this statement, by listing the various groups that he includes among the church's opponents, and by identifying the motivations that supposedly underlie their enmity. The Jews are said to be moved against the church by *aemulatione*, the soldiers for money, domestics "by their nature". *Aemulatione* is often translated by scholars as "rivalry" (Frend 1970: 294, Simon 1986: 119), and quoted as proof of the threat posed by the growing church to the position and status of the synagogue, but "jealousy" or "envy" are much more appropriate renditions here. The distinction is important, because, as we saw above, jealousy was an emotion often attributed by the church writers to the people that they claimed to have displaced as the chosen people of God (see above, "The Envy Of Those Who Have Been Superseded").

In almost any another context this passage would surely be seen as an expression of the rigid and fixed opinions of the speaker, rather than as an objective assessment of the opposition that he faced. Indeed, when Tertullian equates strangers and foes, he tells us a great deal more about the Christian perception of outsiders than he does about the real opposition suffered by the Christians in his day. He is making a statement of principle. The birth of Christianity is here described as the coming into the world of truth. The claim that all those who do not actively recognize this truth somehow stand in the way of its dissemination, and are involved in perpetrating a lie, is quite a natural extension of this line of reasoning "Truth and the hatred of truth came into our world together. As soon as truth appears, it is regarded as an enemy." (*Apology* 7; cf. also Justin, *Dialogue* 110.5).

Cyprian's passing reference to the "menaces of Gentiles or Jews" is another example of the universalizing of opposition. This text is quoted, mostly without much commentary, as evidence of Jewish involvement in the Decian persecution in Carthage in 250 C.E..[49] Once again, however, when the passage is set in context, its perspective shifts, and the self-referentiality of the text becomes evident. The real aim of Cyprian's 59th epistle is to urge strength and firmness in the face of the pressure exerted by a schismatic faction. It is the authority of the church that lies in the balance in this contest. Cyprian is concerned that the strength of episcopal authority be maintained through ecclesiastical discipline. His real preoccupation is in combatting the enemy within. He warns his readers to be *as* resolute in combatting this internal enemy as they are in resisting the enemy without. It is in this context that the Jews make their appearance in the text: "and it is not only against the menaces of Gentiles and Jews that we should be alert and watchful", but turn our firm attention to the real peril from our *own* brethren, for "the Lord himself was laid hold on by His brethren". "Gentiles, Jews and heretics" are all placed in the same category as enemies of the church. The Jews are the pair group to the gentiles in a characterization of the non-Christian world. The reference here is to archetypical groups that define a conceptual reality, and not to living and breathing contemporaries. It seems evident that it was not the synagogue down the road which was Cyprian's focus in his exhortations.

This notion of universal opposition is also revealed in Hippolytus' typological interpretation of the apocryphal story of Susannah. The young woman, who prefigures the church is threatened by two elders, representing Jews and gentiles respectively. Both have designs on her, and they agree to collaborate in betraying her on false charges when she refuses their advances. This text which implies the existence of a conspiracy between Jews and gentiles clearly emerges from the church father's theological vision rather than any literal observations. The common enmity of Jews and gentiles towards the church overrides, in the eyes of Hippolytus, that which divides these opponents, and this opposition forms an implicit alliance between them. Several factors militate against a literal reading of this text.

"There is nothing here about any specific events in any specific places" that would indicate that Hippolytus was referring to events in Rome of his day (Millar 1966:234). Secondly, the tone of the passage highlights the expected,

---

[49] See commentary on the Martyrdom of Pionius above.

universal and perpetual character of opposition to the church. It lacks altogether the urgency and force that one might expect of a charge addressing a
specific and recent injustice. "I am straitened on every side" wails Susannah.
Thirdly, among those who plot against her from "every side" are included the
heretics. Once again, the forces that impinge on the church, whether from
within or from without form, from the Christian perspective, a conceptual
unity. "For the church is afflicted and straitened," explains Hippolytus, "not
only by the Jews, but also by the gentiles, and by those who are called Christians, but are not such in reality. For they, observing her chaste and happy life,
strive to ruin her" (*Commentary on Daniel and Susannah (In Danielem et Su-
sannam)* 22; cf. also Justin, *Dialogue* 131.5).

Finally several passages in the writings of Origen also reveal the tendency
among the church fathers to characterize all those who fall outside the communion of saints as belonging, in conceptual terms, to a unity. In his homily
on Judges, Origen claims that "together with pagans and Jews, even heretics
persecute the church of God" (*Homilies on Judges (Homiliae in Judicum)*
viii.1). In his commentary on the Psalms, the church father describes Jews and
heretics as belonging to the "conventicle of the wicked who build in vain
against the church" (*Selecta on the Psalms (Selecta in Psalmos)* cxxvi.1; cf.
also Clement, *Miscellanies (Stromata)* 7.18). The sweeping nature of these
statements and the fact that they put heretics in the same class as pagans and
Jews indicates that Origen is here affirming theological rather than factual
truths (cf. also *Homilies on Jesu Nave (Homiliae in Jesu Nave)* xv.1).

That the texts alluding to the universality of opposition emerge from the
church's theological vision rather than from its interaction with Jews is confirmed in passages which refer not specifically to persecution but to the beliefs
and practices of non-Christians. When Marcion is said by Tertullian to
"borrow poison from the Jew", this cannot literally mean that the heresiarch
made use of Jewish ideas because the Marcionites stood for the elimination of
all Jewish influences in the church. Tertullian intends to convey, rather, that
Marcion, like the Jew before him, was considered to have fallen into the
"same ditch" in virtue of the fact that both made the most fundamental of errors "in denying that Christ has come" (Tertullian, *Against Marcion (Adversus
Marcionem)* III.7.1; cf. III.8.1; III.23.1).

So in matters of doctrine, just as in discussions referring to the church's
opponents, the Jews are sometimes described as keeping company with all
other outsiders to whom Christ is unknown. Origen likens Jewish and heretical methods of Scriptural intepretation (*Homilies on Jesu Nave* 15.1; cf. 13.3).
The "assembly of the impious" in Psalm 1, serves for Tertullian, to describe
both the historical Jews who deliberated against Christ, and the contemporary

gatherings of heathens, who are no "less impious, less sinners, less enemies of Christ" (Tertullian, *On Spectacles (De spectaculis)* 3).

In sum, there is no basis for the widely held claim that second and third century Jews were involved in the persecution of their Christian contemporaries. On examination, the "charges" against the Jews in the early writings of the church reveal themselves to be theologically motivated affirmations rather than observations of historical fact. The misapprehension among modern scholars about Jews as persecutors is regrettable not only because it serves a hidden apologetic agenda, making Christian antagonism seem justifiable, but because it also implicitly passes judgement on ancient Judaism.[50]

---

[50] See Conclusion.

CHAPTER THREE

INHERITED ANTI-JUDAISM

In the following chapter we will consider two hypotheses about anti-Judaism which are based on the assumption that Christian anti-Judaism was to some extent an inherited phenomenon. (1) The first hypothesis claims that early Christian anti-Judaism was a continuation of pagan prejudices against the Jews. I will examine and criticize this hypothesis under the heading of "Environmental Anti-Judaism". (2) The second hypothesis holds that the anti-Jewish themes found in the works of the second and third century fathers were inherited from the Christian tradition of biblical exegesis. I will defend this hypothesis in the discussion of "Traditional Anti-Judaism". Though the traditional character of the anti-Jewish writings is recognized on some level by most scholars, I propose to show that this aspect of the texts has been underestimated by the conflict theorists in their focus on the social foundation of anti-Judaism.

TYPOLOGY III.1
ENVIRONMENTAL ANTI-JUDAISM

A number of scholars have detected an environmental component in Christian anti-Judaism, assuming that it was absorbed from the cultural environment of the pagan world, and that it was a reflection of the church's assimilation into the gentile world. While (1) some scholars see Christian hostility toward the Jews as a mere extension of pre-Christian pagan prejudices, (2) others see the aversion to Jews among pagans as one among many factors that contributed to the creation of Christian anti-Judaism. I will argue against both these views with those scholars who insist on the peculiarly Christian foundations of anti-Judaism in the early church.

(1) Pagan Hate in Christian Guise

Thomas Idinopulos and Roy Ward define Christian anti-Judaism as an extension of an already existing pattern of rivalry between Pagans and Jews.[1] The source of Christian anti-Judaism, according to Idinopulos and Ward, "is not Christian thinking per se but the political purposes to which it was put" (1977: 209). Their theory emerges, then, from a firm conviction that the antagonism between church and synagogue had its roots "primarily in historical or political events", and only "secondarily in theological ideas". They seem to adopt an almost reductionist approach in which theology is robbed of its power to explain anything on a causal level, and becomes "more expression than cause" (1977: 203-4).

For example, the charge that the Jews were primarily responsible for the crucifixion of Christ, a traditional and recurring theological theme in the early Christian literature, is reduced by Ward and Idinopulos to an apologetic argument with a political purpose. In blaming the Jews, the two scholars argue, the early Christian writers aimed both to allay suspicions about Jesus as an enemy of Rome, and to portray the Jews as the real troublemakers, as the real enemies of both Romans and Christians (Idinopulos & Ward 1977: 199). The deicide charge becomes a "potent weapon" in an "on-going increasingly bloody struggle", rather than a product of the "inner logic of christology itself" (1977: 203). The aim of the two scholars is to show that the church's anti-Judaism was not a "necessary negative translation of the church's confession of the Messiahship of Jesus", and their "acutely political" version of

---

[1] Although they recognize that the Christian-Jewish rivalry was more heated, because the two traditions were closer, and because of the church's need to assert its independence over against the synagogue, they see this peculiarly Christian dimension as secondary (Idinopulos & Ward 1977: 202). It accounts for the intensity of the conflict but not for its source.

the "conflict theory" leads them to the belief in the pagan roots of Christian anti-Jewish hostility.

John Meagher offers a slightly moderated if slightly more confused version of the thesis outlined by Idinopulos and Ward. According to Meagher, the "bulk of surviving evidence" indicates that Jews were viewed with hostility in pagan antiquity,"especially during the period of Christian beginnings",[2] and this provides proof in Meagher's eyes, that anti-Judaism was "not a Christian invention" (Meagher 1979: 4). He appears to be more moderate than Idinopulos and Ward, however, in his concession that "the motives of pagan dislike were not assimilable by the church". While Idinopulos and Ward equate the motives of Christian and pagan hostility toward the Jews, Meagher seems initially to accept the view of Rosemary Ruether that "Christian anti-Judaism grew from quite a distinct motivation" (Meagher 1979: 12; cf. Ruether 1974: 29-30). Unfortunately, this insight is virtually negated as the article progresses, and Meagher argues that while there is discontinuity between Christian and pagan antagonism on the level of ideas, there is much more continuity on the level of sentiment. On a most significant level, Christians are said to be continuing a pagan tradition.

By the time the Christians came on the scene, Meagher claims, hostility towards the Jews "had already been firmly, however unjustly and uncritically, established in public consciousness", and Meagher is eager to ensure that the responsibility for these unjust and uncritical feelings be distributed "more evenly" between Christians and their predecessors. Though he is less specific than Idinopulos and Ward about the motives that fueled pagan anti-Judaism and contributed to the Christian version of it, he appears, ultimately, to adopt a reductionist stance which is very similar to theirs. "I do not believe that theology logically brought the Christians to their unconscionable treatment of the Jews" (Meagher 1979: 23). Meagher reduces theology to a mere rationalization, and robs it of its ability to explain anything meaningful about "real motives". "I believe", he affirms, that theology "was used to whitewash and justify an antagonism that sprang mainly from other sources" (Meagher 1979: 23).

---

2 In fact, pagan attitudes to the Jews were far from uniformly negative. Some pagan authors showed signs of respect and even admiration for Judaism. John Gager talks of a "long history of theological interchange" between Judaism and Paganism, in which the Jews came to be viewed as "in some sense a philosophical sect" (Gager 1983: 102). The physician-philosopher Galen, for example, who lived in the latter half of the second century, "compares Moses with different Greek philosophers and quite explicitly engages him in a philosophical debate on the cause of creation" (Gager 1983: 102; Galen, *On the Function of Parts of the Body* 11.14).

(2) Anti-Judaism as a Product of Both Pagan and Christian Influences

The main scholar to adopt a double-sided approach to understanding the sources of Christian anti-Judaism is Marcel Simon.[3] While Simon recognizes Christian anti-Judaism as a peculiarly Christian phenomenon with Christian roots, he affirms that the "social foundations" on which this Christian outlook was built were pagan. Simon distinguishes two aspects of anti-Judaism: the Christian notion of the Jews as dissidents who rejected Christ, which was "nourished by the bible", and the common complaints of the Gentile public about Jewish nonconformity. The two became "intimately intermingled", argues Simon, when the Christians "retained and took over", or "continued and revived in a more virulent form" the "traditional animosity" of the ancient world (Simon 1986: 207-8,209). When Simon talks of Christian anti-Judaism as a phenomenon with two dimensions, one "secular and popular", the other "ecclesiastical and learned", he seems to have in mind a model of Christian anti-Judaism which gives equal weight to these two key elements (Simon 1986: 208).

Indeed, Simon's conviction that early Christian attitudes to Jews were rooted in social reality leads him to describe the pagan contribution to Christian anti-Judaism as "foundational". Yet there appear to be some contradictions in his views on this matter. When he discusses the actual content of the themes that make up Christian anti-Judaism, he seems all too aware of essential and irreconcilable differences between pagan and Christian anti-Judaism. Simon recognizes, for instance, that the substance of the moral and religious accusations levelled against the Jews by the Christians are fundamentally different in nature from the social accusations common among pagans. "It is not the supercilious insularity of the Jews that chiefly annoys the community. Their primary accusation is that the Jews are addicted to all the vices, and that under cover of their scrupulous observance of the law they are really immoral and irreligious" (Simon 1986: 212).

So Simon acknowledges that pagan and Christian complaints about the law come from very different angles. The pagans objected to the Jewish insistence on observing a law which they despised as exclusive and insular, and without value. The Christians may have believed this law to be outdated and surpassed by a new dispensation, but it remained a God-given law, and one of their chief accusations against the Jews concerned the failure of the people of the Bible to heed the provisions laid down by God in his first dispensation. Simon also acknowledges the uniqueness of the Christian "methods of argument", and re-

---

[3] In his attempt to account for Tertullian's anti-Judaism, David Efroymson also enumerates a number of causes. Aside from peculiarly Christian factors, such as the church's biblical inheritance, and the church's psychological sense of inferiority vis-à-vis the synagogue, he also lists the "culturally inherited pagan anti-Judaism which would naturally have formed part of the outlook of Gentile Christians" (Efroymson 1976: 61-2). See also Grayzel 1946: 84; Lovsky 1955: 160; Oesterreicher 1975: 21-2; Davies 1969: 62-65; Baron 1952: I.194.

fers to these as the "really characteristic contribution of Christianity to anti-Semitism". Whereas the pagans denigrated the Jews "gratuitously and without proof", the Christians backed their accusations "with texts of scripture" (Simon 1986: 215). And because the Christian variety of anti-Judaism was rooted in exegesis, it had "a sanction and a coherence" which its pagan predecessor lacked. It was neither "spontaneous nor unorganized, nor based on hearsay", as were the Gentile objections to the Jews (Simon 1986: 223).

Environmental Anti-Judaism and the "Conflict Theory"

My critique of the notion of "environmental" anti-Judaism is in part a critique of the "conflict theory". Those "conflict" theorists who place importance on the pagan sources of Christian anti-Judaism adopt this view as an extension of their conviction that anti-Judaism was a phenomenon with roots in social reality. When Simon examines the actual substance of the Christian anti-Jewish passages, he makes little mention of the pagan contribution to anti-Judaism, and emphasizes the uniqueness of the church's argumentation against the Jews. Where Simon does attribute a pagan element to Christian prejudices against the Jews, it is a direct function of his prior assumption that anti-Judaism was the by-product of a social conflict. And, as we have seen, those scholars who see the greatest continuity between pagan and Christian anti-Judaisms virtually discount the theological dimension altogether in their explanation of Christian animosity toward the Jews. Ward and Idinopulos go as far as to argue that Christian and pagan antagonism toward the Jews was rooted in the need felt by both communities to stem the tide of Jewish proselytizing (Idinopulos & Ward 1977: 202), a phenomenon which we have already shown to be extremely dubious (cf. Typology I).

The implicit apologetic motive in "environmental" anti-Judaism must also give us pause when judging the credibility of this theory. As Gager rightly points out, "to the extent that the blame for Christian antipathy toward Judaism can be shifted from Christian to Gentile shoulders, to that same extent will Christianity itself be partially exonerated" (Gager 1983: 30; cf. also Flannery 1985: 26).

Finally, the notion that Christian anti-Judaism had its roots in pagan hostility to the Jews also fails to hold up to scrutiny when the objections of the two gentile groups to the people of the synagogue are compared and contrasted, and it is to this that we now turn.

Pagan and Christian Objections to Judaism

The first point to note is that the role played by anti-Judaism in the two gentile traditions is markedly different. While the Jewish question was a crucial issue, a main preoccupation for the early church, this can hardly be said to be true for the pagans, for whom Judaism was a minority religious sect among others. Even on those occasions when the Jews stirred up trouble, the main interest of the Roman authorities was in pacification, not negation or annihilation. They confronted the Jews only to the extent that this was necessary to the restoration of order. Nor is there any evidence of a persistent campaign against Judaism in the pagan writings.[4]

While the Roman authorities were concerned chiefly with order and stability, and while pagan authors vacillated in their views, anti-Judaism played a central role in the writings of the early church. The very centrality of anti-Judaism in Christian thought is a sign, not of a difference in intensity, but of the fact that the source of Christian opposition to the Jews was quite distinct from the sources of pagan antipathy. While the Greeks and Romans objected to the religiously sanctioned exclusivity of the Jews, to the barriers they erected between themselves and other men (Schürer III.1: 152), the Christians had no objections to exclusivity in itself, but claimed merely that the Jews practiced the wrong kind of exclusivity.

Even where parallels seem to exist between pagan and Christian attitudes to the Jews, the contrast in the motives behind what might appear initially as similar sounding objections is striking. Two examples follow:

(1) Although the Greek repulsion against circumcision finds an echo in the deprecation of this Jewish rite in the church fathers, the impetus behind these two anti-Judaisms is quite distinct. The pagans objected to the insularity of the Jews, to the sense in which their observances set them apart from Roman society. The church's main argument against circumcision, on the other hand, was that it was outdated as a sign of election. The Christians did not spurn circumcision as a repulsive and exclusive rite but, quite to the contrary, appropriated it as a symbol and reinterpreted it in a spiritual sense. Since the advent of Christ, it was circumcision of the heart and not that of the flesh which was to be the mark of God's chosen people (Justin, *Dialogue* 12; Irenaeus, *Against Heresies* 3.12.11; 4.16.1).

(2) Jewish misfortune in the wake of the destruction of the Jewish wars, was interpreted by the ancients as a sign of God's displeasure, and the Christians also argued that the political defeat of the Jews was a sign of their disinheritance by God. But while the pagan view was rooted in the equation of good fortune and divine favour, the Christian notion was theologically rooted, and ultimately had little to do with the observation of political and historical realities. If they had been basing themselves on objective facts, the early Christians would have had to acknowledge that the periodic persecutions suffered by the early church were also signs of divine wrath. Quite to the contrary, however, martyrdom was viewed as a great honour, and as a special mark of redemption. Where Jewish misfortune was a seen as a mark of punishment from God, and was portrayed as proof of the synagogue's bankruptcy, the oppression of the church was understood to be a necessary

---

[4] On the themes of anti-Judaism in paganism see Stern 1974-84; Juster 19 14: I.44-49; Wilde 1949: 32-77.

prelude to ultimate victory. That Christians saw no contradiction in holding a double standard of this sort confirms that their views were founded in theological principle rather than objective observation. According to the Christian view, God disinherited the Jews because they were an idolatrous nation whose ultimate crime was the rejection of His only Son, and Jewish hardships were thought to follow upon this. So while in the eyes of the Christians, God's judgement preceded the misfortune of the Jews (which became no more than a confirmation of divine wrath), in the pagan view, it was the hardship *itself* which gave birth to the idea of divine displeasure.

In sum, "when we turn from a Seneca or a Tacitus to a Tertullian or a John Chrysostom, we sense immediately how radically the scene had changed" (Wilken 1967: 318). And this contrast between pagan and Christian objections to the Jews provides evidence of the distinctly theological foundation of Christian anti-Jewish ideas and themes.[5] Indeed, those scholars who emphasize the uniqueness of Christian anti-Judaism define it as a phenomenon with roots in the theological vision of the church. The above examples confirm that "the motives of pagan dislike were not assimilable by the church", and that "essentially, Christian anti-Judaism grew from quite a separate and distinct motivation" in which pagan prejudices played an insignificant role (Ruether 1974: 29-30; cf. also Isaac 1948; 1956). Christian anti-Judaism was of another kind than the pagan variety. Members of the gentile church may well have been subject to the cultural influences of the pagan world, but in the Christian writings that have come down to us, the objections to Judaism clearly have their source in a peculiarly Christian strain of thought and sentiment (cf. Flannery 1985: 27).

---

[5] The church's anti-Jewish motifs shall be considered in greater detail in the section on "theological" anti-Judaism (Typology IV.1).

TYPOLOGY III.2
TRADITIONAL ANTI-JUDAISM

As has already been mentioned, the anti-Jewish writings of the early Christian fathers take the shape of exegetical expositions of the Scriptures, and the most striking features about these arguments is their coherence and consistency (cf. Typology I). As a corpus, they form a theological construct within which three main themes can be distinguished:[6] (1) The exposition of the christological meaning of the Scriptures, in which Christ is shown to be the Messiah long promised and foretold by the prophets. (2) The critique of the Mosaic dispensation, in particular of the ritual law, said to be abrogated in favour of a new spiritual law. (3) The interpretation of salvation history as revealed in the Holy Writings in terms of a dialectic of judgment and promise, which reinterprets past, present and future in terms of the response to Christ, and which describes the election of the gentile church in terms of an antithetical or supersessionary contrast with God's rejection of the sinful Jews. These "basic themes appear already in the first century and vary little thereafter" (Gager 1983: 158), remaining "quite constant from the second to the sixth centuries" (Ruether 1974: 123).

The form and character of the anti-Jewish corpus has led a number of scholars to suggest that the anti-Judaism found in the second and third century fathers was, at least to some extent, the reflection of an inherited literary tradition passed down through the generations of Christian writers. Simon notes the formation of a "portrait of the Jew" in the Christian tradition, "built up by pasting together verses of the Bible". He points to the way Christians collected evidence for the "depravity of the people of God" by removing the prophetic warnings and accusations in the Holy Writings from their context of time and place, and combining them to create a picture of "the eternal Jew". Simon recognizes the sense in which this "eternal Jew" was a "conventional figure, a literary fiction" (Simon 1986: 215).

David Efroymson lists the "traditional image of the Jews as portrayed in the New Testament texts" among the factors that make Tertullian's antagonism towards Judaism intelligible (Efroymson 1976: 61-2). He recognizes that "very little that is original can be found in Tertullian's anti-Jewish accusations", and he attributes this to the fact that "much of the material is biblical and the content if not the attitude has become traditional among Christians by Tertullian's time" (Efroymson 1976; 79). He describes Tertullian's anti-Judaism as "an inheritance" from the church father's "Christian and Roman African roots" (Efroymson 1976; 64).

---

[6] Already stated briefly in Typology I.1. See Simon 1986: 156; Wilken 1971: 15; Efroymson 1976: 2; Gager 1983: 158.

In his study of Cyril, Robert Wilken also recognizes that the church father was "not an inventor in his attitude toward Judaism", but rather formed "part of a tradition which had its beginnings in the primitive church". Wilken refers to both the continuity and the uniformity of the tradition. "Since earliest times, Christian beliefs had taken shape with reference to Judaism, and now attitudes were hardening into a fixed mould" (Wilken 1971: 228; cf. also Davies 1969: 59; Burghardt 1970: 189). I propose to show that the existence of this traditional element raises some hermeneutical questions which pose a direct challenge to the "conflict theory".

In as far as the anti-Jewish passages are said to form part of an inherited tradition, both Simon and Wilken show an awareness of the fact that the contemporary relevance of these passages is cast into doubt. Wilken, for instance, raises the possibility that the anti-Jewish corpus formed part of a literary tradition, and he recognizes that the "mere fact that Christians wrote books of this sort is not sure proof that they were responding to actual Jews. They may represent simply a literary tradition" (Wilken 1971: 18; Simon 1986: 136).

But, though the two scholars call for the need to choose between the "controversy" and "literary" options, neither take the latter seriously as a viable choice. As we have seen, the "conflict theory" prides itself on moving beyond a one-sided preoccupation with the categories of dogmatic theology towards a sensitivity to the power of social and political forces. It would not be an exaggeration to describe this as the main impetus behind the whole modern approach to the patristic anti-Jewish texts, and in this setting, the literary dependence theory doesn't stand a chance. Its emphasis on theoretical continuity is out of fashion at a time when modern scholars are still much preoccupied with refuting the traditional approach of the "doctrinal historians". So the "literary" option is quickly dismissed, despite its ability to account for the abstract, theoretical and consistent character of the anti-Jewish corpus (cf. Introduction and Typology IV). Once again, the determination to search out, at all costs, the social underpinning of the Christian writings, even where it is doubtful that this dimension of reality is revealed, skews the hermeneutical approach to the texts. The path is predetermined from the outset, and the "controversy" option becomes the only way to go.

Ultimately then, when Simon and Wilken raise the possibility of the literary option, they are really presenting the reader with a false dichotomy which serves only to promote the plausibility of the "conflict theory". Simon equates the literary option with the production of "a type of literature" that had "lost, centuries earlier, its justification and purpose" (Simon 1986: 140), and then discounts it in one rhetorical question: "Do men rage so persistently against a corpse?" (Simon 1986: 140). Wilken also sees literary dependence as lifeless, the remnant of a tradition "whose raison d'être had lost its significance" (Wilken 1971: 18; cf. also Hulen 1932: 70; Remus 1986: 73).

Consequently, it is not the *substance* of the persistent themes linking the texts which is granted significance by modern scholars, but the mere *fact* of continuity. The continuity and persistence of the anti-Jewish writings is explained in terms of the "persistence of the same objections and the same methods on the part of the adversary" (Simon 1986: 145). "The persistence of a certain representation through the course of several centuries entitles it to serious consideration", argues Amos Hulen. Although he recognizes that the Christian documents "may be defective in reflecting contemporary attitudes", Hulen maintains that they give us a picture of the "total reaction" of one group towards the other (Hulen 1932: 64). While he can't claim that the documents give detailed evidence of the actual discussions that took place between Jews and Christians at any given time and place, he wants to argue that they give us a sketch of the broad outlines of the debates and disputes.

In order to justify the theory that the persistence of the anti-Jewish writings is a sign of the persistence of the *challenge* posed by contemporary Jews, and a reflection of social and political circumstances, modern scholars are forced to minimize or downplay the consistency in the writings as much as possible. "The monotonous and stereotyped nature of the anti-Jewish literature ought not to be exaggerated" affirms Simon. "It does in fact offer some variety, which is a sign of life" (Simon 1986: 140). Like Simon, Wilken is also convinced that the exegetical and theological writings against the Jews were prompted by the presence of actual Jews, and directed at the problems raised by the influence of this vital and powerful group (cf. Wilken 1971: 36-37). Like Simon, he tries to emphasize the diversity of the anti-Jewish material. "The anti-Jewish literature is more diverse than we have supposed...the discussion varied from place to place and author to author" (Wilken 1971: 37). Stephen Wilson also warns against putting "too much emphasis on the similarity of themes recurring in the literature as a whole" because it fails, according to Wilson, to allow for the "considerable range of tone and emotion" in the writings (Wilson 1986a: ix-x).

It would indeed be surprising if there were no variations in tone and emotion in texts written over nearly two hundred years. But in the anti-Jewish corpus, these variations are minimal, and pale in significance when compared with the striking consistency of themes that extends right through the whole tradition. Indeed, though modern scholars so readily point to what they see as the failings of the literary dependence theory, they remain oblivious to the absurdity involved in their own position. If we buy into the "conflict theory", and accept that the persistence of themes provides evidence of the continued relevance of the same socially-rooted problems, then we have to assume that one model can succeed in explaining the interaction of disparate communities of Jews and Christians living in different places of a vast empire, and over a period of almost two centuries. Can we really believe that ten generations of Jews and Christians living in such different cities as Rome, Sardis and Carthage interacted with one another according to one fixed pattern?

I would suggest that this way of accounting for the persistence of the anti-Jewish literature is sorely inadequate, and that the "literary" option deserves further exploration. If we focus on the substance, on the content, of the anti-Jewish literature, and if we can break free from the presupposition that traditions are by definition devoid of life, then perhaps the anti-Jewish passages themselves can reveal the purpose and raison d'être of the consistency and coherence that characterizes them. It is to this investigation that we now turn in the following discussion on "symbolic" anti-Judaism.

CHAPTER FOUR

SYMBOLIC ANTI-JUDAISM

TYPOLOGY IV.1
THEOLOGICAL ANTI-JUDAISM

We have examined hypotheses about anti-Judaism as it is thought to have been expressed in a religious rivalry between Christians and Jews (Typology I). We have considered theories about the social and political underpinning of this conflict (Typology II). Finally we have looked at assumptions about the environmental factors that are believed to have contributed to hostility against the Jews in the early church (Typology III). In each case, I have argued that the references to Jews and Judaism in the writings of the fathers make much more sense as expressions of an anti-Judaism rooted in theological ideas than as responses to contemporary Jews in the context of an on-going conflict. In this chapter, I propose to explore the theological motivation for anti-Judaism in the early church.

I will begin by reviewing the place accorded by modern scholars of early Christianity to the theological dimension of Christian anti-Judaism. It is generally recognized that the negation of Judaism in the early Christian writings was in part theologically motivated. This theological anti-Judaism is said to emerge from the church's efforts to resolve the contradictions inherent in its simultaneous appropriation and rejection of different elements of the Jewish tradition. The church appropriated the Jewish God and the Jewish Scriptures, but abandoned the law which this God had proclaimed in these very Scriptures. In the words of Marcel Simon: "the position of Christianity itself...made it necessary for the Church, as the new Israel, to establish its rights as against those people whom it claimed to dispossess. It had to explain why, in taking over the heritage, it rejected part of it, accepting the name and the book, but refusing to be subjected to the observances that authenticated that name and that the book laid down" (Simon 1986: 369). Simon devotes a whole chapter of *Verus Israel* to describing the way Christian theology applied itself to addressing and resolving the *logical* difficulties that emerge from the church's debt to Judaism (chapter 3, entitled "The Church and Israel"). The gentile church's debt to Judaism was indeed extensive. "It was from Judaism that it derived its moralism and the substance of its liturgy... And from the same source it derived certain elements of its teaching, its

method of interpreting the scriptures, and, in the form of the LXX, the text of
the scriptures themselves" (Simon 1986: 69). The debt came to be of the
greatest significance because

> at exactly the time when events were combining to put the two religions apart,
> the Church by its affirmation of the value of the Old Testament was acknowledg-
> ing more plainly than ever before its debt to the Synagogue. The Church, then
> made the Jewish canon its own, and clung steadfastly to the book that from the
> beginning had nourished the piety, faith and thought of the Christian communi-
> ties (Simon 1986: 69-70).

The church followed a *via media* between the way of the synagogue on one
side, and the complete rejection of all that was Jewish (as advocated by the
Marcionites), on the other. The anti-Jewish arguments of the church emerged
from the effort to steer and maintain this difficult middle course.

David Flusser describes the source of anti-Judaism in similar terms to those
used by Simon. Early Christian opposition to Jews and Judaism was a function of the emergence of a gentile Christianity that understood itself as "the
heir to Judaism, as its true expression", that saw itself as a church which revered the Holy Scriptures, but to whom it was forbidden to fulfill the commandments of the law of Moses which these Scriptures proclaimed (Flusser
1983: 32). Stephen Wilson expresses it another way: "The Catholic position,
imperiously defending its right to the Jewish God and scriptures, could find
only a negative reason for the continued existence of the Jews" (Wilson
1986b: 58). The church "could not establish the truth of its own faith without
in the same breath denouncing the error and blindness of Israel, that is of the
old Israel" (Isaac 1956: 156; my transl.). Thus was formed a traditional and
caricatural image of the Jews founded in a systematic "teaching of contempt"
(Isaac 1956: 57).

Perhaps inevitably, the anti-Judaism that emerged out of a need to resolve
inherent contradictions in the Christian theological position became woven
into the church's definition of itself. Christianity's commerce with the holy
book led it to take over for itself and itself alone the title of the new and true
Israel, and to deny this inheritance to the people originally chosen by God.
This connection between anti-Judaism and Christian identity is now a widely
recognized insight. Anti-Judaism became for the church an "intrinsic need of
self affirmation" (Ruether 1974: 181). It was a "by-product of Christian self-
definition in which the church was led to deny to Judaism certain central characteristics of its own self-understanding" (Gaston 1986b: 164). John Gager
sums up recent developments in modern scholarship as follows: "The point
has been made repeatedly, from Isaac and Simon to Ruether that the origins of
Christianity within first century Judaism and its painful separation from Judaism meant that its sense of identity and legitimacy took shape within the
framework of opposition to Judaism" (Gager 1983: 135).

The nature of the Christian anti-Jewish passages provides confirmation of the hypothesis that Christian anti-Judaism was theological and self-affirmative in orientation.[1] In their efforts to define the *via media* that came to character-ize the church's position, and to resolve the contradictions in this position, the fathers formulated arguments that justified their claims about the church. As has already been mentioned, these arguments centered around three main themes, namely: (1) christological proofs, (2) the critique of the Mosaic law, and (3) arguments relating to the election of the gentile church, and the judgement of the Jews (cf. Typology III.2). These arguments are striking not only in their consistency over time but in their coherence (cf. Typology I.1, II.3, III.2). They form a theological construct by means of which the church fathers sought to justify the church's own rendition of salvation history. In their attempt to analyze and make sense of this construct, scholars have sought to identify its focal point. The question is which of the arguments described above would have taken centre stage in the church's efforts to assert its claims over against Judaism.

Most scholars place central importance on the question of the law in the formulation of the church's anti-Judaic argument (argument 2 above). Simon, for instance, argues that the greatest difficulty to emerge from the church's attempt to define a middle path was the need to account for and justify the abandonment of the law. After all "The Bible codified the law, or rather, the Bible was the Law" and it remained "the tangible sign of the covenant that God had established between Himself and his people". The question of how the Christians could "claim the Bible as their own and yet empty it of so much of its content?" (Simon 1986: 71-72). is the central one, according to Simon, and he offers a summary of some of the numerous "assaults" made by Chris-tian thinkers on this problem. The authors of the church made subtle distinc-tions between the moral and the ritual law, and talked of the supersession of the old law by a new covenant promulgated for a new people (Simon 1986 73-85). Like Simon, Lloyd Gaston sees the "law-gospel antithesis as the most fundamental root of theological anti-Judaism". Adopting the "antithesis with Judaism as a key hermeneutical principle", was the only way according to Gaston, of "saving the Septuagint as the Old Testament of the Christian church" (Gaston 1986b: 164; cf. also Hare 1979, Meagher 1979).

Rosemary Ruether seems to stand apart. Her central thesis is that the root of anti-Judaism is to be found in the church's christological ideas (argument 1 above). She maintains that anti-Judaism arose as the negative side of the church's exegesis of the Scriptures, and became the "left hand" of the move-

---

[1] In our discussion of the various types of anti-Judaism, one of the objections I have raised against the hypotheses put forward by scholars is that they fail to take proper account of the form and character of the anti-Jewish passages. Theological anti-Judaism avoids this pitfall.

ment's "christological hermeneutic" (Ruether 1974: 123). Ruether has been widely criticized for her focus on the christological question (cf. Gager 1983: 24ff). However, in the context of the attempt to make sense of what lies behind the church's *theological* negation of Judaism, this critique of Ruether is misplaced. Ruether's insistence on the centrality of the christological issue differs in its emphasis from the focus on the law question, but not in its fundamental understanding of the church's theological argumentation. Indeed, when Simon talks about the problems raised by the church's abandonment of the law, and when Ruether links anti-Judaism with the christological ideas of the church, both are seeking to explain the functioning of the same theological construct. They merely approach this task from slightly different vantage points.[2]

Simon's concern is with the logical contradictions that emerge from the church's commerce with the holy book, and in his description of the church's efforts to resolve these contradictions, he naturally turns his focus to the difficult question of the law. Ruether, on the other hand, is concerned more specifically with the internal logic of the anti-Judaic argument as it relates to Christian theological thinking. She is seeking to uncover what lies at the heart of the church's supersessionary language vis-à-vis Judaism, and she traces the source of the anti-Judaic polemic to the "faith principle of the church" (Ruether 1974: 78-79), that is, to the affirmation of faith in Christ. Christology is central because the advent of Christ is the turning point in the story that unfolds in the exposition of the anti-Jewish themes. It is Jesus, as long awaited Messiah, who inaugurates the new covenant, and allows the church to speak of a new spiritual legislation that abolishes the need for, and the validity of, the old law. It is also in Christ, or rather, in the response to Him, that we find

---

[2] Ruether is criticized for paying insufficient attention to Jewish concerns in her study (Meagher 1979: 19), and against her, it is argued that the essential issue that divided the two groups related not to christological beliefs but to Christianity's abandonment of the law. The central importance of christology is dismissed on the grounds that the Jews would have been willing to accommodate non-conformism on the level of messianic claims, and that it was rather serious tampering with the law that they could not tolerate (Hare 1979: 31-2; Gaston 1986b: 166-7; Meagher 1979: 20; Townsend 1979: 88). Scholars may well be right that in the years leading up to the final *separation* of church and synagogue, the "main point of contention" between the two groups, the issue that "produced the parting of the ways" was not the church's unorthodox view of Jesus, but its disregard for the law (Gaston 1986b: 166-7; Hare 1979: 31). The key question that needs to be answered, however, and this pertains directly to the critique of Ruether, is whether the cause of the divorce between church and synagogue was also the issue that *continued* to motivate church thinkers in their systematic negation of Judaism in later exegetical and theoretical texts. Because the conflict theorists take for granted that Christian antagonism, from the apostolic period right up to the conversion of Constantine, was rooted in social reality, they do not even pause to contemplate this question. In my view it should be answered in the negative. Here the discussion pertains not to the anti-Judaism that emerges out of interaction between the two communities but rather to the *internal* sources of anti-Judaism in the church's *theological ideas* (cf. also Typology IV.1).

the fulfillment of the dialectic of promise and judgement—the ultimate proof of the election of the gentile church as the new and true Israel. The promises of the scriptures belong to those who recognize in Christ the Son of God, and heed His word. Judgement and reprobation falls on those whose history of sin culminates not only in their failure to recognize their Lord but in their responsibility for His crucifixion.

So the christological argument resolves the problem raised by the abandonment of the law, and both issues form part of the Christian vision of salvation history. Ultimately, then, to the extent that they are concerned with the theological dimension of Christian anti-Judaism, Simon and Ruether are both making the same kinds of logical connections. Both talk of the way in which the supersessionary argument resolves the problem created by appropriation, whether it be in a discussion of the new law that takes the place of the old, or in a consideration of the nature of Christ. Both kinds of arguments share a "structural dualism" that is "absolutely fundamental to the whole of Christian thought" (Caspary 1979: 107; cf. Dumont 1983: 47).

Let us look briefly at the Christian anti-Jewish arguments, at the logic that unites them, and at the theological problems that they seek to resolve. As we shall see, these arguments, which are "composed of a series of dialectical opposites", are somewhat "circular" in structure. Each argument leads into the next, and one dialectical pair serves as the foundation for the proof of another (Caspary 1979: 107). In "Christian thought letter is to spirit as the Old is to the New Dispensation, as the Old Man is to the New, as the superfluities and externals are to the inner life, as letter is to spirit" (Caspary 1979: 70). The theological dualism expressed in the writings of the church is "capable of almost perpetual self-renewal" (Caspary 1979; 108).

Appropriating the Scriptures, Through the Christological Hermeneutic: Source of Authority for Supersession

The theological teaching of the fathers consists in an exegetical exposition of the Bible, and perhaps the most vital appropriation made by the church was its appropriation of the Holy Scriptures, or its appropriation, rather, of the right to interpret these Holy Writings. This was vital at least partly because the "high antiquity" of the Scriptures claimed "authority for these writings", and though the Christian religion dated from a "comparatively recent period", it could prove its "standing" by demonstrating that it was supported by these, "the oldest which exist" of all writings (Tertullian, *Apology* 21). It was also on the basis of its christological hermeneutic of the Scriptures that the church justified its election as the new chosen people. It became vital then, for the church to secure possession of these Scriptures for itself, but without thereby jeopardizing the integrity of the sacred texts. Once again, christology comes to the rescue. It serves as an interpretive key and provides the unifying principle of scriptural interpretation. Lactantius describes how Jesus opened to his disciples "the writings of the Holy Scriptures, that is, the secrets of the prophets; which before his suffering could by no means be understood, for they told of Him and of His passion". Of the two testaments he tells us: "the Jews make use of the Old, we of the New: but yet they are not discordant, for the New is the fulfilling of the Old, and in both there is the same testator, even Christ, who, having suffered death for us, made us heirs of His everlasting kingdom, the people of the Jews being reproved and disinherited" (Lactantius, *Divine Institutes* IV, 20).

Along with the appropriation of the Scriptures for the church went a denial of them to the Jews. It is the failure of the Jews to read the scriptures on a spiritual level, as a prediction of Christ, that explains the Jewish refusal to believe in Jesus (Origen, *On First Pinciples (In principiis)* 4.1.3-4; 4.2.2). In virtue of this, the Christians claim to dispossess the Jews as sole interpreters and guardians of the sacred writings: "These words were laid up in your scriptures, or rather not in yours but in ours for we obey them, but you, when you read them, do not understand their sense" (Justin, *Dialogue* 29.2; cf. 45-48; 82.1). The Jews, it is argued, are incapable of interpreting their own scriptures, and, with the coming of Christ, all the interpretive gifts are said to be transferred to the Christians (cf. Ruether 1974: 161-2).

The Law: Abrogated with the Old People, and Fulfilled with the New

The problems raised by the abandonment of the law were resolved in a variety of ways by the fathers of the church, but Christ is central here again, and his advent is portrayed alternatively as bringing about the abolition, and the fulfillment of the old law. Sometimes the inadequacy, the shortfalls, of the Mosaic dispensation are emphasized, and it is declared as abolished by the superior law of Christ. "For the old law used to avenge itself by the vengeance of the sword, and to destroy "eye for eye" and inflict retaliatory revenge for injury; but the way of the new law is point to mercy, and to change the old fierceness of swords and spears into peacefulness" (Tertullian, *Against the Jews (Adversus Judaeos)* 3; cf. *Barnabas* 11.2). In other instances, the transition from the old dispensation to the new is portrayed not as a sharp break, but as a natural progression from the incomplete to the perfect. Clement of Alexandria stresses the unity of the old and the new dispensations by claiming that both are given by the one Logos, the former "by the Logos, through his servant Moses" who acted as intermediary, the latter directly by the incarnate Christ (Clement, *The Instructor of Children (Paedagogus)* 1.60.1).

But whether the transition to the new dispensation was viewed as radical or progressive, the Mosaic law was said to remain transitory, a mere prelude to the "definitive law and covenant more binding than all others" given by Christ (Justin, *Dialogue* 11). The Christian writings defended the superiority of the church's new law and covenant partly by claiming its anteriority over the Mosaic law, tracing the origins of righteousness in Christ back to pre-Patriarchal history. Justin argues that if circumcision were really necessary, then God would not have formed Adam uncircumcised, nor would he have accepted gifts from Abel, or been pleased by Enoch (Justin, *Dialogue* 18.3). The Jewish law is thus relegated to an insignificant intermediate period of transition, existing on a lower moral level than the spiritual, patriarchal faith restored by Christ (cf. Ruether 1974: 150-1). "And so truly in Christ are all things recalled to their beginning, so that the faith has turned away from circumcision back to the integrity of the flesh, as it was from the beginning. So too, there is liberty now to eat of any kind of food, with abstention from blood alone, as it was in the beginning. And there is unity of marriage, as it was in the beginning" (Tertullian, *On Monogamy (De monogamia)* 5.1-3).

The fathers also portrayed the supersession of the new dispensation over the old as a spiritualization and universalization of the old prescriptions. The "circumcision of the flesh", was portrayed as an inadequate precursor of the true "circumcision of the heart", and was said to have been imposed on the Jews as a racial mark, given "as a sign to separate the Jews from other nations" (Justin, *Dialogue* 16.2). Tertullian summed up the transition as follows: "Whatever had prevailed in days gone by was either abolished, like circumcision, or completed, like the rest of the law, or fulfilled, like the prophecies, or brought to perfection like faith itself. Everything has been changed from the carnal to the spiritual by the new grace of God which with the coming of the gospel, has wiped out the old completely" (Tertullian, *On Prayer (De oratione)* 1.1-2).

Why then did God prescribe this inadequate legislation? That the law was *intended* by God to be limited in time and place, formed an important element in the church's justification for the abandonment of the law. But the Christians had to account for God's purpose in proclaiming an inferior law which was destined to be surpassed. The answer to this key question was found, conveniently, in the moral degeneracy of the Jewish people. The Jews were a rebellious, hard-hearted and ungodly people, and the law was "given them as a means of mitigating some of these offensive qualities and endowing them with some consciousness of God" (Bokser 1973-4: 120-121). When Trypho inquires of Justin why the Christians don't observe the law, Justin levels the accusation back at him, claiming the prophets as witnesses to the obduracy of the Jews. They offend even against their own commandments (Justin, *Dialogue* 12). Irenaeus explains that God gave the law to the Jews on account of their stubbornness and insubordination (Irenaeus, *Against Heresies* 4.15.2; 4.16.4).

In the discussion of the law, then, the denigration of the Mosaic cult was accompanied by an attack on the people themselves, and, as we shall see, it was in terms of Jewish sinfulness that the church's displacement theory was justified. A natural corollary of the notion of a new law, then, was the notion of the new people for whom this new superior dispensation was intended. We return to the argument in Tertullian's *Adversus Judaeos*, with which we opened this discussion on the law: "Accordingly, we, who were not the people of God previously, have been made His people, by accepting the new law above mentioned, and the new circumcision before foretold" (Tertullian, *Against the Jews* 3).

Salvaging and Appropriating the Jewish God at the Expense of the Jewish People

The abandonment of the law as enshrined in the Holy Scriptures also posed a problem for early Christian scholars on the level of theodicy. How to explain that the God of the Old Testament promulgated a sacred law for his people and then repealed it, without thereby robbing Him either of His justice or omnipotence? Once again, anti-Judaism served an important function here, because the Jewish God was "rescued at the expense of making him anti-Torah and anti-Israel" (Gaston 1986b: 164). The abrogation of the Jewish law was explained in terms of the sinfulness of the Jewish people, thus sparing the Jewish God from charges of weakness and injustice.

Stephen Wilson brings out the logic in this argument very clearly by contrasting it with the Marcionite position. Marcion was condemned in the early church for his denigration of those key elements of the Jewish tradition which the orthodox church had chosen to appropriate (cf. Typology IV.2). He thus dispensed with the Old Testament God as an inferior deity, and his notion of the inferiority of the law was consistent with his view of this inadequate God. Indeed, Marcion made a radical separation between Judaism and Christianity, as was exemplified in his view of two gods. He contrasted the fickle and inconsistent god of the Jews, who ruled the created order through his law, with the redeemer God of the Christians, a god of love and mercy, who was revealed in a completely unprecedented way in the person of Jesus (Wilson 1986b: 48; cf. also Efroymson 1976: 112-146). As Wilson demonstrates, Marcion's sharp break with the Jewish tradition "solved in one bold stroke" the contradictions inherent in the Catholic *via media* (Wilson 1986b: 57). As a result, his anti-Judaism was markedly different from that which emerged from the church's theological arguments.

Though Marcion saw Judaism as inferior, he made no claims on the Jewish inheritance, and was thus able to leave Judaism to the Jewish people. Expressed in simple terms, while Marcion "attacked the symbols" of Judaism, and "left the people alone", the Catholics "took the symbols and attacked the people". Wilson illustrates this contrast by imagining what the Marcionite and the Catholic might each have said to the Jew. Where the Marcionite says:

"Keep your God, your Scriptures, your Messiah, and your law; we consider them to be inferior, superseded in every way by the gospel", the Catholic says: "We'll take your God, your Messiah, your Scriptures, and some of your law; as for you, you are disinherited, cast into a limbo, and your survival serves only as a warning of the consequences of obdurate wickedness". Wilson contemplates briefly which of these two forms of denigration of Judaism constitutes the lesser evil, and though he wouldn't want to "be found defending either view", he suggests tentatively that the position which left Judaism to the Jews might be seen as marginally less objectionable (Wilson 1986b: 58).

The main point for our purposes is the clear and unambiguous connection in the logic of the Catholic position between the church's claim to the Jewish tradition and inheritance, and its chastisement of the Jewish people. "The Catholic position, imperiously defending it proprietal rights to the Jewish God and scriptures, could find only a negative reason for the continued existence of the Jewish people" (Wilson 1986b: 58). It is revealed to us, once again, how the early church's peculiar brand of anti-Judaism emerged from its theological argument.

The Christians salvaged the Creator God from Marcion's scornful dismissal of Him by condemning the Jewish people, and in defending the Jewish God at the expense of the Jews, the church also took possession of the God of the Jews. The christological argument intervenes here once again. This is not only because the rejection of Christ was thought to be foreshadowed in the early apostasy of the Jews against God, but because the refusal to acknowledge the Messiah also became *equated* with an outright denial of God. It was in virtue of their rejection of Christ that the Jews were said to forfeit all claims to address God as father. In the rejection of the "Word, through whom God is made known", the Jews are thought to show their blatant ignorance of God, for the Father cannot be known except through the Son who imparts knowledge of Him. "Therefore have the Jews departed from God, in not receiving His Word, but imagining that they could know the Father (apart) by Himself, without the Word, that is without the Son" (Irenaeus, *Against Heresies* IV.vi.1 & vii.4). In his exposition on the Lord's Prayer, Cyprian expresses this appropriation in no uncertain terms: "We Christians, when we pray, say Our Father; because He has begun to be ours, and has ceased to be the Father of the Jews, who have forsaken Him" (Cyprian, *On the Lord's Prayer (De oratione Dominica)* 10; cf. Tertullian, *On Prayer* 2.3).

Reinterpreting the History Leading up to Christ: Appropriating the Promise, and Assigning the Blame

We have seen that the legitimacy and authenticity of Christ as Messiah was proven by showing how he was prefigured in the Old Testament. The church fathers also sought confirmation in the Holy Writings of the election of those who *followed* Christ. And the reverse side of these supposed prophecies of election were prophecies interpreted as announcements of the disinheritance of those who were to reject the Lord. In appropriating the "Old Testament", the church claimed the right to reinterpret both its warnings of judgement and its promise of forgiveness. Ruether describes how the early church thinkers split the "prophetic dialectic of judgement and promise" in the Scriptures, and claimed that that which was once thought to apply to one people now applied to two: the faithless Jews and the faithful future Christians. "Every negative judgement, threat, or description" was taken out of context and "read mono-lithically as descriptive of the 'Jews'". The positive side of the prophetic mes-sage, on the other hand, that is, "the traits of faith, repentance, and future promise" were said to apply not to the Jews, but to the "future Church" (Ruether 1974: 131). Ironically, the prophets, the "flower of Israel" thus be-came involuntarily responsible for the disinheritance of their own people (Simon 1986: 215).

The whole of scriptural history was reinterpreted by the fathers around their central theological tenet, the divinity of Christ (Blanchetière 1973: 398). In this context the history of the Jews, as recounted in the Scriptures, was rein-terpreted as a history of apostasy, leading up to and making sense of what was defined as the worst and most unforgivable of all crimes. As Ruether explains, the purpose of listing a "catalogue" of Jewish crimes was "to provide the heritage for the final apostasy of the Jews in the killing of the Messiah" (Ruether 1974: 128-9). The rejection and murder of Christ was portrayed, then, as the culmination of a long history of Jewish sin. This history explained why the Jews did not recognize the Messiah who had long been promised to them. In response to Celsus' objection that the Christian God was not recog-nized by the people who had long been expecting him, Origen replies: "In fact, I think that this is enough for anyone who wants an explanation for the Jews' disbelief in Jesus, that it was consistent with the behaviour of the people from the beginning as described in Scripture... You testify by the fact that you disbelieve in Jesus that you are sons of those in the wilderness who disbe-lieved the manifestations of God" (Origen, *Against Celsus* II, 75).[3]

In the church's lore, it was believed, then, that the two people were "predicted" and "anticipated" in the Scriptures (cf. Ruether 1974: 132). Hip-

---

[3] Of course placing sole responsibility on the Jews for the crucifixion was also essential to the church's theological argument. Historically, this is an inaccurate claim. Jesus' crucifixion was ordered and carried out by the Roman authorities in Palestine. We referred earlier to the tendency in the early church to shift the blame for the crucifixion away from the Roman authorities, and onto the Jews as a religious group. We also saw that this is viewed by some scholars as a political ploy to gain favour with the Romans at the expense of the Jews (cf. Ty-pology III.1). I am arguing here that a theological motivation for this culpabilization of the Jews makes much more sense.

polytus explains how Moses knew beforehand that the people would reject the Saviour, because "at all times, they showed themselves enemies and betrayers of the truth, and were found to be haters of God, and not lovers of Him" (Hippolytus, *On Christ and Anti-Christ (Demonstratio de Christo et Antichristo)* 58). In a pastoral treatise exhorting patience, Cyprian tells the story of the Jews to illustrate or epitomize the crime of impatience:

> Why was the Jewish people faithless and ungrateful in respect of the divine benefits? Was it not the crime of impatience, that they first departed from God? Not being able to bear the delays of Moses conferring with God... nor did they even desist from their impatience, until impatient always of docility and of divine admonition, they put to death the prophets and all the righteous men, and plunged even into the crime of crucifixion and bloodshedding of the Lord (Cyprian, *The Advantage of Patience (De bono patientiae)* 19).

Aside from passages affirming the sinfulness of the Jews, there are also many passages in the writings of the fathers testifying to the church's triumphant appropriation of the positive side of the Jewish past (Bokser 1973-74: 208). The church frequently appealed to the imagery of the rival sons of Isaac, Jacob and Esau in its attempts to typify the two peoples (Ruether 1974: 133). Jacob, who prefigured the church, was said to have received the rights of the first-born, because his elder brother had looked on these rights with contempt:

> Even as also the younger nation received Him, the first-begotten, when the elder nation rejected Him... But in Christ every blessing [is summed up], and therefore the latter people has snatched away the blessings of the former from the Father, just as Jacob took away the blessings of Essau (Irenaeus *Against Heresies* IV.xxi.3).[4]

Justin explains that it is the prefiguration of Christ in the Scriptures which entitles His followers to bear the name of Jacob, and of Israel, and to become "the true children of God": "since Christ was referred to as Jacob and Israel, so we who keep his commandments, are, by virtue of Christ who begat us unto God, both called and in fact are, Jacob and Israel and Judah and Joseph and David, and the true children of God" (Justin, *Dialogue* 123.8).

The irony involved in the claim that a gentile people, known in the Scriptures as the heathen idolatrous nations, had superseded the first guardians of these Scriptures, is not lost on the fathers of the church. The handmaid casts out her mistress, just as "the Church of the Gentiles, which though itself a slave and a stranger to the promises, cast out the free-born and lordly synagogue, and became the wife and bride of Christ" (Hippolytus, *On Proverbs*

---

[4] See also Cyprian, *Testimonies (Testimonia ad Quirinum)* I.19; Tertullian, *Against the Jews.* 1; *Barnabas* 13.2-4. The image of the two wives of Jacob was also appealed to by the church writers for purposes of contrast with the synagogue. Cf. Cyprian, *Testimonies* 20; Justin, *Dialogue* 134; Irenaeus, *Against Heresies.* IV.21.3. The gospels also provided raw material for the opposition of church and synagogue. See Tertullian's interpretation of the parable of the prodigal son (Tertullian, *On Modesty (De pudicitia)* VIII and IX).

(In proverbia)). This makes the Jewish rejection of Christ all the more reprehensible, for though they "were shown beforehand all these mysteries ere they
were fulfilled and yet they are always ungrateful" (Justin, *Dialogue* 131.4);
and the election of the gentiles becomes correspondingly all the more noble:
"the faith of the Gentiles is proved to be of a more noble description, since
they followed the word of God without the instruction (derived) from the
(sacred) writings" (Irenaeus, *Against Heresies* IV. xxiv. 1-2).

Essential to the argument here is that the fall of the Jews stems from their
failure to follow the logic of their own tradition, and the main proposition,
which emerges directly out of this, is that "authentic Judaism is really Christianity" (cf. Bokser 1973-4: 98).

Interpreting the Fate of the Two Peoples in the Wake of Christ's Advent

The judgement and promise that are foretold in the Scriptures, and that are
applied to Jews and Christians respectively, find their fulfillment in Christ's
advent. "After Jesus' advent the Jews have been entirely forsaken and possess
nothing of those things which from antiquity they have regarded as sacred,
and have not even any vestige of divine power among them. They no longer
have any prophets or wonders, though traces of these are to be found to a
considerable extent among Christians" (Origen, *Against Celsus* II.8). Just as
the history of the two peoples is said to prepare the way for their different responses to Christ, so the response to Christ itself, it is believed, also seals the
fate of the two peoples, ensuring the triumph of the church, and the defeat of
the synagogue. The Christians use this model not only to interpret the past,
and to predict the future on the Day of Judgement, but also to make sense of
present events. The destruction of Jerusalem, the exile of Jews from their holy
city, and the crushing defeat of the Bar Kochba revolt at the hands of the Romans are attributed to the synagogue's rejection of Christ. Origen's statement
about the dispossession of the Jews continues:

> On account of their disbelief in Jesus and all their other insults to him the Jews
> not only will suffer at the judgement which is believed to be coming, but also
> have already suffered more than others. What nation but the Jews alone has been
> banished from its own capital city and the native place of its ancestral worship?
> They suffered this because they were very ignoble people; and although they
> committed many sins they did not suffer from them any comparable calamities to
> those caused by what they had dared to against our Jesus (Origen, *Against Celsus*
> II.8; cf. also Tertullian, *Against the Jews* 13; Hippolytus, *Against the Jews* 5-7).

We have already referred to the double standard expressed in the writings of
the church fathers. Persecutions suffered by the Jews, it was claimed, were a
sign of divine wrath, while Christians subjected to oppression were believed
to have earned the name of holy martyrs for a cause whose ultimate vindication was beyond doubt. The Christian authors saw no contradiction in this

double claim because it emerged directly from, and served as a justification for, their central theological position.[5]

The Theological Dimension: How Much Can it Explain?

To sum up: We have here a tradition which remains constant over centuries, and forms a coherent body of mutually reinforcing arguments. It functions according to an internal logic in which the invalidation of Judaism emerges as a theoretical necessity in the appropriation of the Jewish God and the Jewish Bible for the church. It is grounded in a hermeneutic of the Holy Scriptures which condemns not the contemporary actions of Jews, but judges them rather in terms of historical crimes with a theological significance. The Jews are judged in particular in terms of their response to Christ as Messiah. The church's portrayal of Judaism is expressed in terms of a dualism opposing Christians and Jews which is built into the very logic and into the very structure of Christian teaching. Recognizing this, scholars have acknowledged, as we have seen, a theological dimension in the formation of the "Adversus Judaeos" tradition, and they have further linked these theological arguments to the formation of Christian identity.

It might appear, at this stage, as though we were merely adding a new dimension to a consideration of the many factors accounting for anti-Jewish ideas and feelings among the early Christians. The need to invalidate Judaism on a theoretical level is seen as complementary to the need to counter the Jews as rivals (Typology I), and as a reinforcement of the resentment generated by the Christian sense of social and political inferiority vis-à-vis Judaism (Typology II). In an earlier chapter we referred to the common assumption among scholars that the early Christians sought to assert their identity on a *practical* level by opposing the secure and established Jewish communities that they came into contact with (Typology II.1). In this chapter we have discussed the sense in which the affirmation of the Christian "self" involved a negation of the Jews on the theological level. These two aspects of identity formation, the practical and the theoretical, might easily be seen as complementary: two motivating factors both contributing to the denigration of Judaism in different dimensions of the church's existence.

As we shall see shortly, most scholars defend this thesis in some form or other. Their aim is to uncover the patterns that governed relations between Christians and Jews on the level of action and perception in the first centuries of the church's existence. In the attempt to come to grips with what is commonly viewed as a complex social phenomenon, scholars have put forward hypotheses and explanations which are, by definition, multi-factorial. Starting with the premise that the relationship between Christians and Jews was a

---

[5] See Typology III.1, and below "The Cultural Perspective".

conflictual one, scholars seek to identify the many different factors that are believed to have fueled and perpetuated this hostility and antagonism. They operate with the unstated assumption that the identification of a large number of factors will automatically lead to a more nuanced, sophisticated, and therefore to a more accurate understanding of the Christian negation of Judaism in the writings of the early church.

A very important step has been overlooked here, however. In their determination to avoid the pitfalls of the theologically over-determined approach, and to uncover the social and political context of early Christian existence, scholars come to their interpretation of the Christian texts on Judaism with a preconceived notion of the level of reality revealed in the writings. Eager to speculate about the social dimension of the church's relations with the synagogue, these scholars proceed to make suppositions about the many aspects of Christian identity without stopping to enquire what aspect of Christian identity is actually revealed in the sources which have come down to us. Taking for granted that the texts give us access to a social phenomenon in all its dimensions, modern interpreters generalize about the complementarity of the ideological and socio-political levels of reality.

Yet clearly, as has been argued in this book so far, it is not Christian identity in all its dimensions that is revealed in the Christian writings. We have access here to one expression of Christian identity—that is Christian identity in as far as it is expressed in the theological, exegetical and pastoral writings of the early church. The key question is, what aspect of Christian identity vis-à-vis Judaism these Christian writings reveal. And this important hermeneutical question must precede any historical investigation. Before we interpret the Christian references to Judaism in the light of externally generated hypotheses about how Christians might have perceived and reacted to their Jewish contemporaries, we must first focus on the content of these references in order to determine what aspect of Judaism they oppose.

This prior hermeneutical question is essential because the various hypotheses about the sources of anti-Judaism put forward by modern scholars are potentially mutually exclusive. To the extent that we define the source of anti-Judaism as stemming from *genuine* theological concerns, and as emerging in a *genuine* way from the need to resolve internal contradictions in the Christian argument, then we identify the references to Judaism as references to a figurative entity. To the extent that the early Christian writers are thought to be concerned with the formulation of Christian identity on a theoretical level, the anti-Jewish myths become abstract creations, stemming directly from the formation of an identity that affirmed itself through the appropriation of the Jewish tradition for the church, and the denial of this tradition to the Jewish people. In other words, then, accepting that the church's writings have a theoretical dimension, which can account for the origins of anti-Jewish ideas, has important implications for our understanding of the references to Judaism in these writings. To the extent that the Judaism portrayed by the church fathers is recognized as a figurative entity which emerges out of Christian theorizing about Christianity, it cannot simultaneously be interpreted as referring to a living Judaism from which useful information can be gleaned about Jewish-Christian interaction. Unfortunately, though, most scholars seem oblivious of the need to make interpretive choices of this kind.

This is not to say, of course, that the answer to the hermeneutical question is predetermined. There are several possible ways of interpreting and understanding the theological references to the Jews in the Christian writings. I am merely making a plea, at this stage, for exploring all the options. In very simple terms, three main options might be distinguished.

(1) The Reductionist Option

One might want to argue that the theological portrayal of Judaism is no more than a rationalization for deep-seated prejudices held by Christians against their Jewish contemporaries. According to this view, the theological language used in the writings of the fathers to denigrate the Jews conveys the fact but not the substance of Christian objections to Judaism. Though the writings ostensibly condemn scriptural Jews, the real source of these anti-Jewish passages is thought to be the social and political tensions between second and third century members of church and synagogue. The scholars who come closest to defending this point of view are those who see Christian anti-Judaism as an extension of earlier pagan prejudices. These scholars essentially reduce anti-Judaism to a political phenomenon in which the theological argument plays a secondary, "whitewashing" role (cf. Typology III.1; Idinopulos & Ward 1977; Meagher 1979).The reductionist thesis is also hinted at elsewhere. In the analysis of Melito's *Paschal Homily*, for instance, the substance of the bishop's objections to Judaism is often ignored altogether in the effort to build a case for social animosity between church and synagogue (see Typology II.1). This reductionist option is rarely defended in its pure form, however.

(2) The Multi-Factorial Option

Most interpreters of the texts under study here are advocates of the multifactorial option. They draw on both theological and social factors in their attempts to account for Christian anti-Judaism. Though the case is never stated explicitly, the consensus seems to be that these factors stem from two mutually reinforcing levels of motivation. In fact however, it is difficult to determine exactly how scholars evaluate the various motivating factors, and what role they grant to each of them. The reason for the lack of clarity is that most interpreters of the Christian texts on Judaism seem unaware of the need to distinguish clearly between orders of motivation in their hermeneutical efforts. They obviously operate on the unspoken assumption that there is no impediment to the accumulation of motivations in the attempt to account for Christian anti-Judaism as a global phenomenon. This is problematic because, as has already been stated, what we have access to here is not a global phenomenon, but one expression, one aspect of what Christians had to say about Judaism. If indeed, we detect in this expression both theological and social objections to Judaism, then we need to be precise about where and how each order of explanation holds true in the writings; about which level of motivation is primary; and about how the secondary factors fit into the picture.

This kind of clarity is essential, because, as we have seen, in as far as we are trying to make sense of specific references in the writings at our disposal, different explanations of what underlies these references come into contradiction with one another. If anti-Judaism is a creation of Christian logic for the purposes of Christian self-definition, then it becomes of limited usefulness to those who seek in it an expression of how Christians typically responded to their Jewish contemporaries in day-to-day interaction. The failure to address any of these issues has led to great deal of confusion, and even to blatant contradictions in the scholarly literature, as I propose to demonstrate shortly.

(3) The Theological or Cultural Option.

A third option sees anti-Judaism, as it is expressed in our writings, as internally generated, a product of Christian theologizing.[6] The denigration of Judaism is seen, according to this view, as emerging from the internal dynamic in the formation of the church's cultural identity. As such, it is thought to arise independently of any contemporary influences. Though some scholars seem to be tempted to move in this direction, this option has been given far too little consideration in attempts to account for the historical sources of Christian anti-Judaism. In the remainder of this section: (1) I will consider the kinds of confusions and contradictions that have resulted both from the failure to distinguish between these options, and from the inability to choose clearly between one option and another. (2) I will then show how this confusion arises from the tenacity of the "conflict theory", and I will review the factors that have prevented scholars from giving serious consideration to the theological explanation as a viable option in its own right. (3) Finally, I will make a defence of the third option. My aim is to show why it offers the most convincing

---

[6] David Flusser defends this view in Flusser 1983 & 1983-4, reprinted in Flusser 1988: 617-64. Parkes also adopts this view in his *Antisemitism* (1963: 62), though elsewhere, he seems to be swayed by the "conflict theory" (cf. Parkes 1969, discussed in Typology II.3).

explanation of Christian anti-Judaism as it is portrayed in the early writings of the church.

(1) Confusions in the Multi-Factorial Option

As we have seen, most scholars who recognize some kind of theological dimension in the anti-Jewish writings are also exponents of the "conflict theory" of Jewish-Christian relations. Though they go part way towards acknowledging the sense in which anti-Judaism emerged from theological self-definition, they clearly don't see how this might be incompatible with the idea that anti-Judaism was a product of active rivalry.[7] Interpreters often move unconsciously from affirming the theoretical dimension of anti-Judaism to a discussion of the competition that is assumed to have characterized the relations between church and synagogue. Nowhere is any attempt made to distinguish properly between these levels of explanation, either to establish an order of priority, or to determine which of the two dimensions is revealed in any given passage.

Marcel Simon, who laid the foundations of the "conflict theory", seems in his discussion of theological anti-Judaism to acknowledge for a moment that he has stepped out of the realm of controversy into the realm of logic. When he sketches the evolution of the fathers' attempt to resolve the contradictions inherent in the church's position, he reminds the reader that he is not tracing an "evolution in time" but uncovering, rather, a "logical progression" (Simon 1986: 447 note 39). He also seems aware on some level that in as far as Judaism was a foil for Christian argumentation, and in as far as anti-Judaism was a product of "subtle reasoning", the references to "Jews" and "Judaism" in the church's writings, must have been used "figuratively" rather than literally: "also included in the charge of Judaism are all those who deviate from officially accepted teaching or profess erroneous positions...Doubtless to call people "Jew" in this fashion was to use the word figuratively" (Simon 1986: 96). Despite this apparent recognition of an exclusively theoretical dimension of anti-Judaism, however, Simon does not really leave room for the "figurative" in his explanation of anti-Judaism.[8] In Simon's view, the "conflict theory" is all encompassing, and the most fundamental cause of anti-Judaism remains the rivalry between the two missionary religions. Ultimately, for Simon, there is only one important level on which the church is thought to have

---

[7] Aside from those scholars discussed below see also Williamson 1982: 89; Flannery 1985: 284-295; Poliakov 1965: 37-38; Lovsky 1955: 114-15, 159, 162; Grayzel 1946: 83-87.

[8] Strangely enough, Simon seems to assume that the "significance" of the figurative "manner of speaking" is that it offers an example of the church's "defensive reaction against Israel after the *flesh*" (Simon 1986: 96-7; my emphasis)!

been preoccupied with Israel, the level of live controversy, and real confrontation.

The confusions found in the work of Simon are also shared by many other scholars of the "conflict theory". Some of the affirmations of these scholars seem to imply that anti-Judaism emerged from the internal and theoretical process of identity formation in the church. Yet elsewhere they appeal to the very same arguments in building a case for the "conflict theory", as providing evidence of Christianity's need to defend itself against attack. In attempting to account for the sources of anti-Judaism, John Gager talks of the church's efforts to "create and maintain a symbolic universe of its own". Christianity's historical origins in, and "painful separation from Judaism meant that its sense of identity and legitimacy took shape within the framework of opposition to Judaism"(Gager 1983: 135). Gager appears here to be acknowledging a theological dimension to the church's anti-Jewish arguments, and, indeed, he describes this as a "factor at once more profound and more elusive than the need to defend oneself against outsiders". Ultimately however, his notion of "symbolic universe" has very little life apart from its defensive function, because it is only cited in the context of an attempt to explain why the "Jewish critique" of the church "could not be left unanswered", and it is placed very firmly in the setting of "competition and conflict with local synagogues" (Gager 1983: 135).

Stephen Wilson also recognizes anti-Judaism as the "reverse side" of the attempt by the church to articulate Christian self-definition, and he seems to attribute this directly to the appropriation by the church of elements of the Jewish tradition: "The adoption of many of the beliefs and structures of Judaism, and above all, of their scriptures meant that it was virtually impossible to assert a Christian understanding of salvation without implicitly denying the Jewish equivalent." Yet Wilson moves without warning from the realm of self-definition to the realm of conflict as he continues in the very next sentence: "Between them (Jews and Christians), too, there was bound to be a degree of animus lacking in their conflict with other competitors". Once again, competition is assumed as a given, and whatever applies to Christian theorizing is automatically and unquestioningly thought to apply equally to the interaction between the two groups. Ultimately Wilson only raises the issue of Christianity's origins in Judaism the better to explain the intensity of the conflict between the groups. "The closer they were, the more intense was the competition" (Wilson 1986c: 95).

Contradictions: Lame Versions of the Theological Option

Some modern scholars seem to be more aware that the attribution of a theological motivation to Christian anti-Judaism involves a reevaluation of the references to the Jews in the writings of the church fathers. These scholars appear to recognize that seeing anti-Judaism as a function of the internal logic of Christian arguments is not consistent with understanding it as a response to the external pressures exerted by a living Judaism. They seem prepared to talk in terms of alternative rather than complementary levels of explanation. Yet even here the "conflict theory" will not be laid to rest. It creeps back into the argument in some guise or other. The idea of conflict has become so much a part of modern presuppositions about the relationship between early Christians and Jews, that scholars seem unable to free themselves of the "conflict theory" altogether, even when reintroducing it involves them in a contradiction of their earlier rejection of it. Part of the problem of course stems from the lack of conceptual clarity in this field. Because the "conflict theory" has never been clearly identified and defined as a concept, there has been no way of measuring the consistency of affirmations relating to it. As a result, blatant contradictions and inconsistencies in the modern interpretation of the ancient Christian texts on Judaism have gone unnoticed and uncorrected.

In the "Retrospect" to a series of articles on *Anti-Judaism in Early Christianity*, Lloyd Gaston makes an attempt to define Christian anti-Judaism, and concludes that "it arises out of an inner theological debate rather than a rivalry with a living Judaism." In other words, it was generated within the church, and neither prompted by a response to contemporary Judaism nor "motivated by personal animosity toward specific Jewish persons" (Gaston 1986b: 163-64). The "Adversus Judaeos" tradition aims not to express hostility towards the Jews, or even to prove Christ to the Jews, Gaston goes on, but "to convince *Christians* that Scripture is compatible with faith in Christ" (Gaston 1986b: 167, my emphasis). Though Gaston seems to be discounting rivalry as a source of anti-Judaism, he refers later in the same article to the controversy over scriptural interpretation as the "main point of contention between Christians and Jews" (Gaston 1986b: 166-7). Gaston does not explain, however, how he comes to identify a "point of contention" in a conflict whose existence he has already effectively dismissed.

On the basis of his study of the writings of Tertullian, David Efroymson also concludes that the church father's anti-Jewish polemic is disconnected from Jews and their actions. The church father's references to Judaism do not seem to arise out of "face-to-face contact" with a living Judaism. Quite to the contrary, Efroymson tells us, the evidence strongly suggests that Tertullian "was dealing with a caricature, with the Jews in his head, not those in Carthage". The references to Judaism lack the specificity and substance that one would expect from allusions to living Jews. In fact, Tertullian appears to have had little or no "authentic personal knowledge" of the Jews of Carthage, "if anything, what seems noteworthy is what he apparently does not know" (Efroymson 1976: 63).

Efroymson concludes then that we can glean little about Judaism per se
from Tertullian's accusations against the Jews or, for that matter, from those
of other Christian writers in the Patristic age. He bases his conclusions both
on the content and on the spirit of Tertullian's writings. Firstly the Jews who
appear in Tertullian's writings are for the most part scriptural Jews. Secondly
they are referred to in a surprisingly indirect and abstract way. Though Tertullian takes on most of his opponents directly, addressing them in the second
person, the Jews are always referred to in the third person. "Roman magis-
trates are 'you'; Tertullian's catholic opponents are 'you'; Marcionites, and
even the dead Marcion himself are all 'you'. But never Jews." "The Jews are
never 'you', the Jews are 'they'". Perhaps, Efroymson proposes, "the abstraction, the caricature, simply will not take on sufficient life or concreteness to
become 'you'...the Jews are not those in the synagogue on the outskirts of
Carthage; they are the Jews in Tertullian's imagination" (Efroymson 1976:
63).

Along with this negative estimation of the contemporaneity and accuracy
of the Jewish references, goes a positive hypothesis accounting for the purpose of Tertullian's polemic against Judaism. Tertullian's anti-Judaism was an
inheritance from his Christian and Roman African roots. "Very little that is
original can be found in the *content* of the anti-Jewish accusations"
(Efroymson 1976: 79), explains Efroymson, but this tradition was kept alive
for a purpose. The Judaism of which Tertullian wrote "seems to have been a
theological abstraction, constructed from a narrow selection of biblical texts
for purposes of *contrast with Christianity*. And this seems to be the rule rather
than the exception, both for the Patristic age and later" (Efroymson 1976: 4).
Therefore Efroymson elaborates, the tradition was kept alive not through personal confrontations,.but because Tertullian "grew to need anti-Judaism" for
internal reasons. Efroymson distinguishes two main objectives in Tertullian's
use of the anti-Jewish tradition. The first, the "rhetorical" use of anti-Judaism
against Marcion and other opponents, shall be considered under the heading
"reaffirmative" anti-Judaism below (Typology IV.2). The second objective
identified by Efroymson relates directly to "theological" anti-Judaism, which
is the subject of this section. According to Efroymson, Tertullian uses anti-
Judaism "theologically, or symbolically, to construct a Christianity, a Christian social identity" (Efroymson 1976: 64).

We might be tempted to conclude from this brief review of Efroymson's
hermeneutical analysis that he has ruled out the "conflict theory". Yet despite
what appear to be clear and unequivocal observations, Efroymson does not
seem able to shake free of the "conflict theory" altogether. In a chapter entitled "Why the Jews?", in which he tries to explain why Tertullian chose the
Jews as his anti-type, Efroymson proposes a number of explanatory factors
and, in doing so, he falls back on some of the familiar notions of the "conflict

theory". Although the evidence won't allow him to speak of an active conflict between Christians and Jews, he cannot seem to escape from setting the anti-Jewish passages in a context of hostility between the church and the neighbouring synagogue. Like most modern scholars, Efroymson assumes that the two groups viewed each other with antagonism and mistrust. In the light of his earlier observations, he can't argue that Jews and Christians physically clashed, so he transfers the conflict to the level of perceptions and feelings. In the true tradition of the "conflict theory", he engages freely in suppositions about the attitudes of both groups.

Though Efroymson questions the claim that Jews were actually involved in the persecution of Christians, he argues that "there is little reason to doubt the fact of Jewish resentment or hostility toward Christianity". On the Christian side, Tertullian was no doubt "quite convinced of Jewish antagonism". He certainly "*believed* there had been Jewish persecution at least of the early disciples of Jesus, and probably *wanted to believe* there was Jewish responsibility for recent and current Christian tribulation" (Efroymson 1976: 55; my emphasis). One might wonder how Efroymson justifies making assumptions about Christian and Jewish perceptions of the other on the basis of texts which he himself has told us were not intended as references to contemporary Jews. What is particularly astounding is not just that he makes assumptions about what Tertullian supposedly "believed" or "wanted to believe" (I wonder about the distinction between these) about his Jewish contemporaries, but that he leaps to conclusions about the hostility of Tertullian's Jewish contemporaries after having told us in no uncertain terms that they make no appearance in the writings of the church father.

Efroymson also seems to buy into the notion of "defensive anti-Judaism". [9] The two groups may not have come into contact, they may not "have engaged in actual disputations", but the Jews "were certainly there", and they constituted a "significant and attractive presence". Here once again Efroymson makes assumptions both about Jews and about Christians. He quotes Robert Wilken to describe the Jews as "a real, active and often effective rival and competitor of Christianity" (Wilken 1967: 313), and he describes Tertullian as responding to this potential threat with feelings of resentment (Efroymson 1976: 55-6). Because Efroymson can't justify the notion of direct and active conflict between the two groups, he talks rather of "an atmosphere of competition or conflict" (Efroymson 1976: 208-9). One might wonder what an "atmosphere" of conflict consists in. It seems to have all the key elements of tension and hostility, despite its apparent lack of a concrete manifestation. It is of course conceivable that a given group should feel hostility towards another on the basis of purely illusory and unfounded perceptions not grounded in

---

[9] Cf. Typology I.2: the defence against the supposed allure of Judaism.

contact, but Efroymson seems to be suggesting here that Christian feelings of hostility were generated by the actual "presence" of Jews and by the implicit threat that this presence posed. How the Jews could be active and effective competitors of the new church without coming into contact with any Christians is difficult to imagine. In addition, we also need to enquire of Efroymson how he arrived at his assumptions about the tensions emerging from an implicit competition on the basis of texts that are, by his own admission, disconnected from real Jews.

Finally, in his brief discussion of the factors contributing to Jewish-Christian hostility, Efroymson also seems to adopt the notion of "reactive anti-Judaism". [10] Like most scholars, he attributes much importance to the contrast in the social status of the two groups. The "privileged civil status of the Jews", he presumes, no doubt fueled Christian resentment against the people of the synagogue. This was particularly true, argues Efroymson, because of the "heavy social and psychological price" that had to be paid by Roman citizens who converted to Christianity. Presumably, the Christian convert's "loss of status" would have made the privileges of the Jews all the more difficult to bear (cf. Efroymson 1976: 58-61).

Efroymson draws on a quotation from Tertullian to back up his claim. The passage is from the *Apology*, and, in it, Tertullian defends himself against the potential charge that Christians are "hiding something" under the *umbraculum*, or protection of Judaism, an *insignissimae religionis, certe licitae*, an illustrious and undoubtedly a lawful religion. Tertullian is thought to be referring here to the fact that Judaism enjoyed the status of a *religio licita* within the empire. Because Efroymson cannot conceive of Tertullian voluntarily expressing anything positive about the Jews, he assumes that the allusion to the illustriousness of Judaism is sarcastic, and derives from Tertullian's irritation at the legal status of the synagogue, a status Tertullian would have wanted for the Christians (Efroymson 1976: 59). This interpretation strikes me as extremely dubious, however, and Efroymson seems to realize this also because he makes his suggestion quite tentatively. Let us look at the passage again within its larger context:

> But having asserted that our religion is supported by the writings of the Jews, the oldest which exist, though it is generally known, and we fully admit that it dates from a comparatively recent period—no further back indeed than the reign of Tiberius—a question may perhaps be raised on this ground about its standing, as if it were hiding something of its presumption under shadow of an illustrious religion, one which has at any rate undoubted allowance of the law (*Apology* 21.1-2).

This passage opens the twenty-first chapter of Tertullian's *Apology*. The question at issue here is the "standing" of the church, and the basis of its bold

---

[10] Cf. Typology II.1: the negative reaction to the "power" and "prestige" of the synagogue.

claim to possess the truth. Tertullian argues that despite its relative youth, the Christian religion is backed by the most ancient and, therefore, by the most venerated of all authoritative sources, the Jewish Scriptures. It is in Tertullian's interest therefore to point to both the illustriousness and the legality of the Jewish religion. This is the very religious tradition upon which the claims of Christianity are based, the tradition which "supports" the authority of the church. Tertullian would have been defeating his own purpose, therefore, if he had used the adjective "illustrious" in a sarcastic tone in this context. What is striking about his reference to Judaism is not its negative, but its positive overtones. Tertullian sings the praises of Judaism in this passage because the Judaism of which he speaks here is an appropriation of Christianity. He is not thinking of a live and independent religion, but of the tradition out of which Christianity emerged, and from which his church derived its antiquity, and therefore its authority. This is a perfect example of the theological symbolization of Judaism in the name of Christian self-affirmation.[11]

So while Efroymson recognizes the role of the anti-Jewish motifs in the formation of the church's vision of itself, he is too much a prisoner of the premises of the "conflict theory" to be able to abandon the idea of Judaism as adversary of the church. He is unwilling to make the choice between defining anti-Judaism as an exercise in internal fortification, on the one hand, and identifying it as part of a polemical strategy directed specifically against Jews, on the other (cf. Efroymson 1976: 64; 80; 112).

We turn finally in this discussion to the work of Rosemary Ruether. Her aim, in *Faith and Fratricide* is to uncover the theological roots of Christian anti-Judaism, and she traces these to the internal logic of the church's christological hermeneutic. It appears at first as though she sees anti-Judaism as a purely internally generated phenomenon, as an "intrinsic need of Christian self-affirmation" (Ruether 1974: 181). Like Efroymson, she also comments on the "somehow insubstantial" quality of the portrayal of Judaism in the Christian writings (Ruether 1974: 164). The "present day synagogue is largely ignored" states Ruether, and she notes the absence of any direct appeal to the Jews in the texts (145 & 148). Like Efroymson, she asserts that the "simplified stereotypic form of the Christian rejection of the law" suggests a "meagerness of actual knowledge" about Judaism on the part of the authors of the early church (Ruether 1974: 156).

---

[11] Simon translates "umbraculo" as "protection", and also argues that the passage refers to Christianity's inferior, less secure position in the Roman world (Simon 1986: 107). But as I have argued, Tertullian seems less concerned here with legal issues than he does with establishing the church's religious authority and legitimacy. (Cf. also Tertullian *To the Nations*. I, 10; Origen, *Against Celsus* 21). On positive references to the Jews as evidence of the church's appropriation of the Jewish tradition, see end of this chapter: "Reevaluating the Jewish Question".

Though Ruether is praised for having "intensified the debate on the sources of Christian anti-Semitism" (Gager 1986: 103). and for having "redefined the problem itself" (Davies 1979: xvi),[12] most scholars are reluctant to accept fully the implications of her work, and she has been widely criticized for what is thought to be her "monocausal" explanation of anti-Judaism. In her study, she explores the theological foundations of anti-Judaism and, in doing so, she uncovers the intrinsic link between the church's theological argumentation and the anti-Jewish motifs in the church writings. Consequently, she has been called to task for not taking enough account of social and political factors, and for not giving enough consideration to Jewish concerns in her portrayal of anti-Jewish ideas in the church. She is thought to pay insufficient attention to the "nature of the dynamics and reciprocal relationship" between Christians and Jews (Meagher 1979: 19), and to the complex and varied causes that contributed to anti-Jewish sentiments among the early Christians (Hare 1979: 31; Wilson 1986a: ix; Gager 1983: 24).

The sustained critique of Ruether's central claims can be explained in terms of the implicit threat that her thesis is seen to pose to the "conflict theory". Even so, Ruether's analysis is not as monocausal as it might at first appear. Her focus in *Faith and Fratricide* is certainly theological rather than historical. She is interested in the logic of Christian theology, rather than in the *historical* causes of anti-Judaism in the early church. But perhaps because her interest is primarily theological, she does not proceed to examine the historical implications of the intrinsic link that she makes so clearly between Christian anti-Judaism and the formation of Christian identity. Though her critics seem unaware of this, to the extent that Ruether does make passing allusions to the historical causes of anti-Judaism, she is in full agreement with the consensus view of Jewish-Christian relations.

In the very quote in which she describes anti-Judaism as "intrinsic to Christian self-affirmation", she expresses her readiness to consider other motivating factors. "For Christianity, anti-Judaism was not merely a *defence against attack*...The "Adversus Judaeos" literature was not created...primarily to *attack Jews*..." (Ruether 1974: 181; my emphasis). Elsewhere she makes an unequivocal endorsement of the "conflict theory". The "Adversus Judaeos" tradition is a "tool of active polemic". "It expresses Christian self-affirmation in the face of a live and proselytizing Judaism that continued to challenge Christianity" (Ruether 1974: 123).

Further on in her argument Ruether proceeds to an outright defence of the "conflict theory" against doubts that might be raised by the abstract quality of the Jewish references. Though the words attributed to Jews in the Christian dialogues represent "what Christians thought Jews would say" rather than rep-

---

[12] Cf. also Meagher 1979: 23-4; Hare 1979: 27; Efroymson 1979: 98.

resenting authentic arguments, this should not undermine our belief in the polemic behind these texts, Ruether affirms. The insubstantial quality of the Jews as represented in the writings "should not lead us to suppose that the disputes were not real and that Christians were not in fact replying to a real polemic that was taking place between the two faiths" (Ruether 1974: 166). So, far from attributing everything to christology in her attempts to explain or account for the *historical* sources of Christian anti-Judaism, Ruether seems to agree wholeheartedly with those conflict theorists who trace the causes of anti-Judaism to an on-going rivalry between Jews and Christians in the early centuries of the Christian era.

How to explain the tenacity of the conflict theory? What can account for the reluctance of scholars to explore the theological option, to take it seriously as a genuine and self-sufficient explanation for Christian anti-Judaism? There is both a specific and a general reason for this.

(2) The Tenacity of the "Conflict Theory": Stuck in Refutational Mode

This reluctance has something to do, I believe, with the spirit that gave birth to the "conflict theory". The "conflict theory" emerged, as we have seen, as part of a drive towards a more contextualized and deconfessionalized reading of the ancient Christian writings (cf. Typology I and II). The "doctrinal historians" of the nineteenth and early twentieth centuries treated the interpretation of the early Christian texts as a purely intellectual discipline, and they viewed the historical development of the early church as an evolution of systematic theological doctrines. In an age acutely sensitive to the power of social and political forces, this one-sided preoccupation with the categories of dogmatic theology has been deemed highly unsatisfactory. The traditional approach has been criticized not only for falling prey to the theological presuppositions of the texts it set out to interpret (cf. Simon's critique of Harnack in Typology I and Typology II.1), but also for conceiving of Christian history purely as a history of ideas to be understood in conceptual terms, and for thereby reducing Christian reality to the unfolding of an abstract, objective cognitive system. This approach certainly produced a unidimensional view of early Christian existence, and the move towards a more contextualized, socially-rooted reading of the Christian writings as a whole has no doubt led to a more balanced and more accurate understanding of early Christian development.

The "conflict theory" was born of a desire to measure up to the more rigorous standards set by modern scholarship. These scholars aspire in their study of Jewish-Christian relations, to break free from the dry and abstract categories of the traditional theologians towards a more socially-attuned understanding of the references to Judaism. After such great pains have been taken to free hermeneutical methods from the fetters of theological thinking in the name of a greater sensitivity to the social dimension, it becomes difficult to rule out altogether any consideration of social and political factors. This explains, perhaps, the popularity of the "conflict theory", and why its hold remains strong even on those scholars who recognize in principle that Christian anti-Judaism, as expressed in the writings of the church, was motivated by internal theological questions rather than external social pressures. Scholars are stuck in a kind of "refutational mode". Still busy combatting the overly-theoretical approach of Harnack, these scholars are unable to move beyond their aversion to abstract theological categories in order to allow the theological language of the early church's objections to Judaism to speak for itself. Convinced that their interpretation remains incomplete without attention to social context, they do not stop to ask whether the texts that have come down to us are actually amenable to social enquiry.[13] But there is also a more general reason which explains why the theological dimension has been overlooked and underestimated.

Culture as a Residual Category in Modern Sociology

The reluctance to view the theological as a genuine order of motivation, able, in its own right, to account for early Christian anti-Judaism, also fits in with a wider trend in sociological theory. The story of sociological theory since the Second World War is the story of the rise and fall of the "Parsonian empire" (Alexander 1987: 281). Talcott Parsons dominated English language social theory in the post-war period until the mid-60s. His "structural functionalism" has come under severe criticism ever since, but his importance has meant that many modern social theorists define their theory as a challenge or refutation of the Parsonian synthesis. Parsons developed a picture-type, static model of social interaction, in which behaviour was determined by socially shared patterns, for the sake of socially agreed on purposes (cf. Malina 1982: 234). Parsons saw the social world in terms of ideas, particularly in terms of norms and shared values, and he constructed an immense abstract theoretical framework which claimed in principle to be able to account for all social action. Part of the impetus behind the challenge to Parsons arose, however, out of the sense of functionalism's inability to encompass the new empirical conflicts and the new ideological themes that have characterized post-war society. Founded on the early hopes of stability and prosperity in the postwar era, structural-functionalism was felt to be inadequate in efforts to understand a society in which change, conflict and constraint played an intrinsic role. The Parsonian synthesis found it difficult to withstand the combined challenge posed by such developments as the rise of the "new economic and racial conflicts, the instability of the third world, the rise of existentialism and critiques of confor-

---

[13] Cf. Introduction and Typology III.2

mity, and the emergence of revolutionary youth culture" (Alexander Alexander, Jeffrey, C. 1987: 118).

Indeed, sophisticated theories of conflict, and a full appreciation of the power of individualism are absolutely essential to any real understanding of our rapidly evolving, turbulent modern world. Unfortunately however, the reaction to Parsons' overemphasis on the collective order and the status quo, has also been accompanied by an underemphasis of the "normative" dimension which was so central to Parsons' theory. In effect, post-Parsonian theories have made culture into a "residual category" (Alexander 1987: 284). Interestingly, it is precisely from these post-functionalist theories that modern scholars of the biblical and post-biblical Christian texts have derived their interpretive models, and one might even draw some parallels between the reaction to Parsons in sociological theory and the anti-theological thrust in biblical and post-biblical hermeneutics.

(3) Restoring Autonomy to the Cultural Sphere

There is however one strain of post-Parsonian theory that has tried to right this imbalance. It is called hermeneutical theory. The tradition from which this theory springs has its roots in German idealism and in the reaction against the individualistic and rationalistic tendencies of the English and French Enlightenment. One of the tradition's early exponents was the German philosopher Wilhelm Dilthey, who wrote in the late nineteenth and early twentieth centuries. Dilthey argued for the need to interpret and understand the world as a realm of collective meaning, as a common sphere of outer reality, into which our lives as individuals are woven (Dilthey 1976: 191, 221-2). In its modern versions, hermeneutical theory criticizes Parsons from quite a different angle than other post-Parsonian theories. Rather than accusing Parsons of undervaluing the individual, the hermeneutical critique accuses him of not recognizing the true importance of the collective cultural realm (Alexander 1987: 285). The most important figure in this cultural critique of Parsons is the cultural anthropologist Clifford Geertz. In some respects, Dilthey's notion of "outer reality" or "objective mind"[14] is an old-fashioned version of the "cultural system" that Geertz has fought to gain recognition for (Alexander 1987: 290).[15]

---

[14] Dilthey's concept of "objektiver Geist" is borrowed from Hegel.

[15] Geertz has recently become popular among New Testament scholars (eg. Esler, MacDonald), and his ideas are occasionally appealed to in the modern interpretation of the patristic texts on Judaism. David Efroymson adopts Geertz's concept of "cultural patterns" as "models of" and "models for reality", in his elucidation of Tertullian's anti-Judaism (Efroymson 1976: 223; Geertz 1966: 6 & 9). But that in as far as these concepts stand alongside the "conflict theory" of Jewish-Christian relations, the central premise of Geertz's critique of modern sociological thinking seems to have been missed altogether.

Let us examine Geertz's cultural theory (in particular as it applies to religion), and the critique of current cultural anthropology that emerges from this theory. Geertz defines culture as a series of symbols or "inherited conceptions expressed in symbolic forms, by means of which men communicate, perpetuate and develop their knowledge about and attitudes toward life" (Geertz 1966: 3). In the religious realm, these symbols "formulate conceptions of a general order" which dispose men towards certain kinds of actions and attitudes (Geertz 1966: 4). Religious beliefs help to make sense of the world, argues Geertz, but they also transform everyday existence, by imbuing the dispositions that they induce in men with a prior authority which is peculiar to them (Geertz 1966: 9).

Geertz describes the unique source and direction of the religious perspective on the world through a contrast with a perspective derived from commonsense. The common-sensical perspective bases itself on the realities of every day life, and seeks to act upon them. The religious perspective, on the other hand, moves beyond these mundane realities to wider ones which correct and complete them, and its aim is not to act on these realities but to accept them, to have faith in them (Geertz 1966: 27). The religious realm has an objective observable quality to it, and Geertz affirms the importance for the anthropologist of recognizing its autonomy. It not only interprets social relations and "psychological events", but also shapes them, and it serves as a source of "distinctive concepts of the world, the self and the relations between them" (Geertz 1966: 40).

In emphasizing the centrality of the religious dimension, Geertz is not adopting an idealist position. He is not arguing against the influence of other dimensions of reality, but stating rather that religion cannot be reduced to them, that it needs to be considered in its own right. "No matter how deeply interfused the cultural, the social and the psychological may be in the everyday life of houses, farms, poems, and marriages, it is useful to distinguish them in analysis" (Geertz 1966: 6) Accordingly, Geertz defines the anthropological study of religion as a two-stage operation. In the first stage, an analysis is undertaken of the "system of meanings embodied in the symbols which make up the religion proper". Only once this dimension has been explored, should the second stage be embarked upon, in which the systems of meanings are related to social-structural and psychological processes.

Geertz's purpose, in distinguishing these two phases, is to point to a key problem in "much of contemporary social anthropological work in religion". In their concern with the second stage of investigation, scholars neglect the crucial first stage, and in doing so, they take "for granted what most needs to be elucidated" (Geertz 1966: 42). Regrettably, our understanding of symbolic action is paltry when compared with our analysis of social and psychological action. "Only when we have a theoretical analysis of symbolic action comparable in sophistication to that we now have for social and psychological action, will we be able to cope effectively with those aspects of social and psychological life in which religion...plays a determinant role" (Geertz 1966: 42).

Geertz's general critique of methodology in social anthropological study applies equally to the interpretation of the patristic texts on Judaism. As we have seen, the primary focus of scholars in this area has been the social and psychological dimensions of Christian antagonism towards the Jews. Here too, therefore, Geertz's first stage of study has been sadly neglected. To the extent that the theological dimension of the church's denigration of Judaism is even recognized, it is incorporated into the "conflict" model of Christian-Jewish relations. In attempts to account for the sources of Christian anti-Judaism, the theological order of motivation inevitably takes on a secondary role to, or becomes confused with, social and political factors. The sense in which the anti-Jewish myths embodied systems of meaning that made sense of the world for the early Christians is never examined or explored in its own right, but always related back to religious rivalry, or social and political conflict.

Along with his negative critique of current methodology, the positive aspect of Geertz's work, his overall approach and his definition of a cultural system, can also be useful to our investigation. His approach is helpful to our particular endeavour because it brings the focus back from general hypotheses about group interaction to a study of the texts themselves, and asks us to take seriously the language and concepts conveyed in these texts. Hermeneutical methods, as distinct from scientific ones, are "interpretive" rather than "explanatory". As Geertz explains, "the analysis of culture" is "not an experimental science in search of law but an interpretive one in search of meaning" (Geertz 1973: 5). The interpretive approach does not seek to arrive at general rules about patterns of behaviour, but attempts, through its study of man, to make sense of the "webs of significance" in which man is "suspended" and which "he himself has spun" (1973: 5).

Cultural Analysis versus "Empathetic Reconstruction"

Cultural analysis is distinct not only from the scientific approach but also from the psychological perspective, an important distinction in the interpretation of the texts under study here.[16] Where psychological reconstruction focuses on the attitudes, perceptions, and feelings of authors and their audiences as they are revealed incidently, the initial focus of cultural interpretation is on the central message of the writings themselves.

---

[16] As we have seen, many scholars of the patristic texts on Judaism seek, through empathy, to penetrate the hearts and minds of the early Christians, and to discern something of their perceptions and attitudes.

This is not to say that efforts at "empathetic reconstructions" of the world of the early church should be discounted altogether. In the area of New Testament studies, where this approach forms part of a new focus on the "social world" of early Christianity, scholars have spelled out very clearly what they hope to accomplish, and how they aim to proceed (Smith 1975: 21). The psycho-social perspective is described as an attempt to improve on what is perceived as the elitism of the traditional approach to the study of early Christian literature. Scholars seek, in other words, to shift the focus away from the "ideas and self-understanding of the leaders and writers" of the early Christian texts, towards a greater concern with the people for whom these texts were written, and who made use of them (Meeks 1983: 2; cf. Best 1983: 183). The aim of these scholars is to arrive at a much more nuanced, well-rounded and rich understanding of early Christianity, to discover "what it felt like" to become and be an ordinary Christian, rather than focussing solely on the concerns of a small group of thinkers and theorizers (Meeks 1983:2; Gager 1975: 5; Best 1983: 181; Smith 1975: 21).

This approach sounds promising and, indeed, it has produced some interesting results in the study of the New Testament texts. In the study of the patristic texts on Judaism, however, efforts at "empathetic reconstruction" have led, as we have seen, to some faulty assumptions and misleading conclusions. This is partly because interpreters of the anti-Jewish texts have set a much more ambitious task for themselves. It is one thing to focus on texts produced by and for a given group, and to attempt to uncover the social reality which these texts unconsciously and unintentionally convey. It is quite another matter, however, to focus on references touching on the "other", and to assume a priori that these references provide insight into the everyday perceptions and feelings of the group vis-à-vis this "other".

Secondly, in New Testament interpretation, the focus on the social dimension of the Christian canonical writings is founded on a long tradition of literary-critical studies. An isolated passage would never be interpreted with complete disregard for the integrity and focus of the text as a whole. Indeed, a number of New Testament scholars engaged in social reconstruction have attempted to integrate some form of textual analysis into their sociological method of enquiry. John Elliott, for example, characterizes his approach as a form of "sociological exegesis" (Elliott 1981:7). He is aware of the need to ensure that the literary text remains the "primary focus" and "starting point" of any study, so that it might serve as an "empirical control of sociological analysis" (Elliott 1981: 8; cf. Best 1983: 192). Philip Esler refers to his methodology as "socio-redaction criticism", and he calls for the need to give due consideration to "unique theological intentions" alongside the study of social and political factors (Esler 1987: 2-3,6).

In the study of patristic texts as they refer to Judaism, on the other hand, little attention has been paid to the genre of the texts in which these references are found, or to the theological language in which these references are couched. Convinced that Melito was ranting against contemporary Jews, scholars do not consider that anti-Jewish motifs would inevitably form an integral part of any interpretation of the history behind the church's Easter tradition (cf. Typology II.1). Convinced that Pionius is berating his Jewish neighbours for their collaboration in Roman persecutions, scholars overlook the real nature of the martyr's appeal and how it made sense as an urgent call to steadfastness at a time when the church was being put to the test (cf. Typology II.3). The preoccupation with the psychological predispositions of the anti-Jewish writers has prevented scholars from really listening to the words that these authors have left us with, and from hearing these words in the spirit in which they were intended.

Cultural analysis, on the other hand, provides a useful hermeneutical tool for the study of the patristic texts on Judaism. Because it focuses on the "cultural order", that is, on an observable collective reality that functions on a symbolic level and that is transmitted and perpetuated over generations, the cultural model can account for and explain the theoretical character and traditional content of the anti-Jewish passages in the Christian writings. Because it grants a living dynamic autonomy to the cultural or theological sphere, the cultural approach allows us to interpret the fathers' references to Judaism without removing them from the theoretical context in which they appear, without underemphasizing their coherence and consistency, and without translating them out of the theological language in which they are couched. It is no longer necessary to assume that the theological inadvertently or deliberately conceals a more "objective", more concrete, social or psychosocial reality.

The cultural approach allows us to appreciate for example the great importance placed by Christian authors on biblical exegesis when they adjudicated questions of vital importance to the church. In their appropriation of the Scriptures, the early Christians declared that the Holy Writings of the Jews embodied all that was authoritative for the church. It was according to the truths contained and elucidated in these Holy Scriptures that church thinkers chose to define their movement and the world in which they lived. It is perhaps difficult for us as moderns to understand the mind-set of the ancients, but for the early Christians, the Bible was much more than an occasional guide for select problems, more than a source of quaint aetiological tales, and certainly more than a source of ammunition to be used against their enemies. "For all ancient biblical scholars, Jews and Christians, the Bible contained implicitly every idea believed and propounded" (De Lange 1976: 106). This was in part because "it was usual to think that all issues bearing on human life and destiny had been settled definitively in ancient times" (Barton 1986: 140). And when Christian scholars delved into this rich tradition, it was to find answers to the central questions that required elucidation (cf. Blanchetière 1973: 370).

Most scholars of the early Christian texts recognize the importance attached by Christian authors to the consultation of the biblical writings. However, the conflict theorists have tended to underestimate how integral the biblical language and biblical orientation of the anti-Jewish passages really were to early Christian argumentation. In as far as modern interpreters believe that the main preoccupation of the fathers vis-à-vis Judaism was to discredit the Jews and disarm the Jewish threat, these scholars are inclined to view the exegetical dimension of the anti-Judaic arguments as a superficial technique adopted the better to discredit the church's Jewish opponents. Simon, for instance, talks of Christian anti-Jewish exegesis in these terms: "The Old Testament was an *arsenal* which they (the Christian authors) made free use of. Their accusations are supported by invective drawn from holy writ" (Simon 1986: 215; my emphasis). Interestingly, however, when these exegetical passages are examined as a body, when their biblical idiom is taken seriously, their orientation and their central preoccupation shifts away from Judaism as such and toward internal Christian concerns. If the Jews who make their appearance in the Christian writings are portrayed as biblical figures, this is because these figures play a crucial role in the unfolding of the church's scriptural history as interpreted and related by the Christian writers. If, for instance, Ignatius refers to Jews and Jewish ways in his efforts to bring around the Docetic heretics within the church, it is not because he is combatting Jews per se, but because it was second nature for him and his fellow Christians to draw on biblical imagery and analogies in the elucidation of all questions of importance to the church (cf. Typology I.2)

Finally, an appreciation of the theological dimension is important on another level. It is only in taking the theological dimension seriously that we can do justice to the sense in which the horizon of the early Christian writings extends beyond the finite horizon of their authors. This enables us to see the anti-Jewish literature as purveyor of cultural and religious symbolism; to recognize the sense in which the themes in this literature were transmitted historically; and to come to grips with the enduring significance of these themes, not just for the Christians of the first centuries, but for the modern Christian today (See concluding chapter).

The Mandate of the Fathers

We have seen how Geertz's theory of religion suggests the way to a new her-meneutical approach. But Geertz's notion of the cultural order, and his under-standing of the vital role of religious symbolism, can also help us in the actual interpretive task itself. With the aid of his model, we can come to see theological anti-Judaism as conveying, in itself, something worth noting, even vital about early Christian reality. Geertz's definition of culture seems very apt here. The anti-Jewish motifs of the early church can be seen as "historically transmitted symbols" by means of which the early writers of the church sought to "communicate, perpetuate and develop" their own distinctive conception of the world (Geertz 1966: 3). The Christian fathers were clearly preoccupied with their own conception of the world, and their mode of expression is theological in its essence. No doubt, in their eyes, theology was not a dry, lifeless endeavour removed from reality. It is unfortunate that, most often, when the anti-Jewish passages are seen as expressions of social reality, they are disconnected from this central preoccupation with theological motifs.

It is surely no accident that the Jewish references leave us with the sense that they deal in the abstract rather than the concrete, and in generalities rather than specifics. This is an indication that the anti-Jewish motifs emerge from, and are linked to, the overall theological focus of the works as a whole. In his study of Origen, J.W. Trigg talks about Origen in his role as ethical rigorist. The church father was always moralizing, but "his fulminations are against sin in general rather than against particular sins". It is the nature of sin that Origen seeks to expound on, and the central theme of his homilies is "the soul's attainment of unity with God". His writings therefore contain little circumstantial detail, and on the historical front they are dismissed as a "poor source of information on Christian life in Caesarea". Trigg even goes as far as to say that "Origen always assumed that any purely historical information was irrelevant" (Trigg 1983: 179-81)[17]

Robert Smith speaks of Origen's homilies in very similar terms, arguing that the church father's allegorical interpretations should be understood on a symbolic rather than a practical level: Origen addressed his audience "not by reference to his own personal experiences or even to those of others around him but by the internal and inherent power of the ideas he developed" (Smith 1974: 95; cf. also Macleod 1971: 365). The anti-Jewish passages are no exception to this general hermeneutical principle. On the contrary, these passages make much more sense when understood as historically transmitted cultural symbols, which form part of the whole theological vision of the fathers, than when they are used as evidence in efforts at social and political reconstruction.

Aside from being moral preachers and teachers of ethics, the church fathers were the "founders of ecclesiology" (Judant 1969: 261), and it would

---

[17] When it comes to the Jewish references, however, Trigg opts wholesale for the "conflict theory" without recognizing that he has contradicted himself cf. Trigg 1983:183-185 and Typology I.1.

seem that they deliberately took on this role as part of the mandate that they defined for themselves. To them fell the task of interpreting salvation history, of defining the movement to which they belonged, of tracing its origins, and of elaborating how this fit in with God's plans for His church. More importantly, they no doubt saw the transmission of these ideas to be of vital importance, and, to borrow the language of Geertz, they sought in their writings to "communicate, develop and perpetuate" this Christian cultural reality. The anti-Jewish references make sense as part of this endeavour, because, as we have seen, the church's insistence on preserving its Jewish roots meant that the affirmation of "self" could only be made at the expense of the negation of Judaism.

Simon who, like most scholars, is convinced that the church's claims about Christ were formed under constant criticism from the Jews, expresses surprise that the anti-Jewish references touching on Christ's status "reflect faithfully" the development of christological doctrine in general (Simon 1986: 158 & 160). Yet surely this is no coincidence. That the anti-Jewish passages are consistent with the general theological ideas of the church is an indication that anti-Judaism emerges from this very doctrinal development. We have evidence here of the intimate connection between anti-Judaism and the theological conceptualizing of the church. Nicholas De Lange hints at this very connection when he affirms that Origen's rejection of the requirements laid down in the Mosaic law depends on other wider theological concerns. Origen's argument against the law belongs in the context of the church father's expectation of "the coming of a new age", and of his conviction that in the old scriptures, "a new meaning" was revealed (De Lange 1976: 96). Unfortunately, De Lange does not go on to explore the implications for our understanding of anti-Judaism of this intimate connection between Origen's negations and affirmations.

The Cultural Perspective

Recognizing that in their anti-Jewish passages the fathers saw themselves as conveyors of Christian cultural reality involves a radical shift of focus in our approach to the Christian texts on Judaism. As we saw, the psycho-social approach emphasizes the polemical and apologetic bent of the Christian writings. It portrays the early Christian community as an insecure and beleaguered minority, suffering from its sense of inferiority vis-à-vis an influential and well-established synagogue. Yet if we start our investigation not with socio-political models of group interaction, but with the tone, language and content of the texts themselves, and if we take the message conveyed in these texts seriously (as a depiction of a certain dimension of the church's existence which is worthy of examination in its own right), then our perspective on the impetus and direction of early Christian anti-Judaism undergoes a dramatic reversal.

The hypothesis that the Christian references to Judaism are polemical in nature involves the presupposition that the early Christians were outwardly directed, concerned with countering the Jewish challenge, and anxious to win points against the Jews with the pagan populace and the Roman authorities. As I have already argued in the discussion of "recriminatory" anti-Judaism (Typology II.3), the Christian writings on Judaism betray a preoccupation with matters of intra-mural significance rather than a concern with justification and defence vis-à-vis contemporary Jews. The psycho-social theory's emphasis on the church's insecurity and inferiority complex is unjustified when the anti-Jewish references are interpreted within their original theoretical context. The assuredness with which the early church authors make their pronouncements not only emerges in a striking and forceful way from their writings but also clearly permeates their whole vision of their movement and of its relationship to the Judaism they oppose.

This is revealed, for instance, in the double standard maintained by the church fathers in their depiction of the sufferings of church and synagogue respectively.[18] While the defeat and exile of the Jews was interpreted as a sign of God's disfavour, the authors of the church felt no compunction in arguing that the persecutions experienced by their own movement provided confirmation of the rightness of their cause. It is certainly not in writings such as these that we find evidence that the early church viewed itself as an oppressed, beleaguered minority, intimidated by the overbearing and all-powerful synagogue. In their theological writings, the Christians show no apparent need to gauge their success according to such external standards as the size or social rank of their community. The certainty of their ultimate victory was intrinsic to their message, and it carried far more weight when they compared themselves with the Jews, than any amount of social wealth or political influence.[19]

Bolstered by the certainty of ultimate victory, the fathers could find comfort and seek reassurance even in the "hindrance of governors and populace", who "oppose the gospel and those who believe in it". For the belief in itself that "the Word of God is mightier than them all" turns the hindrance into "nourishment" by which the Word advances and wins more souls (Origen, *Against Celsus* IV.32). In effect, then, the oppression suffered by the church was thought to contain within it the seeds of the future growth and expansion of the church. In his famous "semen est sanguis Christianorum" (The blood of

---

[18] See discussion on the substance of the anti-Jewish arguments at beginning of this chapter, and Typology III.1.

[19] On the assumption that the social and political contrast was all important in generating anti-Judaism, see Typology II.1

Christians is seed), Tertullian expresses his assurance that witnesses to the death of martyrs will "feel shaken by the sight", and be intrigued to "seek out what lies behind the mystery" (Tertullian, *Apology* 50.13-15). Origen tells us that even his pagan opponent, Celsus must recognize that

> those who serve the supreme God and often face countless dangers and deaths for the sake of worshipping Him and for the laws believed to have been given by Him, should not have been overlooked by God, but that some revelation should have been made to them (Origen, *Against Celsus* VIII.53).

The certainty and confidence expressed in the writings of the church fathers emerges directly from the bold claims made in these texts to universalism, to the possession of a definitive and final truth. What the Christian theologians "may have lacked in vigor or fairness, they tended to make up in self-confidence. They no longer looked upon the Jewish community as a contributing party in the holy history that had produced the church" (Pelikan 1970: 87-89), and in virtue of this they felt free to dismiss Judaism and declare it defunct. Christians, it was argued, opted to live by "an everlasting and final law" within a "covenant more binding than all others, which must now be respected by all those who aspire to the heritage of God", and which "voids" all those that came before it (Justin, *Dialogue* 11). When Celsus charges the Christians with failing to adhere to any of the traditional long-standing customs of the recognized nations, Origen responds that the "better and more divine laws" of Christ supplant all those "customs which have existed in each locality from the beginning" (Origen, *Against Celsus* V.32). Irenaeus also explains that the validity of the Christian "rule of truth" cannot be subverted by differing opinions, for it comes intending neither to "tolerate" nor to "preserve each man's idea regarding God rooted in him of old" (Irenaeus, *Against Heresies* III.12.6-8).

That the early church had universal aspirations, and that its members were keenly aware of the uniqueness and exclusive nature of the movement to which they belonged is commonplace. However, scholars have apparently failed to appreciate the importance of this aspect of early Christian existence in their attempt to come to terms with the church's anti-Judaic arguments. Indeed the exclusiveness that characterized the church's perspective on the world is often taken for granted, as though it were a given. Yet the church's sense of its own distinctiveness played an essential role not only because it coloured the Christian view on all matters of importance, but because it was in itself part of what made the Christian movement unique, part of what distinguished this minority religion from other groups in the pagan world.

We take for granted today that adherence to a religious group constitutes an exclusive commitment, but the development of differentiated religious groups was a relatively slow and gradual process in antiquity. If the Roman state was willing to accept and find room for a wide variety of religious cults, it was in part because the notion of alternative religious systems, which called for an act of commitment that cut new adherents off from their old allegiances, was a foreign concept in the traditional system of Rome (North 1979: 85). While the Roman way of life in the Republican period was "saturated with religious observances and religious rules, there were no major institutions which were religious in their central purpose" (North 1979: 96). The practice of religious life was something automatic, integral to all areas of life, and not dependent on separate religious institutions, or on the necessity of effective religious choices.

The church was born into a Roman society whose religious life was in the process of radical transformation. According to John North, this was a period that witnessed the retreat of religion from certain areas of life, as well as the simultaneous "emergence of religious associations devoted to religious purposes and bearing a particular religious message" (North 1979: 96-97). This was a time for the emergence of exclusive religious choices and, as North explains, it was in Christianity, possessing an "autonomous institution capable of carrying its own hierarchy, its own value-system and asking the total commitment of its members", that this transformative process "reached its fulfillment" (North 1979: 96).

It is no doubt the church's unique sense of exclusivism which Tessa Rajak has in mind when, weighing the differences between Christians and Jews as religious groups in a pagan world, she comments on the paradoxical fact that "while Christianity discarded the (supposed) rigours of the law and of Jewish piety requirements...it was among Pauline Christians that the drawing of boundaries appears sharper and more complete, the alternative language, value-system and structure overwhelming" (Rajak 1985: 249). Of course, we have no way of knowing for sure to what extent average Christian believers differentiated themselves in their daily interactions with Jews and pagans in the ancient world. But there can be no doubt that a firm and uncompromising belief in the church's uniqueness and distinctness from the non-Christian world is communicated in the writings of the early church. This consciousness of exclusivity inevitably played an important role in the church writers' definition of their movement's relationship with Judaism, and it is to an examination of this aspect of the early Christian perspective that we now turn.

In his evaluation of the impact of the church on the moral and spiritual world of late antiquity, Peter Brown states that it was not the moral message of the church that constituted its most important contribution, but rather the movement's exclusive and all-embracing sense of unity. Indeed, "in moral matters", Brown estimates, "the Christian leaders made almost no innovations", and essentially sought to encourage practices which "pagan and Jewish moralists had already begun to preach" (Brown 1987: 259). This may have been recognized on some level by the church fathers themselves for they show a willingness to acknowledge on occasion the sense in which the church's moral preachings reflect a general moral order.

Origen argues for the compatibility of the law in Christ with a kind of natural law, self-evident to any "rational person", who acts after careful "deliberation" (Origen, *Against Celsus* V.38-40). Justin also implies that Christianity aspires to adhere to the laws of nature (Justin, *Dialogue* 23.3). This sense of a shared morality was also said, by the fathers, to extend to the teachings of the Jews, (the church's so-called rival). Justin and Trypho agree on the qualities that make up a righteous life— steadfastness, continence, and temperance— the very virtues which are also praised and encouraged in the teachings of the philosophers (Justin, *Dialogue* 1.8). Origen too admits his admiration for the "deeper wisdom" of the Jews, "free from all superstition". Had they not fallen into sinful ways, he continues, they might even have aspired to Plato's heavenly city (Origen, *Against Celsus* V.43).

Hence, Brown affirms, "the rise of Christianity altered profoundly the texture of the late Roman world" not because of the revolutionary content of the church's moral teachings (as many would assume), but because the Christians created a new group with an "exceptional emphasis on solidarity" (Brown 1987: 259). The new Israel saw itself as a "gathering in" of the nations, in which all previous social and religious categories faded into insignificance in the name of a "single-hearted solidarity" (Brown 1987: 256; 259). Paul's famous maxim "there is neither Jew nor Greek" (*Galatians* 3.28) continued to move and inspire the leaders of the church in later generations: "the middle wall which separated the Greek from the Jew is taken away, in order that there might be a peculiar people. And so both meet in one unity of faith; and the selection out of both is one" (Clement, *Miscellanies* VI. 13). The bond that united Christians was even thought to have an organic quality to it: "Them that believe in Him" are proclaimed "as men of *one soul* and one synagogue and one church, the Word of God addressed as Daughter, namely the Church which came into being from His name and shares His name" (Justin, *Dialogue* 63.5; 123.8, my emphasis).

Brown goes on to suggest that it was somehow in virtue of its emphasis on solidarity that the church was able to ensure that its members actually lived up to the ethical standards espoused by moralists in general in the ancient world (Brown 1987: 259). The interesting point to note here is the insistence on the priority of the unifying bond, a priority which emerges very clearly in the Christian writings. If other groups and traditions were considered to have legitimacy only as pale imitations or as outdated precursors of the truth embodied in Christian fellowship, it was because of the firm belief that morality was dependent on a willingness to accept the rule of the gospel in the name of a single-hearted loyalty to Christ.

Indeed, genuine and enduring righteousness were thought to be attainable only through faith and unity in Christ, and reform was said to *follow on* conversion, even for those who converted "with a very simple faith" (Origen, *Against Celsus* I.9). Faith and morality both stemmed, then, from the act of giving oneself over to Christ (Origen, *Against Celsus* IV.27). It was Christ who was said to purify the souls of believers (*Against Celsus* VII.8), for those who are now the "limbs of Christ" cannot be made into the "limbs of a harlot" (*Against Celsus* IV. 26). When asked about the salvation of judaizing Christians, Justin states two essential conditions on which there can be no compromise: the judaizer must make no error about the genuine *source* of righteousness, and must participate fully and without reservations in the *communion* of believers. "In my opinion such a man will be saved, remembering that these laws contribute nothing to the practice of righteousness and of piety... Nor should (he) abstain from communion or convince others to do so" (Justin, *Dialogue* 47.1).

It is in this context that we should understand the importance placed on the act of conversion in the Christian writings. Modern sociologists refer to the crucial unifying role played by the conversion experience itself, and they refer to it as a form of "radical resocialization" which essentially involves a nihilation of the convert's "former social and cultural worlds" (Remus 1986: 68, 70). Certainly, for the Christians, baptism, the rite of initiation into the community, was seen as an act of purification which washed away all sins once and for all (and was contrasted with what were described as the inferior, ephemeral forms of ritual purification in Judaism, e.g. Tertullian, *On Baptism (De baptismo)* XV.3). The powerful moral message of the church, the promise of spiritual rejuvenation that it offered (one of the main elements in Christianity that is thought to have appealed to educated pagans (Gager 1983: 66)), were thought to be rooted in the act of conversion, in the act of becoming a member of a new people, a new body that henceforth gave definition and meaning to the life of the new convert.

The early church's sense of exclusiveness, its triumphalism, and the self-referentiality that this bred, all emerge very clearly in the Christian writings. This is not to say that all Christians lived their daily lives free from all doubts, and focused only on the internal concerns of the church. My point is that we cannot really have access in the anti-Jewish passages to the perceptions and preoccupations of the average Christian believers. But we can generalize about Christian identity as it is revealed in the theological and exegetical expositions of the church on Judaism, that is, about the church's identity on a symbolic level. And on this level, the church's exclusivity and its claim to a monopoly on righteousness are primary. More particularly, these factors play a determinative role in the church's portrayal of the religious tradition from which it stemmed, a tradition which church thinkers freely adapted, appropriated and negated as they saw fit.

Reevaluating the Jewish Question

The Jewish question clearly remained an issue of central importance in the church, but it was not the size and prestige of the contemporary Jewish community that made it so. The Judaism which the Christian fathers negated was not a formidable community, or a powerful religious group which was feared and resented. The church's theological vision left no room for the recognition of any other tradition, and Judaism in particular was robbed of its legitimacy in the church's supersessionary arguments. The "conflict" scholars have been tempted to stress the apologetic element in the these arguments, to see them as justifications for the church's need to counter and undermine the challenge posed by the synagogue. Yet clearly, as has already been argued, when the church fathers declared the law null and void, and when they claimed that the old people had been disinherited and surpassed, this was no mere justification developed to meet immediate apologetic concerns. It was central to the whole theological argumentation of the church, and to Christian self-affirmation. This must be kept in mind in any attempt at determining what aspect of Judaism is actually negated in the writings.

Rather than seeing the negation of Judaism as an attempt by the fathers to undermine an existing tradition, we should see it as an indication of how complete and unabashed the Christian appropriation of Judaism really was. When they laid claim to the Jewish tradition, the Christian fathers also appropriated the right to make free use of that tradition in their account of the holy history of the church. In as far as they defined themselves in opposition to a certain form of "Judaism", it was not an independent entity that they had in mind. The "Judaism" which they opposed stood rather, in Christian theological language, for that which Christianity had left behind. The anti-Jewish passages should not be seen, then, as referring to an independent religious tradition, but only to one aspect of that tradition. It would be inappropriate to try and situate the Jews negated in the Christian writings chronologically either in the present or the past. "Judaism", in as far as it was opposed by the fathers of the church, was the theological representation of the reverse side of Christianity. It occupied the negative side of the dialectical dualism that was so intrinsic to Christian thought. It represented that aspect of scriptural history and tradition which the church had abandoned or rejected or disowned. It was, in the real sense of the word, a theological foil for Christian self-affirmation.

Max Weber's notion of an "ideal type" can shed some light on what is being described here, both through similarity and contrast. Weber defined an "ideal type" as being formed "by the synthesis of a great many diffuse, discrete, more or less present and occasionally absent concrete individual phenomena, which are arranged according to those one-sidedly emphasized viewpoints into a unified analytical construct", and which "cannot be found empirically anywhere in reality" (Weber 1968: 90). Weber's concept applies here, in that the Judaism negated in the Christian writings formed a "unified analytical construct", shaped by a one-sided emphasis on certain characteristics which existed nowhere in reality. However there is also an essential difference between Weber's "ideal type" and the Christian portrayal of Judaism. Because the "ideal type" was formed on the basis of social phenomena, Weber saw it as ultimately useful in explaining social change. In the case of the early Christian portrayal of Judaism, on the other hand, the "synthesis" was not formed on the basis of social reality, but created from a one-sided interpretation of the scriptural tradition. It was thus twice removed from contemporary reality. The source on which the Christian writers drew in their negation of "Judaism" was neither a living Judaism, nor even Jewish history, but a truncated version of Jewish tradition, more specifically, that part of the tradition which the church had abandoned or disassociated itself from in the Christian account of salvation history.

As we have already mentioned, the fathers split the prophetic message contained in the Scriptures and, in the writings of the church, the Jews came to represent one side of the people of the "Old Testament"; the side that was said to have disobeyed God and to have earned His wrath; the side that committed idolatry and was judged by the prophets; the side that was destined to murder Christ as a culmination of its history of crimes. The "Judaism" that emerged out of this interpretive process, was equated with, or reduced to, certain quintessential characteristics or traits. These were all the negative traits ascribed to the people of the Bible, which accounts for the tendency among Christian authors to describe certain qualities as peculiarly "Jewish". Envy, jealousy, pride, blindness, hardness of heart, impatience, ingratitude were all "ideal-typical" aspects of the "Judaism" negated by the church. And because "Judaism", in as far as it was negated in the church writings, represented that aspect of the Jewish tradition which the church claimed to have abandoned, and to have moved beyond, the most quintessentially Jewish quality of all, and the one which was central to all the others, was Jewish obsolescence.

In the writings of the church, the "Judaism" that was *not* at the source of Christian tradition, became synonymous with that which had been surpassed. For example, the charge of *vetustas*, or "oldness", the "perseverance in a dead past", constitutes the axis of Tertullian's accusations against Judaism. It has even been said that "if Tertullian has a theology of Israel or Judaism, it can be called a *theologia vetustatis*" (Efroymson 1976: 44). The passage below is typical. In it, Tertullian explains the separation of gospel and law in terms of the obsolescence or *vetustas* of the Jewish legislation:

> I have long since established the fact that this termination of the ancient things
> was rather the Creator's own promise made actual in Christ, under the authority
> of that one same God to whom belong both the old and the new (*vetera et
> nova*)...Christ separated the newness of the gospel from the oldness (*vetustate*) of
> the law...In that sense we admit this separation, by way of enlargement, of prog-
> ress...so also the gospel is separated from the law, because it is an advance from
> out of the law, another thing from the law (Tertullian, *Against Marcion* IV.1.9-
> 11; cf also *On the Resurrection (De resurrectione mortuorum)* 50.7; *Against
> Marcion* I.20.4-6; V.2.1-4; V.8.4-5).

Correspondingly, the few positive references to Judaism in the Christian
writings refer to those aspects of Jewish tradition which the orthodox church
identified as belonging to its *own* past. When Celsus challenges the authority
of the ancient prophets who the Christians claim foretold Christ, Origen defends the strength and resolve of the people who gave rise to these prophets.
These ancient Jews are praised for having "endured countless sufferings to
avoid renouncing Judaism and their law" (Origen, *Against Celsus* III.3). In
their appropriation of the Jewish scriptures, the Christians claimed to rely on a
source of authority far more ancient and venerable than that of the revered pagan philosophers, and the fathers sometimes acknowledged the Jews as the
original guardians of this tradition. Origen describes the Jews as possessing a
deeper wisdom even than the philosophers (*Against Celsus* V.43), and he
praises the high moral standards observed by the Hebrews who were rescued
by God from Egypt (*Against Celsus* IV.31).

In his *Exhortation to Martyrdom* (*Exhortatio ad martyrium*), Origen calls
on the faithful to live up to their title as "the true Hebrews" by imitating the
holy men who stood up to Nebuchadnezzar's threats (33). Surely if the church
had been involved in a dispute with the Jews over the right to the guardianship
of the Scriptures, if Origen had indeed identified his Jewish contemporaries as
the chief opponents of his movement, he would not have afforded himself the
luxury of praising them in this way. A polemicist involved in an intense competition for converts, or feeling resentment against the power and prestige of a
rival group, would be making a serious tactical error in ceding any ground to
this rival whatsoever. Yet the church fathers felt free to alternately praise and
condemn Judaism without fear of contradiction. These laudatory comments
can only confirm, therefore, that the references to "Judaism" in the writings of
the church were not meant to identify an independent community, but allude
rather to aspects of a tradition that the Christians had selectively appropriated
and rejected (See also Origen, *Homilies on Jeremiah (Homiliae in Jeremiam)*
XII.13). Irenaeus actually articulates this fundamental principle in his *Against
Heresies*. "In regard to the position of the Jews as seen in Scripture, we ought
not to be their prosecutors but rather look at that of which they are a symbol"
(*Against Heresies* 4.31.1). Not only does this passage confirm that the references to Judaism had a symbolic meaning, but it testifies to the fact that the

church fathers adopted this symbolic approach in a deliberate and self-conscious manner.

In the next two sections on "reaffirmative" and "illustrative" anti-Judaism, we will look for confirmation of the theological foundation of Christian anti-Judaism, by examining the important function fulfilled by anti-Judaic symbolism in the church. "Reaffirmative Anti-Judaism" refers to the use of the anti-Jewish myth in the reaffirmation of the Christian vision against Marcion. "Illustrative Anti-Judaism" refers to the sense in which the anti-Judaic corpus became a source of tradition in its own right, used in the illustration of intramural doctrinal and pastoral issues.

TYPOLOGY IV.2
REAFFIRMATIVE ANTI-JUDAISM

Over several generations, the church fathers took on the challenge issued to
orthodox Christian theology by Marcion and his followers. As was noted earlier (cf. Typology IV.1), Marcion repudiated the Catholic *via media*, and insisted on a sharp break between the church and all the symbols connected to
Judaism. He saw the God of the Old Testament as an inferior deity, lacking in
wisdom and justice, and he denigrated both the Scriptures and the law that
were associated with that God. He denied the authority of the "Old" Testament as a Christian holy book, and, as a result, he dismissed the notion, so
central to the orthodox view, that Christ was the Messiah prophesied and
foretold in the sacred Jewish writings. The Marcionite Jesus was a new and
unprecedented figure who revealed a hitherto unknown deity of love and
mercy.

Against Marcion, the Catholic church had to defend its notion of the
Creator God as one, just and omniscient; of the authority of Scriptures as
source of revelation; and of Jesus as the Messiah long promised to the Jews,
whose coming was revealed in the Holy Books (cf. Efroymson 1979: 100;
Wilson 1986b: 48; cf. also Harnack 1923: 135-59; Blackman: 1948: 66-80;
Aland: 1973: 420-47; Campenhausen: 1972: 73-102). In some senses, then,
the repudiation of Marcion amounted to a rescue operation: in the face of
Marcion's denigration of all that pertained to Judaism, the church had to rescue those Jewish symbols that it had appropriated as its own.

Though the repudiation of Marcion amounted to a defence of certain
aspects of Jewish tradition, the attack on the Marcionite heresy also
summoned the church's own form of anti-Judaism. The connection between
the rebuttal of Marcion and anti-Jewish arguments is by no means accidental.
As Efroymson has pointed out, "the largest block of anti-Jewish material in
Tertullian" is to be found not, as might be expected, in his *Adversus Judaeos*,
but in his later *Adversus Marcionem* (Efroymson 1979: 100), and there is even
a certain overlap between the two works (cf. Evans 1972: xix). There are also
links between anti-Judaism and anti-Marcionism in Justin's writing. His
Dialogue with the Jew Trypho shows clear signs of the defence against
Marcion (Stylianopoulos 1975: 20-32). Pierre Prigent suggests that the
Dialogue is an extract, even an abridged version of Justin's lost anti-heretical
work (mentioned in *First Apology* 26.8), the *Syntagma Against All Heresies*
(Prigent 1964: 9-12). Whether or not this theory is correct,[20] the fact that it
can be seriously entertained indicates how closely connected were the anti-
Marcionite to the anti-Judaic arguments in the early orthodox church.

---

[20] For a critique cf. Stylianopoulos 1975: 23.

In traditional considerations of the church's response to Marcion, the anti-Judaism that emerged from the church's refutation of Marcion received little attention. More recently, however, scholars have begun to puzzle over the connection between what they see as two polemical fronts in the early church: one internal, against an influential Christian heresiarch, the other external, against the Jews. This sort of connection between anti-Marcionism and anti-Judaism is inappropriate, however. Anti-Judaism played a role in the polemic against Marcion because it was intrinsic to the orthodox church's concepts of God, of Christ, and of the Scriptures, concepts which Marcion challenged directly. The use of the anti-Judaic tradition against Marcion provides confirmation not of a polemic directed at distinct groups, but of the theological foundation of anti-Judaism within the church. Anti-Judaism, as was argued above (Typology IV.1), was central to Christian self-affirmation not just in an incidental way, but in that it gave coherence and consistency to the theological construct that defined the church as the new Israel. Marcion's view of Christianity challenged and undermined this theological construct directly, and it forced the Christian writers to reaffirm their vision of the creator God, of Jesus as long prophesied Messiah, and of the Scriptures as holy and authoritative. The church's own brand of anti-Judaism was of course essential to this enterprise, and the anti-Jewish arguments were restated all the more vehemently against Marcion, to prove, for instance, that it was not the God, but rather the people of the Old Testament who were fickle and unworthy. I refer to the anti-Judaism used against Marcion and his followers as "reaffirmative" anti-Judaism, because it formed an integral part of the "reaffirmation" of the *via media* in the face of Marcion's threat to sever the church completely from its Jewish roots.

In an article entitled "The Patristic Connection", considering a wide range of patristic authors, David Efroymson appears to recognize this kind of substantive connection between anti-Marcionism and anti-Judaism.[21] Efroymson explains how the anti-Judaic themes came to play a *central role* in combatting Marcion's challenge to the orthodox church. Against Marcion's attack, the anti-Jewish myth came to be employed to salvage the God of the Hebrew Bible, to retrieve Jesus for traditional Christianity and to preserve the authority of the Scriptures. In response to Marcion's denigration of those aspects of the Jewish tradition that the church had appropriated for itself, the church fathers could answer that the fault lay not with the symbols but with the people.

However, while Efroymson clearly recognizes a theological dimension to the anti-Judaism that emerged from the attack on Marcion, he seems to suggest here that it was not until the church responded to Marcion that the anti-

---

[21] Efroymson 1979; cf. also Gager 1983: 160-67 who repeats Efroymson's insights.

Judaic themes began to "congeal" around central theological conceptions (Efroymson 1979: 108). He doesn't go as far as to say that Marcion created or invented the "problem" of anti-Judaism, but he does seem to imply that Marcion's challenge was responsible for appending the anti-Judaic themes to the central theological ideas of the church "in ways that came perilously close to permanence" (Efroymson 1979: 105). "Antagonism between Judaism and Christianity may have been unavoidable; but after Marcion and the defence against him, Christianity was thinking of God, its Christ, its Bible, and itself, in anti-Jewish ways", tells us Efroymson (Efroymson 1979: 108).

I do not agree. The threat posed by Marcion may have played a role in *refining* the church's theological vision by creating the need for greater clarity and coherence in the face of challenge, but anti-Judaism was integral to the church's theological conceptions, quite apart from Marcion. If the traditional anti-Jewish themes were appealed to in the attempt to refute Marcionism, it is precisely because they were so central to the theological construct which Marcion opposed. The best weapon against Marcion's anti-Judaism, was the church's own brand of anti-Judaism. Against Efroymson's suggestion that the church began to think of God and Christ in anti-Jewish ways in the response to Marcion, I would maintain, rather, that Marcion's challenge to the church's theological vision compelled the fathers to "reaffirm" their own notion of an anti-Jewish God and of an anti-Jewish Christ.

Let us look briefly at some examples. The most problematic area for the church in its defence against Marcion was the argument concerning the cessation of the Mosaic law. Marcion denigrated all Jewish symbols, and the Jewish law was no exception. He saw it as beneath all dignity, worthy only of the inferior god of the Old Testament. Though the orthodox church wished, like Marcion, to dispense with the "old" law, the early Christian theorists had to account for the fact that this outdated, abrogated law had been promulgated by a God who they believed to be infinitely just and omniscient, the same God who was revealed in Christ.[22] Justin Martyr, who is thought to be the first major Christian writer to have responded to Marcion's challenge (Stylianopoulos 1975: 26; Efroymson 1979: 105), devoted a lengthy section of his *Dialogue* to a discussion of the law, providing "proofs" of its cessation, and more importantly describing its purpose in God's plan (*Dialogue* 10-30). The law, explains Justin, has no permanent value, but was given by God as a temporary measure to restrain the sinfulness of the Jews. So, the argument continues, the fact that this law was inferior, and is now obsolete reflects badly, not on the God who decreed it of old, but on the people for whom it was decreed. Justin's argument, supposedly directed against a Jew, serves

---

[22] Cf. Typology IV.1: "Salvaging and Appropriating the Jewish God at the Expense of the Jewish People".

quite conveniently to respond to the Marcionite challenge. That he has Marcion in mind in this dissertation on the law is confirmed by his graphic and detailed defence of the Creator God of the Scriptures, a defence that would presumably have been unnecessary had he really been discussing with a Jew.

> There will never be another God, Trypho, and there has never been one from the beginning...than the one who created and gave shape to this universe. Furthermore, we do not claim that our own God is different from yours, for He is the God, who, with a strong hand and an outstretched arm, led your forefathers out of the land of Egypt. Nor have we placed out trust in any other (for, indeed, there is no other) but only in Him whom you have also trusted, the God of Abraham and of Isaac and of Jacob (*Dialogue* 11).

Justin is all too aware of what hangs on his argument about the inferiority of the law and of the Jewish people. It is the Christian view of God that is at stake in this discussion:

> But if we do not admit this, we shall be liable to fall into foolish opinions, as if it were not the same God who existed in the times of Enoch and all the rest, who neither were circumcised after the flesh, nor observed Sabbaths, nor any other rites, seeing that Moses enjoined such observances; or that God has not wished each race of mankind continually to perform the same righteous actions: to admit which seems to be ridiculous and absurd. Therefore we must confess that He, who is ever the same, has commanded these and such like institutions on account of sinful men, and we must declare Him to be benevolent, foreknowing, needing nothing, righteous and good (*Dialogue* 23).

Justin blames the Jews for the inferiority of the law, and "in a brilliant *tour de force* he argues that Judaism is responsible for Marcion" also (Donahue 1973:165). The very fact that the Jews made the promulgation of this law necessary makes them indirectly responsible for the calumnies against the creator God spread by Marcion:

> But impute it to your own wickedness, that God even can be accused by those who have no understanding, of not having always instructed all in the same righteous statutes. For such institutions seemed to be unreasonable and unworthy of God to many men, who had not received grace to know that your nation were called to conversion and repentance of spirit, while they were in a sinful condition and labouring under spiritual disease (*Dialogue* 30).

And further, God will be slandered unless you show that you were commanded to observe the Sabbath, and to present offerings, and that the Lord submitted to have a place called by the name of God, in order that, as has been said, you might not become impious and godless by worshipping idols and forgetting God, as indeed you do always appear to have been (*Dialogue* 92).

Tertullian was the most thorough of Marcion's critics, and he refutes the Marcionite heresy in a systematic and elaborate way in his *Adversus Marcionem*. Like Justin before him, Tertullian engages in a "reaffirmation" of the church's theological vision against Marcion, and he does this partly through a denigration of the Jewish people. His defence of the God of the Old Testament in Book II is reminiscent of Justin's argument: "This law was not laid down because of its Author's hardness, but by reason of that supreme kindness which preferred to tame the people's hardness, and smooth down with exacting obligations their faith, as yet unpracticed in obedience" (*Against Marcion* II.19.1). In Book III, it is the church's traditional image of Christ that Tertullian defends, the Christ that was "ordained" and "announced" and foretold by the Creator God of the Bible. Against Marcion's objection that Christ cannot be the Messiah of the Jewish scriptures, as the Jews themselves did not recognize him, Tertullian turns the Jewish rejection to his own advantage:

> But seeing there were also prophecies that the Jews would not recognize Christ and would therefore destroy him, it at once follows that he who was unrecognized by them, he whom they put to death, is the one whom they were marked down beforehand as going to treat in this fashion (*Against Marcion* III.6.4).

The church's notion of a new dispensation in Christ was also vulnerable to attack by Marcion, because it could easily be interpreted as a concession to the radical separation between old and new that Marcion himself had called for. This made the emphasis on the unity of God and on the continuity of His work all the more essential.

> I do admit that there was a different course followed in the old dispensation under the Creator, from that in the new dispensation under Christ. I do not deny a difference in records of things spoken, in precepts for good behaviour, and in rules of law, provided that all these differences have reference to one and the same God, that God by whom it is acknowledged that they were ordained and foretold (*Against Marcion* IV.1).

The question of the unity of God continued to preoccupy Christian thinkers into the third century. In his treatise *On First Principles*, Origen declares his aim to "refute those who think that the Father of our Lord Jesus Christ is a different God from him who gave Moses the sayings of the law and sent the prophets, and who is the God of the fathers Abraham, Isaac, and Jacob" (*On First Principles* II.4.1). Origen's main contribution to the anti-Marcionite debate is in the realm of scriptural interpretation (cf. Efroymson 1979: 107). He calls for a spiritual reading of the scriptures, and accuses Marcion of understanding the holy writings "according to the sound of the letter" in the manner of the "hard hearted and ignorant members of the circumcision". The Marcionites are thus likened to the Jews in their disbelief, because neither perceive in Scripture "that rule and discipline which was delivered by Jesus Christ to the apostles and which they delivered in succession to their followers who teach the heavenly Church" (Origen, *On First Principles* IV.2.1-2). Apart from the use of anti-Jewish argumentation in the defence against Marcion's claims and Marcionite influence, the fathers occasionally try to discredit the Marcionites not by using the anti-Jewish myths to counter them, but rather by *likening* them to Judaism and Jewish ways. This rhetorical ploy is evidenced in the above passage of Origen's as well as in the following passage from Tertullian's *Adversus Marcionem*. Marcion's belief in the wholly unprecedented nature of Jesus allies him, in Tertullian's eyes, with the Jews who refuse to recognize the prophecies foretelling Christ in the Jewish scriptures.

> So then, since heretical madness was claiming that a Christ had come who had never been previously mentioned, it followed that it had to contend that the Christ was not yet come who had from all time been foretold: and so it was compelled to form an alliance with Jewish error, and build up an argument for itself, on the pretext that the Jews, assured that he who has come was an alien, not only rejected him as a stranger but even put him to death as an opponent, although they would beyond doubt have recognized him and have treated him with all religious devotion if he had been their own (Tertullian, *Against Marcion* III.6).

These kinds of arguments would no doubt have greatly irked the Marcionites who defined themselves as the eradicators of all Jewish influences from the church, and it was probably to that precise end that they were used. Though used against Marcion here, this sort of anti-Judaism fits more properly into the next section on "illustrative" anti-Judaism, to which we now turn.

TYPOLOGY IV.3
ILLUSTRATIVE ANTI-JUDAISM[23]

I argued, in the discussion of theological anti-Judaism, that the anti-Jewish themes expressed in the Christian writings stemmed from the church's appropriation of certain elements of the Jewish tradition, and from the attempt by the early thinkers of the church to define their movement in fundamental opposition to those aspects of the Jewish tradition that had been rejected or abandoned. I defended the notion, therefore, that the Jews portrayed in the texts of the fathers were symbolic figures in a theological argument. I argued that the anti-Jewish corpus was a system of symbols which identified "Judaism" with the ideal-typical aspects of a reprobate and obsolete people (cf. Typology IV.1). In the section on "reaffirmative" anti-Judaism, we saw how this theological anti-Judaism served an important function in the struggle against Marcionism (cf. Typology IV.2). In this section, I propose to examine yet another function served by the symbolic portrayal of the Jews in the writings of the church. There is evidence in some of the anti-Jewish passages found in the works of the fathers of a secondary stage of symbolization.

One of the striking features of the anti-Judaic corpus, as we have seen, is its persistence over the centuries. The same anti-Judaic themes are repeated and transmitted in the works of the Christian fathers throughout the period under consideration here, and even beyond it. This is no doubt in part because fundamental theological questions of this sort were thought to be in constant need of reformulation, refinement and reinforcement within the church. The anti-Jewish myths formed part of the church's vision of salvation history, and it is to be expected that these myths should be told and retold through the generations. In addition, as we have seen, the theological construct which formed the very basis of Christian identity needed to be defended against the direct challenge posed by Marcion and the Gnostics. The latter rejected the orthodox church's *via media* between appropriation and rejection, and proposed to sever all ties with the Jewish tradition, dismissing the Jewish God, the Jewish Messiah and the Jewish bible. But the persistence of the themes that make up the anti-Jewish corpus is significant for another reason, a reason that goes beyond the needs of defence and reinforcement.

Though the anti-Jewish exegetical tradition may have been developed in the effort to defend the church's supersessionary claims, it persisted also as a system of symbols, which became incorporated in its own right into the tradition to which the church turned in its deliberations on matters of importance.

---

[23] I am partly indebted to David Efroymson for this concept. He has noted the use of the anti-Jewish myths in the works of Tertullian, for what he refers to as "rhetorical" purposes, but as I shall try to show in my own analysis, he puts too much emphasis on the contrast with Judaism, and is unable, in my view, to appreciate the real intentions behind this technique.

As a body of exegetical passages, it came to form part of the officially-sanctioned interpretive tradition of the church, a tradition which, as we have already seen, was capable of perpetual renewal. In our review of the Church's anti-Jewish themes, we examined some of the motifs that formed part of the Church's *Heilsgeschichte*. This Christian version of the history of salvation was foundational to all the claims made by the Christian movement. It authenticated the church's pedigree, as well as its claim to antiquity and legitimacy, it confirmed the church's claim to sole possession of the Truth revealed in the Scriptures, and it affirmed the inevitable triumph of Christianity. But it also provided the church with some key symbols which, even when removed from their salvation historical context, served to illustrate the Christian way in matters of discipline and doctrine. In this context, the anti-Judaic corpus became a source of tradition and authority in its own right, a tradition drawn on by the thinkers of the church for a variety of purposes. This was a source of tradition to which the writers and leaders of the church appealed in their deliberations on matters of moral, pastoral, and doctrinal importance, and which was not directly connected to the church's relationship with Judaism, whether living or symbolic, or even to the denigration of Judaism per se. These anti-Judaic symbols and themes were particularly useful in that they provided an archetypical contrast to right action and correct belief as defined by the pastoral leaders of the church.

This type of anti-Judaism is unlike the other types discussed so far, in that it makes no claim to account for anti-Judaism, to explain the motivation behind the church's need to oppose and denigrate the Jews. It is itself, rather, a product of the anti-Judaic tradition, an extension of the theological anti-Judaism so central to the church's view of itself and of the world. I have included it here in the typology of hypotheses about anti-Judaism because, in as far as it emerges from "theological" anti-Judaism, it provides further support for the view that the anti-Judaic corpus formed part of a coherent body of arguments that played a central role in the formulation of Christian identity.

We will begin in IV.3.1 by looking at some more straightforward examples of this "illustrative anti-Judaism", used in exhortations to virtue, and in attempts to rationalize and explain some of the standard practices of the church. I call this "fortifying anti-Judaism". Next, in IV.3.2 we will look at another sub-type of "illustrative anti-Judaism" which I call "associative anti-Judaism". "Associative" anti-Judaism refers to the adaptation of anti-Judaic symbols by the writers of the early church in attempts to discredit views within the church which they oppose.

TYPOLOGY IV.3.1
FORTIFYING ANTI-JUDAISM

"Fortifying Anti-Judaism" refers to the use of anti-Judaism by the authors of
the church for purposes of internal fortification, in efforts to strengthen the
moral fibre of their congregations through the promotion of Christian virtues,
and through exhortations to steadfastness in Christian practice.

The Christianization of Virtue

In their attempts to encourage and inculcate the Christian virtues, the church
fathers defined or illustrated these partially by means of contrast with corresponding Jewish vices. The tales of Israel's apostasy provided a rich source of
illustrative material in the exhortatory works of the fathers. Though they draw
on different scriptural stories, the following passages from Tertullian and
Cyprian both seek to foster patience through the characterization of its opposite, impatience. They provide evidence of the richness and versatility of the
anti-Jewish tradition, and of the free use made of this tradition by the early
church writers in their efforts at persuasion:

> Is it not clear that Israel itself, through its impatience, was always sinning against
> God? Forgetting the heavenly arm whereby it had been rescued from the afflic-
> tions of the Egyptians, it demanded of Aaron gods to be its leaders... For it had
> borne without patience the delay necessitated by Moses meeting with the Lord.
> After the rain of manna as food, after the water that followed and flowed from the
> rock, they gave up hope in the Lord, unable to endure a three-day's thirst... But
> not to range over individual instances: never would they have been destroyed if
> they had not fallen into sin by impatience. Why did they lay hands on the Proph-
> ets, except that they could not bear to listen to them? And more than that: they
> laid hands on the Lord himself, being unable to endure even the sight of him. But
> had they acquired patience, they would now be free (Tertullian, *On Patience (De
> patientia)* 5.22-25).

> Why was the Jewish people faithless and ungrateful in respect of the divine
> benefits? Was it not the crime of impatience, that they first departed from God?
> Not being able to bear the delays of Moses confessing with God...nor did they
> even desist from their impatience, until impatient always of docility and of divine
> admonition, they put to death their prophets and all the righteous men, and
> plunged even into the crime of crucifixion and bloodshedding of the Lord
> (Cyprian, *The Advantage of Patience* 19; cf. Typology IV.1).

It is important to note that it is patience rather than impatience that is the focus
of the fathers' concerns here. In both of these texts, the illustration of impatience through a characterization of the "most impatient of all people", follows
on, and provides a stark contrast to, the epitomization of patience in Christ.
The patience of Christ is described by Tertullian as "patience such as...no
mere man had ever practiced" (Tertullian, *On Patience* 3.10). Cyprian also
looks for the epitomy of patience in Christ, and he find it in the manner of the

Lord's death. The passion was a dramatic moment, and Christ might easily have been tempted to reveal his power and majesty, overshadowing even the natural signs that accompanied His crucifixion. His unrivalled patience is demonstrated in His great humility even at this most trying time:

> And when at the cross of the Lord the stars are confounded, the elements are disturbed, the earth quakes, night shuts out the day, the sun, that he may not be compelled to look on the crime of the Jews, withdraws both his rays and his eyes, He (Christ) speaks not, nor is moved, nor declares His majesty even in the very passion itself (Cyprian, *The Advantage of Patience*, 7).

The structural dualism so central to Christian thought serves here in the inculcation of a Christian virtue. The virtue of patience, and the corresponding vice of impatience, are given new life, and a new more concrete meaning when they are explained and illustrated against the background of scriptural history. Patience is encouraged not just because it is obviously morally good and right, but because it is said to be quintessentially Christian. Falling prey to impatience, on the other hand, is thought to put a person in diametrical "opposition to the peace and charity of Christ", "after the likeness of the Jews", in the manner of that people, in other words, who the early Christians learnt in their teachings were the archetypical sinners and rejecters of Christ (Cyprian, *The Advantage of Patience*, 19).

In his discussion of Tertullian's characterization of impatience, Efroymson rightly concludes: "Thus it is somehow Jewish to be impatient, just as it is Christian to be patient". But he puts the emphasis in the wrong place when he proceeds to describe Tertullian's aim in the following terms: "The only thing to be demonstrated is the key role of impatience in the list of well-known and widely-deplored Jewish crimes" (Efroymson 1980: 27). Tertullian was seeking to warn his fellow Christians, according to Efroymson, "that it would be 'Jewish' to adopt the alternative to the moral or disciplinary position" which he was espousing (Efroymson 1980: 26).

Yet clearly Tertullian is not interested here in "alternatives" or in "counter-positions". It would be absurd to suggest that Tertullian is offering a choice between patience and impatience. He does not need to win his audience over to the idea that patience is in itself a virtue but merely to encourage the practice of it. Also, Tertullian's manner of speech makes it even more plain that neither he nor his audience are tempted by the "Jewish" way as an option. His focus is rather on the positive task of strengthening the resolve of his community, and in order to accomplish this, he draws on some of the widely-used imagery from church tradition, for purposes of illustration. Jewish crimes per se are not of interest here, nor is anything being proven specifically about Judaism.

I have chosen the title "fortifying" anti-Judaism to describe the use of anti-Jewish motifs in the illustration of Christian virtues,[24] precisely because it shifts the emphasis away from the false notion of alternatives, and stresses rather the positive reinforcing intent of these passages. In texts illustrating Christian virtues and non-Christian vices, the fathers drew on anti-Jewish motifs the better to fortify the church.

Tertullian's efforts to encourage the virtues of frugality and modest living in Christian women provides another good example of the way in which the scriptural tradition could be adapted to serve a purely illustrative purpose, one which remained quite free of any deliberate attempt to denigrate the Jews. In *On the Rites of Women (De cultu feminarum)* II, Tertullian exhorts his "blessed sisters" to cast away their ornaments, so that they may not be distracted by the glitter of gold from their true calling as followers and imitators of Christ. The "iron" of martyrdom provides a stark and effective contrast to the "gold" of wealth and apostasy:

> Do not love gold—that substance which caused the very first sins of the people of Israel to be branded with infamy. You should hate that which ruined your fathers, that gold which they adored when they abandoned God, for even then gold was food for the fire. But the lives of Christians are never spent in gold, and now less than ever, but in iron. The stoles of martyrdom are being prepared...(Tertullian, *On the Rites of Women* II.13.5-6).

Just as gold idols led the people of Israel to "abandon" God, warns Tertullian, so now do gold ornaments threaten to lead the wealthy women of the church astray. Stuck on his idea of "guilt by association", Efroymson suggests that Tertullian is attempting here to "conjure up a vision of "Jewishness", with which his "blessed sisters" would be tainted if they did not abandon gold ornaments and ready themselves for martyrdom" (Efroymson 1976: 87). I disagree strongly. Certainly Tertullian's language is very rigid and uncompromising. He likens the love of gold trinkets to no less a crime than "infamy" against God. He drives home his point forcefully by drawing on scriptural tradition to illustrate the intimate connection between the pursuit of gold and apostasy against the Lord. There is no indication in this illustrative use of the holy writings, however, that he is conjuring up an image of "Jewishness", nor that he is seeking to liken anyone to the Jews. In fact, the Jews make no appearance in this passage at all. Though Tertullian does allude to the people of Israel who "adored" gold and "abandoned God", he identifies this people to the women he addresses as *"your* fathers". In as far as he makes reference to Jewish tradition at all, then, it is to an Israel and to a people that he counts among the ancestors of the Christians. Tertullian's use of this Old Testament imagery is clearly illustrative and instructive rather than polemical

---

[24] Though Efroymson's "pastoral" anti-Judaism is also a possibility.

vis-à-vis Judaism in any way. And the free use of anti-Jewish motifs for pastoral purposes provides further evidence of just how disconnected from any form of living Judaism the church fathers' negation of Judaism had become.

TYPOLOGY IV.3.2
ASSOCIATIVE ANTI-JUDAISM

We have seen how the anti-Jewish tradition served in the exhortation to virtue, and in the promotion of the Christian way of life, but it also played a role in efforts by Christian scholars to refute their opponents within the church. Here Efroymson's notion of "rhetorical" anti-Judaism makes more sense.[25] He describes this rhetorical use of anti-Jewish motifs as one of the major "operational objectives" of Tertullian's anti-Judaism, namely the "association" of opponents with Judaism, as a means of showing up the "weakness" of their position. Efroymson refers to this technique as "Guilt by Association" (Efroymson 1976: 79-80; cf. 1980: 25).[26]

When a Christian author associated or tainted an opponent with "Judaism" or Jewish ways, he was not seeking to say anything about the actual connection or similarity of that opponent to Judaism proper. In associating an opponent with Jewish traits or characteristics, the authors of the church symbolically associated a position with the typical traits known from salvation history as characteristic of that which was archetypically obsolete and typically wrong. It seems evident, then, that the fathers were not intending, through these associations, to imply any actual similarities with or connection to Judaism as such. It was not Judaism itself which the early Christian writers had in mind in these passages, nor even strictly speaking any real characteristics of Judaism. They were seeking to encourage certain kinds of practices or to defend and justify their own position against alternative ones within the church.

What better way to accomplish this than to identify the vice being discouraged or the opposing point of view with any one of the "ideal-typical" aspects of a "Judaism" which stood, by definition, in the church for that which was obsolete. The substance of this opposing view clearly mattered little and imposed no limitations on the use of the technique. The opponent's position

---

[25] But unfortunately, he does not make any distinctions between the various uses of the anti-Judaic tradition, and thus detects none of the subtle variations in focus in the different passages.

[26] Once again, however, it seems to me that Efroymson misplaces the emphasis in his characterization of Tertullian's tactics. He implies at times that "Judaism" represented a real opponent rather than a tradition used for purposes of illustration.

need bear no *actual* resemblance to Judaism or Jewish ways in order for the technique to be used effectively. This is confirmed by the fact that associations of this kind were made from both orthodox and heterodox standpoints, and, as we shall see, the same author might find himself on both ends of this practice, seeking to associate an opponent with "Judaism" in one instance, and being forced, on another occasion, to defend himself against the same charge. Some authors even used this associative technique as a way of warning members of their own congregation against falling short of the church's rigorous ethical standards.

The most interesting and noteworthy facet of "associative" anti-Judaism, is its versatility as a technique, a versatility which enabled it to be used from many different perspectives, to defend varying and even contradictory points of view within the church. This versatility provides further evidence of just how disconnected from Jews and Judaism, the anti-Judaic tradition within the church could become.

Association From Every Perspective

The versatility of the technique is exemplified, for instance, in the work of Tertullian, where we find evidence of the use of associative anti-Judaism from all possible angles. Tertullian feels free to associate his opponents with "Judaism" both in his capacity as defender of orthodoxy, and again later as a proponent of heterodoxy. He drew on the anti-Judaic tradition, for instance, when arguing against the Monarchian heresy. In his Montanist period, once he made a formal break with the church, he felt equally at ease, and equally justified, in making the same associative charge against the orthodox practices of the church. The significant point here is that he clearly saw no contradiction or conflict in adopting the associative technique from very different perspectives. This free use of the anti-Judaic tradition would not have been seen as problematic in any sense by Tertullian's contemporaries either. No one group or faction within the church had a monopoly on the associative use of the anti-Judaic tradition. Because it was a source of tradition which belonged to the Christian movement as a whole, the anti-Judaic corpus could be used for purposes of illustration to prove a variety of arguments, even conflicting arguments. It is interesting that, on occasion, Tertullian, our most expert user of the associative technique, should also find himself on the defensive, rather than on the attack, forced into the position of the one being associated rather than that of associator; forced to counter the implication that his own position is marred by the "oldness" of Judaism. Let us now look at the variety of perspectives represented in Tertullian's work:

(1) Tertullian Against the Heretics:

> Finally it would be practically of Jewish faith so to believe in one God as to ref-
> use to count in with him the Son, and after the Son, the Spirit. For what other dif-
> ference would there be between us and them except that disagreement? What
> need is there of the gospel..? It was God's will to make a new covenant for the
> very purpose that in a new way his unity might be believed in through the Son
> and the Spirit, so that God, who had previously been preached through the Son
> and the Spirit might now be known in his own proper names and persons
> (Tertullian, *Against Praxeas (Adversus Praxean)* 31.1-2).

Anxious to preserve the unity ("monarchy") of the deity, the Monarchians rejected the Trinity and refused to acknowledge the full divinity of Christ. Tertullian here likens the Monarchian beliefs to the Jewish faith, not because
there are any real similarities between the two, but because he wants to argue
that in refusing to "count in" the Son and the Spirit with the Father, the Monarchians are going against the most central tenet of the Christian faith, much
as the Jews did in their time. If the Monarchian affirmations are accepted, says
Tertullian, then all the central symbols of the church— the gospel and the new
covenant—are deprived of their purpose and meaning. It is in virtue of the
fact that he styles himself as the defender of that which is *essentially* Christian
that Tertullian's argument has punch to it, rather than because he "maintains"
and "emphasizes" the "difference between Judaism and Christianity" (as
Efroymson would have us believe, cf 1980: 26).

(2) Tertullian as Heretic Against the Orthodox Church:

In his Montanist period,[27] Tertullian wrote a series of moral works in which
he insisted on the necessity of a stringent ethical puritanism (Evans 1972:
xix). The very titles of these works betray his central concern: *Exhortation to
Chastity, On Monogamy, On Modesty, On the Veiling of Virgins,* and *On
Fasting.* In these treatises, Tertullian expressed a consistent concern about
what he saw as the laxity of the church at large. In an effort to encourage the
maintenance of strict moral standards, Tertullian turned once more to the anti-
Judaic tradition. He illustrated his argument by "associating" laxity with the
old Jewish law which had been surpassed, and he defended the severity he
himself espoused as belonging to the new way in Christ (Efroymson 1980:
31).

It is interesting that Tertullian turned to the anti-Judaic material to bolster
his argument, even in this instance, when the traditional themes of anti-
Judaism might not seem, at first glance, to lend themselves readily to his point

---

[27] Montanism was an apocalyptic movement living in expectation of the speedy outpouring
of the Holy Spirit on the church, which won Tertullian's allegiance circa 206 C.E. It developed
ascetic traits, particularly in North Africa, disallowing second marriages, condemning existing
regulations on fasting as too lax, and forbidding flight in persecution.

of view. The "Jewish" way of life is associated in these passages with laxity, and yet the Mosaic law was hardly renowned among early church members for its leniency. Quite the opposite. It was considered to be overly burdensome, and the Christian abandonment of the law was often described as a form of liberation from tiresome burdens. From the time of Paul, Christian texts make reference to a new "freedom in Christ": "When Christ freed us, he meant us to remain free. Stand firm, therefore, and do not submit again to the yoke of slavery" (*Galatians* 5.1). Of course this new found freedom was not deemed to entail an antinomian permissiveness (cf. *Galatians* 5.13ff), and the church developed the notion of a new and greater law in Christ, which was certainly freer but was also considered to be more righteous, fuller than the Mosaic dispensation.

Tertullian made the most of this notion of a fuller righteousness, and it was this aspect of Christian morality that he emphasized in his defence of a rigorous rule of conduct, describing Christian law as "more comprehensive in its scope and more exacting in its details" (*Exhortation to Chastity (de Exhortatione Castitatis)* 7.2). Clever rhetorician that he was, he even succeeded in reconciling the idea of a release from burden with his own plea for a fuller discipline, and a strict adherence to the principles of "chastity", "purity" and "modesty". In his treatise against remarriage, Tertullian argues as follows:

> To clarify the subject, we declare that the law is abrogated in the sense that the burdens which it imposed no longer rest upon us, the burdens, according to the apostles, which "not even our fathers were able to bear" (*Acts* 15:10). However, those of its precepts which have to do with righteousness not only continue in force but have even been extended, so that our "justice may abound more than that of the scribes and pharisees" (*Matthew* 5:20). If this holds true of justice, it also holds true of chastity" (Tertullian, *On Monogamy (De monogamia)* 7.1).

Tertullian made a further clarification in his *On Modesty (De pudicitia)*: "The yoke of works has been cast off, not the yoke of moral precepts; freedom in Christ has done no injury to virtue. There remains in its entirety the law of piety, sanctity...chastity...and purity" (6.3). Tertullian's aim here was to justify his ethical puritanism as being in harmony with the church's concept of the new dispensation in Christ. In order to accomplish this, Tertullian had to give grounds for moral rigourism, without making it appear that he was arguing for a resumption of the "burdens" which characterized the Mosaic law. In the passages quoted above he tried to show that a genuine "freedom in Christ" involved adhering to a new and fuller and more extensive righteousness. He even developed an historical model in which the period of the church came to be characterized as the time of the flowering of true "justice": thought to have been in its "infancy" during the period of the law and the prophets, "through the gospel it blossomed into youth, and now, through the Spirit it is composed in maturity" *(On the Veiling of Virgins (De virginibus velandis)* 1.7).

If anti-Judaism played a role in Tertullian's portrayal of the emergence of the Christian ethical tradition, it is because he identified this emergence with the supersession of the Mosaic law. It is not Jews that Tertullian had in mind when he wrote these passages, nor was he concerned specifically with the question of Christianity's superiority over Judaism (as Efroymson argues 1980: 33). This superiority was assumed as a given in Tertullian's debate with the orthodox church. The real source of disagreement between the two parties lay in defining exactly what that superiority entailed; and the fact that both parties clearly made free use of the anti-Judaic corpus in the attempt to establish their own superiority should not lead us to the mistaken assumption that this was anything but a *purely Christian* matter.

(3) Tertullian on the Defensive:

We find the very same issues at stake in a treatise promoting frequent and extended fasting practices, but this time, we encounter Tertullian on the defensive. Evidently, not all members of the church were converted to his insistence on austerity, and, in expressing their opposition to the strict practices that he encouraged, these opponents challenged him on the level that mattered most—his claim to the support of the Christian tradition. Despite his attempts to balance his rigourism with the affirmation of a "freedom in Christ", Tertullian's notions of "greater justice", "fuller discipline" and "more extended righteousness", made him vulnerable to the charge that his way represented no real advance over the "legalism" that the church was supposed to have surpassed. It was against the charge of "judaizing" that Tertullian had to defend himself.[28] This charge clearly did not imply that he was drawn to Judaism or even that his position resembled Judaism in any shape or form. Rather, it was another way of saying that Tertullian's emphasis on strict rules of conduct was out-dated, belonged to the old ways, and worst of all was backward-looking, one of the most damning of charges in a movement that described itself as irrevocably transformative, and revolutionary. Tertullian and his critics are here arguing over who has the better claim to the authority of Paul, and in their haggling over Christian tradition, it is obviously not Judaism, strictly speaking, that either party has in mind. Against the charge of being stuck in the "old" way, Tertullian bemoans the failure of his opponents to recognize his real role as "innovator" in the church.

> In observing these times and days and months and years, are we Judaizing, doing what the Galatians did? Indeed we would be, if you could show that we were observing *Jewish* ceremonies, or *legalistic* solemnities. These things the apostle teaches against, attacking that hanging on to an old covenant buried in Christ, then there must be new solemnities; otherwise, if the apostle had done away

---

[28] Another example of the very broad use of this term in the early church, cf. Typology I.2.

completely with all devotion connected with times and days, why do we celebrate
Easter?... What is ridiculous here is your own unfairness, in using the charge of
"vetustas" against us in trying to condemn us for innovation (Tertullian, *On
Fasting (De jejunio)* 14.1-4).

Turning the Associative Technique Inward as Warning

Occasionally the associative technique was turned inward and used by the
church writers as a way of galvanizing those members of their congregations
who had fallen into complacency and who had become lax or remiss in practice. A number of church fathers addressed a warning to those who they
feared had allowed their certainty of future triumph to lull them into a false
sense of security. Thus Cyprian explains that any who take God for granted,
even though they be of the elect, could easily go the way of the Jews, and he
urges the new "children of God" to be *worthy* of their right to the kingdom.
"But there is need of continual prayer and supplication, that we fall not away
from the heavenly kingdom as the Jews, to whom this promise had first been
given, fell away" (Cyprian, *On Prayer (De oratione)* 14).

Origen bemoaned what he saw as the inevitable decline that he felt had accompanied the expansion of the Christian movement (*Homilies on Jeremiah*
IV,3). He regretted the passing of the days when the faithful were few in
number but "true", following on the narrow and hard path that led to life. His
exhortations to steadfast courage in the face of trial and persecution intimate
that the election of the church lies in the balance. Playing on the imagery in
Jeremiah of the people as a "waistcloth" put on by the Lord, Origen quotes
Jeremiah 13.10-11 (which speaks of the "waistcloth" of the "whole house of
Israel and the whole house of Judah" as being "good for nothing"), as confirmation of the status of the church as the new chosen people, the *new*
"waistcloth" of the Lord. But, like Cyprian, he warns Christians not to use
their new found status as an excuse for complacency. The Jews, though de-
scended from Abraham were divorced by God for their sins. Will He be more
lenient with a people who have only just abandoned idols and the worship of
many gods, and who now subject themselves to demons anew?

> He rejected the first people, the "whole house of Judah and the house of Israel", a
> people that is "worth nothing", because God no longer wears them as a waist-
> cloth. God has put on a new one in its place, because after having discarded his
> waistcloth, he did not remain naked, but he wove another waistcloth for Himself.
> This waistcloth is the church, made up of the nations. Let them know that if God
> did not spare the first, how much less will He be inclined to spare the church if
> she falls into sin (Origen, *Homilies on Jeremiah* XI.6).

Clearly, the Jews and Jewish tradition make their appearance in these passages for illustrative purposes alone. The Jews are the people well-known in
Christian lore for having forsaken their favoured status with God. The fathers
of the church saw in the allusion to these traditional stories, an ideal oppor-

tunity for driving home to their Christian contemporaries just how precarious their own position as a newly founded movement was, if even the Jews, who had such an illustrious heritage, were not spared by God.

To sum up: The versatility of the associative technique is manifested in its use to champion both orthodoxy and heterodoxy. In defending their various positions within the church, Christian authors could find themselves alternatively on the giving and on the receiving end of the "association" with "Judaism" and the "Jewish" way. Many situations and different contexts were thought to warrant these sorts of analogies. Though the "Jews" make an appearance in these passages, it is clear that the focus is not on Judaism, but on a purely Christian problem which the reference to "Judaism" or Jewish traits serves to illustrate. The associative charge was not meant to imply any real connection with a living Judaism. It provides evidence, rather, of intra-mural disputations in the early church over the correct interpretation of Christian tradition. The representatives of various Christian factions sought both to claim the authority of this tradition for themselves and to deny it to their opponents. They also appealed to members of their congregations not to take for granted the inheritance of this tradition and its promise of election.

CONCLUSION

In this book I have presented a critique of the current approach to the interpretation of the anti-Jewish passages in the writings of the early church fathers. I characterized the approach commonly adopted by scholars seeking to explain early Christian anti-Judaism as the "conflict theory" of Jewish-Christian relations. I defined this theory as based on the notion that church and synagogue were involved in an active and undying rivalry for converts and for political supremacy in the pagan world. I argued that the theory's presumption about Jews as active proselytizers is founded in Christianizing preconceptions about ancient Judaism. I then reviewed some of the current hypotheses, generated by the "conflict theory" which have been put forward by modern scholars to explain and account for anti-Judaism in the early church. I examined what are considered to be the religious, social and political, environmental and theological dimensions of the Jewish-Christian conflict. My aim in identifying and categorizing these hypotheses was to demonstrate that these theories are not only based in dubious historical assumptions, but have themselves generated faulty and unjustified notions concerning the perceptions, motivations and actions of Christians and Jews in the Roman world. In addition, I argued that the "conflict theory" lacks confirmation in the very writings which it claims to interpret. The hypotheses put forward by modern scholars to defend the notion of a socially rooted conflict between church and synagogue have resulted in a distorted reading of the early Christian anti-Judaic passages.

Although for the most part, scholars of the Christian anti-Jewish passages define their work as historical in focus, as we have already seen, the need to come to grips with Christianity's contribution to the history of anti-Semitism provides a wider context, lends a theological significance to these historical findings. The horrors of the Holocaust faced Christians with a profound theological crisis which shook the foundations of Christianity, and which "made theologians take a new look at their Christian past" (Baum 1974: 1; Davies 1969: 35-51; Davies 1979: xiii-xiv; Gager 1983: 33). Rather than laying the foundations for a thorough investigation of the Christian past, and for a real appraisal of the origins and nature of Christian anti-Judaism, the "conflict theory" obscures these important issues. It fails, in other words, to provide satisfactory answers to the very theological questions that provided the impetus for the reappraisal of Christian beginnings in the post-war period. I propose in this concluding chapter to allude briefly to some of the important theological ramifications of the historical and hermeneutical errors made by the "conflict" theorists. The "conflict theory" fails as a theory theological explanation firstly (1) because it remains prisoner to the theological presuppositions found in the very texts which it claims to be investigating, and secondly (2) because it tends to superficialize the nature of early Christian anti-Judaism.

(1) Perpetuating Anti-Judaic Prejudices

As has already been stated, Simon's aim in his elaboration of the "conflict theory" was the defence and resuscitation of ancient Judaism against Harnack's denigration of it (cf. Introduction). But while Simon has been widely praised as a corrector of long held prejudices about Judaism in traditional scholarship, we saw at the beginning of the first chapter that his approach tends to impose the Christian model of development on ancient Judaism. Regrettably, and this despite his good intentions, Simon's model of Jewish-Christian relations is itself ultimately based on the assumption of Judaism's inferiority because it contains within it the seeds of Jewish "defeat" and failure.

In his conclusion, Simon not only implies that Christianity earned its victory and power in the empire through its inherent superiority, but he paints a very condescending and unattractive picture of Judaism at the time of the church's triumph. We see this, for instance in Simon's description of what he sees as the irony of the Jewish defeat. "Judaism had all the advantages in the beginning". It possessed some valuable assets, including "a legally defined and advantageous status" in Roman society. Yet in spite of these "external advantages", and in spite of its "vitality", the synagogue was "vanquished", tells us Simon (Simon 1986: 378). And there can be no doubt about the cause of the synagogue's retreat in Simon's eyes: "the deciding factor in Judaism's gradual development towards total retrenchment was Christian competition" (Simon 1986: 371). "Judaism's withdrawal stemmed", according to Simon, "from the acknowledgement of its own powerlessness" in the face of Christian successes (Simon 1986: 384).

For Simon, Jewish defeat is described as a kind of "retrenchment", and he means this both in a physical and in a spiritual sense. As long as it is assumed that both Judaism and Christianity were active proselytizing movements, their success is made contingent on their ability to expand, and it is in terms of expansionism, also, that their universalistic aspirations are defined. The battle between church and synagogue is one in which the most successful missionary religion not only gets the prize that both supposedly covet, but also establishes its claim to a more mature and unqualified universalism. Simon describes the options open to Judaism in very stark terms. Either Judaism reaffirmed its universalistic ambitions through continued expansion, or it abandoned these aspirations and atrophied. And in the supposed rivalry between the two communities, Simon portrays Christian success as the cause of what he characterizes as Judaism's retreat into a defensive battle for survival. Christianity robbed Judaism of its constituency, according to Simon, and brought about the "collapse" of "Hellenistic Judaism".

Simon thus identifies the rise of "Talmudic rabbinism" as a purely reactive phenomenon (Simon 1986: 374-5), described in negative terms, as an "ineluctable necessity", a "remedy" against absorption: Judaism "seized on to" the law "by a sure instinct of self-preservation", to "keep it firm against the Church's onslaught" (Simon 1986: 374). It is perhaps inevitable, given his extremely narrow view of religious development, that Simon should see this "legalism" as a sign of "impoverishment" that "turned the ancient world's intelligentsia away from Judaism", and "hardened" the "religious thinking" of the Jews (Simon 1986: 376). It is indeed unfortunate that Simon's portrait of Talmudic Judaism falls prey to some of the traditionally held misconceptions among Christian scholars about the religion of the Rabbis.[1] He characterizes Judaism as a religion suffering from a "legalistic ossification" and a corresponding "poverty of doctrine" (Simon 1986: 379). "Jews progressively cloistered themselves in a more passive and occasionally suspicious attitude, to which they had always been prone" (Simon 1986: 383). By contrast, Christianity is thought to have profited from the struggle with the synagogue. "By defending itself so fiercely, Judaism had helped to make her rival, in Justin Martyr's phrase, into 'another Israel'" (Dialogue 123.5; Simon 1986: 384).

So while Simon justifies his whole approach by claiming it constitutes an advance over Harnack's Christianizing, when it comes down to it, one might well say that Simon's real disagreement with Harnack is that Harnack failed to portray the Christian "triumph" as a real fight. Both scholars portray the Christians as emerging victorious. But while for Harnack the Jews were out of the race after their first set-back at the hands of the Romans in 70 C.E., Simon insists that the Jews admitted defeat only after an intense and prolonged struggle, which nevertheless ended with a definitive triumph for the church (when imperial legislation began to reflect the fact that the church was "yoked with the state") (Simon 1986: xvii). Simon certainly doesn't take the Christian "victory" for granted, and he represents the supposed conflict between church as synagogue as a bona fide challenge, but, in doing so, rather than leaving us with a picture of a genuinely vital and vibrant Judaism, he ultimately succeeds only in making the church's victory seem all the more glorious, and Judaism's defeat all the more ruinous.

Ironically, both scholars end up sharing a key theological preconception unconsciously derived from the early church fathers themselves. Like Harnack, Simon ultimately portrays the church as having a monopoly on genuine universalism. In fusing the universalism of the messianic hope with the ideological universalism of the ecumenical empire (Ruether 1974: 234), the church not only arrogantly claimed for itself a "pseudo-universalism" (Ruether 1974: 233), but also contrasted this achievement with a Jewish "particularism" which it assumed to be bad (Ruether 1974: 235). It thus

---

[1] On the unfortunate persistence of these views in modern scholarship see Sanders 1977: 33-58.

falsely claimed a monopoly on a quality which it only possessed partially, and it remained blind to the universalism of Judaism which rested (and continues to rest) on the universality of God as Creator (Ruether 1974: 237).

In his concluding remarks about the nature of a "vanquished" Judaism, Simon spells out the logical implications of the "conflict theory". In as much as the "conflict theory" pits Jews and Christians against one another in a struggle for a single prize, in as much as it describes this struggle as ending in a victory for the church, it inevitably contains within it the notion of a Judaism that failed and was found lacking. These views are not explicitly adopted by recent exponents of the "conflict theory", but nor are they explicitly criticized by those who laud Simon as a corrector of the traditional denigration of Judaism. In addition, in as far as these conflict theorists also accept Simon's "winner-loser" model as an explanation of the outcome of the Christian-Jewish rivalry, their hypotheses implicitly contain the theological presuppositions which are so clearly and bluntly laid out by Simon. Simon simply brings out into the open the Christianizing assumptions that underlie, and are inherent to the notion of conflict. It is unfortunate that scholars seeking to identify and account for the root causes of anti-Judaism, should fall prey themselves to some of the denigrating ideas which they aim to eradicate.

(2) Christian Responsibility for Anti-Judaism

Aside from the fact that the "conflict" theory implicitly contains anti-Jewish biases, it also fails as a theory of theological explanation on another level, that is as a theory seeking to identify the roots of Christian anti-Judaism. As we have seen, the conflict theorists take for granted that in the early Christian texts they have access to a social phenomenon in its many dimensions, in all its aspects. They further assume that underlying Christian teaching on Judaism are the social tensions that bred hostility between church and synagogue. They therefore underemphasize the theological element, and take little account of the substance and coherence of the anti-Judaic corpus, all in the name of a primary preoccupation with the so-called "local hostilities" between Christian and Jewish communities. This approach is sorely inadequate when it comes to determining Christianity's role in the propagation of anti-Semitic prejudices. The question of Christianity's responsibility for anti-Semitism is "not simply whether individual Christians had added fuel to modern European anti-Semitism, but whether Christianity itself was, in its essence and from its beginnings, the primary source of anti-Semitism in Western culture" (Gager 1983: 13). Christian theologians are faced with the difficult question of whether they can continue to express and affirm the "central symbols of their faith" without lapsing into the anti-Jewish overtones of the past." (Davies 1979: xiv-xv; cf. Williamson 1982: 105).

This is precisely the question which Ruether sets out to tackle in her *Faith and Fratricide*,[2] and, as a result, her focus is not so much on the external factors that might have contributed to tensions between Christians and Jews, as on the substance of Christian anti-Judaic teaching as it continues to make its influence felt into the modern day. If she seeks to interpret the anti-Judaic themes developed in "the classical age of Christian theology", it is in order to evaluate the way in which these themes laid the basis for prejudicial "attitudes and practices" in the centuries that followed (Ruether 1974: 226).[3] Ruether's focus, in other words, is on the "basic structures of the anti-Judaic myth" (Ruether 1974: 228).

If Ruether sees anti-Judaism as intrinsic to Christian self-affirmation, it is not simply that she traces anti-Jewish motifs back to the early beginnings of the Christian mission, nor simply that she believes that the early Christians needed to assert themselves over their Jewish contemporaries,[4] but that she perceives that anti-Judaism was woven into the very core of the Christian message. She seeks to "analyze and reconstruct the basic dualisms" built into the Christian message which deny legitimacy to Judaism, and which are "deeply ingrained in Christian language" and Christian teaching (Ruether 1974: 228-9). That which must be examined is the sense in which "eventually all dichotomies of salvation between spirit and flesh, light and darkness, truth and falsehood, grace and damnation, life and death, trust and self-righteousness, were projected on the opposition between Church and Synagogue until the Jewish people became the embodiment of all that is unredeemed, perverse, stubborn, evil, and demonic in this world" (Baum 1974: 12-13).

As Gregory Baum explains in the introduction to Ruether's book, the aim is to "expose the ideological deformation of the Christian religion in a thorough-going way" (Baum 1974: 18), and this can only be accomplished, according to Baum, by submitting "Christian teaching to a radical ideological critique" (Baum 1974: 7). Baum identifies two potential traps in this difficult and disturbing endeavour. First, he emphasizes just how deeply implanted the anti-Jewish roots of Christian teaching really are, and he warns against the temptation to "interrupt the negative critique too soon" through an overly superficial examination of the problem. Only an extensive and probing critique of Christian teaching on Judaism will be sufficient to the "raising of consciousness that is required to redeem Christianity from its anti-Jewish

---

[2] Though Ruether herself seems to confuse the social and theological dimensions of the church's negation of the synagogue (cf. Typology IV.1).

[3] See survey by C.Y. Glock and R. Stark on the continuing power of theological anti-Judaic myths in modern America (Glock & Stark 1969).

[4] Hare obviously misunderstands Ruether's main point. He describes her notion of the church's "intrinsic need of self-affirmation" over against Judaism (Ruether 1974: 181) as a kind of "psychologizing" (Hare 1979: 41). Clearly Ruether is talking about something much more substantial.

virus and its absolutizing trend" (Baum 1974: 18). The second temptation referred to by Baum is the desire, in the examination of the Christian past, to excuse Christianity and to attenuate Christian responsibility for the propagation of anti-Jewish prejudices. It is absolutely crucial, Baum affirms, that the Christian theologian be "willing to let the documents of the past say what they have to say, without softening their meaning to make them a little more acceptable to modern ears" (Baum 1974: 21). Unfortunately, the conflict theorists have fallen into both these traps, in their identification of the sources of early Christian anti-Judaism, and in their virtually exclusive focus on the social "context" of early Christian anti-Judaism.[5]

The Outward Focus of the "Conflict Theory"

The Second World War brought about an important shift in Christian attitudes to anti-Judaism. Whereas prior to 1945, "antisemitism was typically seen as a Jewish rather than a Christian problem", the Holocaust brought home to many Christians the need to turn inward and look for the roots of anti-Judaic prejudices in their own movement (Davies 1979: xiii; cf. also Flannery 1985: 285-6). Regrettably, the "conflict theory" unwittingly slips back into the pre-war perspective, albeit in a much more subtle and sophisticated form. Although the conflict theorists ostensibly look for the roots of anti-Judaism in Christian perceptions, attitudes and motivations, the emphasis they place on Jewish "vitality" (or pseudo-vitality)[6] shifts the entire focus of their interpretive work outwards. Indeed, their theory has a marked external focus in its attempt to explain what lay behind Christian opposition to the Jews. For it is the power and influence of Judaism that is said to provide the trigger for Christian antagonism, and it is to Judaism that these scholars look in developing their hypotheses about the genesis of the church's anti-Judaic arguments. Though the fact that Christianity gave birth to anti-Jewish prejudices is not questioned, this observation is deemed to be "insufficient": "we need to ask why Christianity responded to Judaism in the fashion it did" affirm the conflict theorists, and it is the supposed status and orientation of Judaism that is believed to provide the answer to this puzzling and disturbing question. "The virulence of Christian anti-Semitism is a sign of the vitality of Judaism in the later empire. And for the historian this is worth noting" (Wilken 1967: 327-28).

The historian or sociologist seeking to make sense of racial prejudice and hatred must tread an extremely fine line. On the one hand, it is unsatisfactory simply to condemn without making any attempt at understanding the human reality behind the phenomenon. We are no further advanced if we demonize, or unquestioningly attribute prejudice to the intrinsically evil nature of the

---

[5] This explains the conflict theorists' inability to accept Ruether's insights, as well as their need to criticize her work.

[6] "Pseudo" because it is ultimately only temporary and because it is measured according to purely Christian standards (see beginning of this chapter).

hater. It is incumbent on the analyst to try to explain (in as far as possible), the mechanisms, whether social or ideological, that have generated and perpetuated this hatred. On the other hand, attempts at rationalization should in no way excuse or diminish the destructiveness of hatred and prejudice. The conflict theorists show no conscious awareness of these challenges in their own interpretation of Christian anti-Judaism, and perhaps precisely because they haven't thought these issues through, they slide into making the second error.

Indeed, the focus on Judaism as stimulator of antagonism effectively suceeds in shifting the focus away from internal soul-searching in the Christian camp, in order to distribute the blame and divide the responsibility in accounting for the generation of prejudice. For if anti-Judaism is described as emerging out of a social conflict, then it can be characterized as the by-product of an historical rivalry in which both parties might be said to be equally involved, and equally responsible. Anti-Judaism can come to be viewed, in this context, as a legitimate and natural part of a fair struggle in which the "Jews gave as good as they got" (Trigg 1983:185), and in which there is ostensibly as much to blame in the Jewish camp as in the Christian (Meagher 1979: 19). "For the Jews have never been backward in attack" (Lukyn Williams 1935: xvi). Conveniently, both parties are said to have a share in generating the polemic that is believed to have created and perpetuated animosity and prejudice.

This tendency is especially pronounced among those scholars who defend the notion of "recriminatory" anti-Judaism, who portray Christian hostility to the Jews as an understandable, even justified response to Jewish provocation and involvement in persecution (cf. Typology II.3). These scholars tend to lay the brunt of responsibility for hatred of Jews on the synagogue itself, and thus shift the blame almost entirely away from the church. After all, how can one not expect the Christians to react negatively to a group that supposedly participated in efforts to suppress their movement? Interestingly, in their language and tone, these scholars betray that, far from being engaged in detached historical reconstruction, they seek, through their analysis, to further their own agenda, namely the disculpation of Christianity. This becomes evident in the moralizing and judgemental tone adopted by these scholars in their description of the supposed actions and motivations of the Jews as so-called persecutors.

Simon is among those who describe the actions and intentions of Jews in ethically loaded terms. In their anxiety to dissociate themselves from the new sect, the Jews, he claims, "were not always able to be scrupulous in their choice of methods". In their attempt to defend their tradition against Christian preaching, the Jews "might sometimes have gone further than they were supposed to do" (Simon 1986: 117). The Jews gave assistance, "often in a very active and spiteful way" to the pagan persecutors (Simon 1986: 121). W.H.C. Frend also insinuates that the Old Israel was prepared to sell its soul, by providing assistance to the Roman persecutors, in order to save its skin. Israel

entered into an unholy alliance with the pagan authorities, "at the cost of for-
feiting for ever its claim to the universal allegiance of mankind" (Frend 1965:
194).

The need to condemn or absolve Jews for actions they may or may not
have committed over a millennium ago indicates the inability of commentators to free themselves from the theological prejudices communicated in the
texts themselves, texts which they claim to be examining and interpreting in a
critical manner. While the church is depicted by these scholars as "standing
singlehanded in its holy struggle against paganism and the kingdom of evil",
"the Jewish community's part in the political and intellectual reality of this
world" is not only "forgotten", but Judaism is "regarded as a disembodied
soul, whose inheritance in heaven" seems rather "doubtful" (Baer 1961: 80).
The early church's theological vision of the world is appropriated by these
conflict theorists and presented as historical fact.

Anti-Judaism as an Adventitious and Diffuse Syndrome

There is another important respect in which the "conflict theory" detracts from
the important task of investigating the role of Christian teaching in the generation of anti-Judaic prejudices. The focus of the "conflict theory" on competition as the primary source of the Christian negation of the Jews not only
attenuates Christian responsibility for anti-Jewish prejudices, but actually obscures the roots of Christian anti-Judaism. The notion that anti-Judaism was
rooted in social reality has encouraged scholars to accumulate as many factors
as possible in their efforts to cover all the angles, to provide a comprehensive
picture of what is viewed as a varied and complex phenomenon. As we saw in
the preceding typology, the alleged causes of anti-Judaism among the early
Christians are said to vary from the psycho-social to the environmental. When
taken together, these multiple factors are thought to describe a many-sided and
diffuse phenomenon that originates in external circumstances rather than in
the internal belief structures of the church. However, as long as anti-Judaism
is portrayed as emerging out of social tensions, it becomes an *adventitious*
phenomenon, made contingent, not on internally generated ideas, but on specific and finite social and political conditions. The sense in which anti-
Judaism was a theological choice, built into the church's vision of itself and of
the world, and intrinsic to Christian teaching, is dissimulated by the "conflict
theory". It proves unable to account in a genuine and convincing way for the
continuing power and hold of anti-Judaic prejudices in a world where the external conditions created by conflict no longer prevail. It thus fails not only in
its claims to illuminate the anti-Judaic texts, but fails, more importantly, to
explain the continuing impact through the Christian centuries of the ideas
which these texts have perpetuated.

BIBLIOGRAPHY

A. Texts And Translations

Didascalia Apostolorum, intro. and transl. R.H. Connolly. Oxford, 1929.

Die griechischen christlichen Schriftsteller den ersten drei Jahrhunderte. Leipzig, 1897ff.

Justin, *Dialogue avec Tryphon*. introd., trad. et notes, Georges Archambault. Paris: Alphonse Picard, 1909.

Melito of Sardis: "On Pascha" and Fragments. ed. Stuart George Hall. Oxford: Clarendon Press, 1979.

Migne, J-P., ed. *Patrologia Graeca*. Paris 1857ff.

———, *Patrologia Latina*. Paris 1841ff.

Origen, *Contra Celsum*. transl. with intro. Henry Chadwick. Cambridge: Cambridge University Press, 1953.

———, *An Exhortation to Martyrdom, Prayer, and Selected Writings*. transl. & ed., Rowan A. Greer. Preface by Hans Urs von Balthasar. New York: Paulist Press, 1979.

———, *Homilies on Genesis and Exodus*. transl. by Ronald E. Heine. Washington: Catholic University of America Press, 1982.

Origène, *Homélies sur Jérémie*. introd. et trad., Pierre Nautin et Pierre Husson. Sources chrétiennes 232, 238. Paris: Editions du Cerf, 1976.

———, *Homélies sur Saint-Luc*. éds., Henri Crouzel, François Fournier, et P. Pernichon. Sources chrétiennes 87. Paris: Editions du Cerf, 1962.

———, *Homélies sur le Lévitique*. introd., trad. et notes, Marcel Borret, s.j. Sources chrétiennes 286-287. Paris: Editions du Cerf, 1981.

———, *Homélies sur L'Exode*. éds., P. Fortier et H. deLubac. Sources chrétiennes 16. Paris: Editions du Cerf, 1947.

———, *Homèlies sur les Nombres*. éd. André Méhat. Sources chrétiennes 29. Paris: Editions du Cerf, 1951.

———, *Homélies sur Josué*. éd. Annie Jaubert. Sources chrétiennes 71: Paris: Editions du Cerf, 1960.

Roberts, Alexander and James Donaldson. *Anti-Nicene Christian Library: Translations of the Writings of the Fathers Down to A.D. 325*. Edinburgh: T & T Clark, 1869.

Tertullian, *Adversus Marcionem*. ed. and transl. Ernest Evans. 2 vols. Oxford: Clarendon Press, 1972.

The Apostolic Fathers. ed. and transl. Kirsopp Lake. 2 vols. Cambridge, Mass.: Harvard University Press, 1976-77.

The Acts of the Christian Martyrs. intro. and transl. Herbert Musurillo. Oxford: Clarendon Press, 1972.

B. Secondary Literature

Abel, Ernest L. (1975) *The Roots of Anti-Semitism*. London: Associated University Press.

Abrahams, Israel. (1924) *Studies in Pharisaism and the Gospels*. Cambridge: Cambridge University Press. Vol. 2.

Aland, B. (1973) "Marcion: Versuch einer neuen Interpretation" *Zeitschrift für Theologie und Kirche* 70: 420-47.

Alexander, Jeffrey, C. (1987) *Twenty Lectures: Sociological Theory Since World War II*. New York: Columbia University Press.

Allard, Paul. (1894) *Histoire des persecutions pendant la première moitié du IIIème siècle*. Paris: Lecoffre, 2ème éd.

Alvarez, J. (1975) "Apostolic Writings and the Roots of Anti-Semitism" *Studia Patristica* XIII: 69-76.

Aubé, B. (1885) *L'eglise et l'état dans la seconde moitié du IIIème siècle*. Paris.

Baer, Y. (1961) "Israel, the Christian Church and the Roman Empire from the time of Septimus Severus to the Edict of Toleration of A.C. 313" *Scripta Hierosolymitana* 7: 79-149.

Bamberger, Bernard, Jacob. (1939) *Proselytism in the Talmudic Period*. Cincinatti.

Barnard, L.W. (1966) *Studies in the Apostolic Fathers and their Background*. Oxford: Blackwell, pp. 19-30.

Barnes, Timothy David. (1967) "Hadrian and Lucius Verus" *Journal of Roman Studies* 57, 65-79.

——, (1968) "The Pre-Decian Acta Martyrum" *Journal of Theological Studies* 19: 509-531.

——, (1969) "Tertullian's *Antidote to the Scorpion's Bite*" *Journal of Theological Studies* XX: 105-132.

——, (1971) *Tertullian. A Historical and Literary Study*. Oxford: Clarendon Press.

Baron, Salo W. (1952) *A Social and Religious History of the Jews*. New York: Columbia University Press. 2 Vols.

Barrett, C.K. (1976) "Jews and Judaizers in the Epistles of Ignatius" in Robert Hamerton-Kelly and Robin Scroggs, eds. *Jews, Greeks and Christians: Religious Cultures in Late Antiquity*. Leiden: Brill.

Barth, Frederik (1970) *Ethnic Groups and Boundaries: The Social Organization of Cultural Difference*. Bergen-Oslo, Norway: Universitets Forlaget.

Bartlett, David (1978) "John Gager's 'Kingdom and Community': A Summary and Response", *Zygon* 13: 109-22.

Barton, John (1986) *Oracles of God: perceptions of ancient prophecy in Israel after the Exile*. London, Darton, Longman & Todd.

Baum, Gregory (1974) "Introduction" in Rosemary Radford Ruether *Faith and Fratricide: The Theological Roots of Anti-Semitism*. New York: Seabury Press, pp. 1-22.

Berger, Peter L. and Thomas Luckmann (1966) *The Social Construction of Reality: A Treatise in the Sociology of Knowledge*. New York: Doubleday.

Best, Thomas F. (1983) "The Sociological Study of the New Testament: Promise and Peril of a New Discipline" *Scottish Journal of Theology* 36: 181-194.

Blackman, E.C. (1948) *Marcion and His Influence*. London: SPCK.

Blanchetière, F. (1973) "Aux sources de l'anti-Judaisme chrétien" *Revue d'histoire et de Philosophie Religieuses* 53: 353-398.

Blumenkrantz, Bernhard (1946) *Die Judenpredigt Augustins*. Basel: Helbing & Lichtenmahn.

Bokser, Ben Zion (1973-4) "Justin Martyr and the Jews" *Jewish Quarterly Review* 64: 97-122, 204-211.

Bonner, Campbell (1940) *The Homily on the Passion by Melito, Bishop of Sardis*. Studies and Documents XII. Philadelphia.

Botermann, Helga. (1990) "Die Synagoge von Sardes. Eine Synagoge aus dem 4 Jahrhundert?" *Zeitschrift fur die Neutestamentliche Wissenschaft*. vols 1-2, 103-121.

Bratton, Fred Gladstone (1969) *The Crime of Christendom: the Theological Sources of Christian Anti-Semitism*. Boston: Beacon Press.

Braude, William, Gordon (1940) *Jewish Proselytizing in the First Five Centuries of the Common Era*. Providence: Brown University Studies, vol. 6.

Brown, Peter (1987) "Person and Group in Judaism and Early Christianity" in Philippe Ariès and Georges Duby, eds. *A history of Private Life*. Vol 1: From Pagan Rome to Byzantium. Cambridge Mass: Harvard University Press, pp. 253-267.

Burghardt, Walter, J. (1970) "Jewish-Christian Dialogue: Early Church versus Contemporary Christianity" in Joseph Papin, ed. *The Dynamic in Christian Thought*. Villanova: Villanova University Press.

Burke, Peter (1980) *Sociology and History*. London: Allen & Unwin.

Cadoux, Cecil John (1938) *Ancient Smyrna*. Oxford: Blackwell.

Campenhausen, Hans, von (1958) "Bearbeitungen und Interpelationen des Polycarpmartyrium" *ad Sitzungberichte der Heidelberger Akademie der Wissenschaften* 3: 1-48.

——, (1972) *The Formation of the Christian Bible*. Transl. J.A. Baker. Philadelphia: Fortress Press.

Caspary, Gérard (1979) *Politics and Exegesis: Origen and the Two Swords*. Berkeley: University of California Press.

Collins, A.Y. (1985) "Insiders and Outsiders in the Book of Revelation and its Social Context" in J. Neusner and E.S. Frerichs, eds. *"To See ourselves as Others See Us". Christians, Jews, 'Others' in Late Antiquity*. Chico: Scholars Press. pp. 187-218.

Craib, Ian (1984) *Modern Social Theory: From Parsons to Habermas*. New York: St. Martin's Press.

Daniélou, Jean and Henri Marrou (1964) *The First six hundred years*. Transl. Vincent Cronin. London: Darton, Longman & Todd.

Davies, Alan T. (1969) *Anti-Semitism and the Christian Mind*: The Crisis of Conscience After Auschwitz. New York: Herder & Herder.

——, (1979) "Introduction" in Alan T. Davies, ed. *Antisemitism and the Foundations of Christianity*. New York: Paulist Press.

De Lange, Nicholas R.M. (1976) *Origen and the Jews: Studies in Jewish-Christian Relations in Third Century Palestine*. Cambridge: Cambridge University Press.

De Vos, George and R. Ross (1975) *Ethnic Identity*. Mansfield.

Den Boeft, Jan and Jan Bremmer (1985) "Notinculae Martyriologicae III" *Vigilae Christianae* 39: 110-130.

Dilthey, Wilhelm (1976) "The Construction of the Historical World in the Human Studies" in H. P. Rickman, ed. *Dilthey: Selected Writings*. Cambridge: Cambridge University Press.

Donahue, Paul Jerome (1973) *Jewish-Christian Controversy in the Second-Century: A Study in the "Dialogue" of Justin Martyr*. Unpublished Ph.D. dissertation, Yale University, Religion.

——, (1978) "Jewish Christianity in the Letters of Ignatius of Antioch" in *Vigilae Christianae* 32: 81-93.

Dumont, Louis (1983) *Essais sur l'individualisme: Une perspective anthropologique sur l'idéologie moderne*. Paris: Editions du Seuil.

Edwards, O.C. (1983) "Sociology as a Tool for Interpreting the New Testament" *Anglican Theological Review* LXV.4: 431-448

Efroymson, David, P. (1976) "Tertullian's Anti-Judaism and its Role in his Theology". Unpublished Ph.D. dissertation, Temple University.

——, (1979) "The Patristic Connection" in Alan T. Davies, ed. *Antisemitism and the Foundations of Christianity*. New York: Paulist Press, pp. 98-117.

——, (1980) "Tertullian's Anti-Jewish rhetoric: Guilt by Association" *Union Seminary Quarterly Review* 36: 25-37.

Elliott, John H. (1981) *A Home for the Homeless*. A Sociological Exegesis of 1 Peter, its Situation and Strategy. Philadelphia: Fortress.

——, (1986) "Social Scientific Criticism of the New Testament: More on Methods and Models". in John H. Elliott, ed. *Social Scientific Criticism of the New Testament and Social World*. Atlanta: Scholars Press, pp. 1-33.

Erikson, Eric H. (1963) "The Legend of Hitler's Childhood" *Childhood and Society*. New York: Norton, pp. 326-58.

Esler, Philip, Francis (1987) *Community and Gospel in Luke-Acts: The social and political motivations of Lucan Theology*. Cambridge: Cambridge University Press. Evans, Ernest, ed. & transl. (1972) *Tertullian: Adversus Marcionem*. Oxford: Clarendon Press. 2 vols.

Finkelstein, I. (1925-6) "The Development of the Amidah" *Jewish Quarterly Review* 16: 156-7.

Fiorenza, Elizabeth Schussler (1976) *Aspects of Religious Propaganda in Judaism and Early Christianity*. Notre Dame: University of Notre Dame Press.

Flannery, Edward H. (1985) *The Anguish of the Jews. Twenty-Three Centuries of Anti-Semitism*. New York: Paulist Press.

Flusser, David (1983) "The Jewish-Christian Schism", part I, *Immanuel* 16: 32-49.

——, (1983-4) "The Jewish-Christian Schism", part II, *Immanuel* 17: 30-39.

——, (1988) *Judaism and the Origin of Christianity*. Jerusalem: Magnes Press.

Fox, Robin Lane. *Pagans and Christians*. Harmondsworth: Viking, 1986.

Fredouille, Jean-Claude (1972) *Tertullien et la conversion de la culture antique*. Paris: Etudes Augustiniennes.

Frend, W.H.C. (1958) "The Persecutions: Some links between Judaism and the Early Church" *Journal of Ecclesiastical History* IX: 141-158.

——, (1967) *Martyrdom and Persecution in the Early Church. A Study of the Conflict from the Maccabees to Donatus*. New York: New York University Press.

——, (1970) "A Note on Tertullian and the Jews" *Studia Patristica* X: 291-6.

Freyne, Sean (1985) "Vilifying the Other and Defining the Self: Matthew's and John's Anti-Jewish Polemic in Focus" in Jacob Neusner and Ernest Frerichs, eds. *"To See Ourselves as Others See Us": Christians, Jews, "Others", in Late Antiquity*. Chico: Scholars Press, pp. 117-144.

Gager, John. G. (1975) *Kingdom and Community: The Social World of Early Christianity*. Englewood Cliffs, New Jersey: Prentice Hall.

——, (1982) "Shall We Marry Our Enemies? Sociology and the New Testament" *Interpretation* 36:256-65.

——, John G. (1983) *The Origins of Anti-Semitism: Attitudes Toward Judaism in Pagan and Christian Antiquity*. Oxford: Oxford University Press.

——, John G. (1986) "Judaism as Seen by Outsiders" in Robert A. Kraft and George W.E. Nickelsburg, eds. *Early Judaism and its Modern Interpreters*. Philadelphia: Fortress Press.

Gaston, Lloyd (1986a) "Judaism of the Uncircumcised in Ignatius and Related Writers" in Stephen G. Wilson, ed. *Anti-Judaism in Early Christianity*. Vol. 2. Waterloo: Wilfrid Laurier, pp. 33-44.

——, (1986b) "Retrospect" in Stephen G. Wilson, ed. *Anti-Judaism in Early Christianity*. Vol.2. Waterloo: Wilfrid Laurier, pp. 163-174.

Geertz, Clifford (1966) "Religion as a Cultural System" in Michael Barton, ed. *Anthropological Approaches to the Study of Religion*. London: Tavistock, pp. 1-46.

——, (1973) *Interpretation of Cultures: Selected Essays*. New York: Basic Books.

Georgi, Dieter (1986) *The Opponents of Paul in Second Corinthians*. Edinburgh: T & T Clark.

Glock, C.Y. and R. Stark (1969) *Christian Beliefs and Anti-Semitism*. New York.

Goodman, Martin (1989) "Proselytizing in Rabbinic Judaism", *Journal of Jewish Studies* 38: 175-185.

——, (1992) "Jewish Proselytizing in the First Century" in J. Lieu, J. North, and T. Rajak, eds., *The Jews among Pagans and Christians: In the Roman Empire*. London and New York: Routledge, pp 53-78.

Goppelt, L. (1954) *Christentum und Judentum im ersten und zweiten Jahrhundert*. Guntersloh.

Grayzel, Solomon (1946) "Christian-Jewish Relations in the First Millenium" in Koppel S. Pinson, ed. *Essays on Antisemitism*. Jewish Social Studies, publ. no. 2. New York: Conference on Jewish Relations, 79ff.

Gregg, John, A.F. (1897) *The Decian Persecution*. Edinburgh: Blackwood.

Grosser, Paul E. and Edwin G. Halperin (1983) *Antisemitism: Causes and Effects, An Analysis and Chronology of 1900 Years of Anti-Semitic Attitudes and Practices*. New York: Philosophical Library.

Hall, Stuart George (1979) *Melito of Sardis: On Pascha and Fragments*. Oxford: Clarendon Press.

Hansen, Adolph (1968) "The Sitz im Leben of the Paschal Homily of Melito of Sardis with special reference to the Paschal Festival in Early Christianity". Unpublished Phd. dissertation, Northwestern University. (Diss. Abstracts 29 (1969) 2343 A).

Hare, Douglas, R.A. (1967a) *The Theme of Jewish Persecution of Christians in the Gospel According to Matthew*. Cambridge: Cambridge University Press.

——, (1967b) "The Relationship between Jewish and Gentile Persecution of Christians" *Journal of Ecumenical Studies* IV: 446-56.

——, (1979) "The Rejection of the Jews in the Synoptic Gospels and Acts" in Alan Davies, ed. *Antisemitism and the Foundations of Christianity*. New York: Paulist Press.

Harnack, A. von (1883) "Die Altercatio Simonis Judaei et Theophili Christiani, nebst Untersuchungen uber die anti-judische Polemik in der alten Kirche" *Texte und Untersuchungen* 1,3.

——, (1908) *The Mission and Expansion of Christianity in the First Three Centuries*. Transl. & ed. by James Moffatt. New York: Putnam. vol. 1.

——, (1921) *Marcion: Das Evangelium von Fremden Gott*. Leipzig: J.C. Hinrichs.

——, (1923) *Neue Studien zu Marcion*. Leipzig: J.C. Hinrichs.

——, (1958) *Geschichte der Altchristlichen Literatur bis Eusebius*. Teil II, Band 2. Leipzig: J.C. Heinrichs.

Harrington, Daniel (1980) "Sociological Concepts and the Early Church: A Decade of Research" *Theological Studies*. 41/1: 181-90.

Hilhorst, A. (1982) "L'Ancien Testament dans la polémique du martyr Pionius" *Augustinianum* XXII: 92ff.

Holmberg, Bengt (1978) *Paul and Power: the Structure of Authority in the Primitive Church as Reflected in the Pauline Epistles*. Lund: CWK Gleerup.

Horbury, W. (1982) "The Benediction of the Minim and Early Jewish-Christian Controversy" *Journal of Theological Studies*, n.s. xxxiii: 19-51.

Hulen, Amos B. (1932) "The 'Dialogues with Jews' as Sources for the Early Jewish Argument against Christianity" *Journal of Biblical Literature* 51: 58-70.

Idinopoulos, T. & R.B. Ward (1977) "Is Christology anti-semitic?" *Journal of American Academy of Religion* 45: 197ff.

Isaac, Jules (1948) *Jésus et Israel*. Paris.

——, (1956) *Genèse de l'Antisémitisme*. Paris: Calmann-Levy.

——, (1964) *The Teaching of Contempt: Christian Roots of Anti-Semitism.* Transl. Helen Weaver. New York: Holt, Rhinehart & Winston.

Jacobson-Widding, Anita (1983) "Introduction" in Anita Jacobson-Widding, ed. *Identity: Personal and Socio-Cultural.* Uppsala: Almsquist and Wiksell Int., pp. 13-34.

Jeremias, J. (1958) *Jesus' Promise to the Nations.* London: SCM.

Johnson, Sherman (1961) "Christianity in Sardis" in Allen Paul Wikgren, ed. *Early Christian Origins.* Studies in honor of Harold R. Willoughby. Chicago.

Judant, Denise (1969) *Judaisme et Christianisme: Dossier Patristique.* Paris: Editions du Cèdre.

Juster, Jean (1914) *Les Juifs dans L'Empire Romain: Leur Condition Juridique, Economique et Sociale.* Vols. I & II. Paris: Paul Geuthner.

Katz, S.T. (1984) "Issues in the Separation of Judaism and Christianity after 70 C.E.: A Reconsideration" *Journal of Biblical Literature* 103/1: 43-76.

Kee, Howard, Clark (1989) *Knowing the Truth: A Sociological Apporach to New Testament Interpretation.* Minneapolis: Fortress Press.

Kimelman, Reuven. (1981) "Birkath Ha-Minim and the Lack of Evidence for an Anti-Christian Prayer in Late Antiquity" in E.P. Sanders, A.I. Baumgarten, Alan Mendelsohn, eds. *Jewish and Christian Self-Definition.* Vol. 2. Aspects of Judaism in the Greco-Roman Period. Philadelphia: Fortress.

Kraabel, A.T. (1968) "Judaism in Western Asia Minor". Unpublished Phd. dissertation, Harvard Divinity.

——, (1971) "Melito the Bishop and the Synagogue at Sardis: Text and Context" in D.G. Mitten, J.G. Pedley, J.A. Scott, eds. *Studies Presented to George M.A. Hanfmann.* Cambridge: Fogg Art Museum, pp. 77-85.

——, (1979) "The Diaspora Synagogue" *Aufstieg und Niedergang der romischen Welt* II, 19: 477-510.

——, (1982) "The Roman Diaspora: Six Questionable Assumptions" *Journal of Jewish Studies* 33: 445-464.

——, (1983) "The Impact of the Discovery of the Sardis Synagogue" in "The Jewish Synagogue and the Jewish Community" in George M.A. Hanfmann, ed., *Sardis from Prehistoric to Roman Times.* Cambridge, Mass: Harvard University Press, pp. 178-191.

——, (1985) "Synagoga Caeca: Systematic Distortion in Gentile Interpretations of Evidence for Judaism in the Early Chrisitan Period" in Jacob Neusner and Ernest Frerichs, eds. "To See Ourselves as Others See Us" *Christians, Jews and 'Others' in Late Antiquity.* Chico, California: Scholars Press.

Kraft, Robert and George E. Nickelsburg (1986) *Early Judaism and its Modern Interpreters.* Philadelphia: Fortress Press.

Laeuchli, S. (1974) "The Drama of Replay" in *Searching for the Syntax of Things.* Philadelphia: Temple University Press.

Langmuir, Gavin (1963) "The Jews and the Archives of Angevin England: Reflections on Medieval Anti-Semitism" in *Tradition* XIX: 183-244.

Lightfoot, J.B. (1889) *The Apostolic Fathers.* Part II, Vol. 1. London.

Lightstone, Jack (1986) "Christian anti-Judaism in its Judaic mirror: the Judaic context of early Christianity Revised" in Stephen Wilson, ed. *Anti-Judaism in Early Christianity.* vol. 2, pp. 103-132.

Lovsky, Fadiey (1955) *Antisémitisme et mystère d'Israel.* Paris" Albin Michel.

Lukyn Williams, A. (1935) *Adversus Judaeos: A Bird's-Eye View of Christian Apologiae until the Renaissance.* Cambridge: Cambridge University Press.

Macdonald, Margaret Y. (1988) *The Pauline Churches: A Socio-historical Study of Institutionalization in the Pauline and Deutero-Pauline Writings.* Cambridge: Cambridge University Press.

MacLeod, C.W. (1971) "Allegory and Mysticism in Origen and Gregory of Nyssa" *Journal of Theological Studies* n.s. XXII: 362-379.

Malina, Bruce (1982) "The Social Sciences and Biblical Interpretation" *Interpretation.* 36: 229-42.

Manis, Andrew, Michael (1987) "Melito of Sardis: Hermeneutic and Context" *Greek Orthodox Theological Review* 32, no. 4: 387-401.

McKnight, Scot (1991) *A Light Among the Gentiles: Jewish Missionary Activity in the Second Temple Period.* Fortress Press.

Meagher, John C. (1979) "As the Twig Was Bent: Antisemitism in Greco-Roman and Earliest Christian Times" in Alan T. Davies, ed. *AntiSemitism and the Foundations of Christianity*. New York: Paulist Press.

Meeks, Wayne A. and Robert L. Wilken. (1978) *Jews and Christians in Antioch In the First Four Centuries of the Common Era*. Ann Arbor: Scholars Press.

Meeks, Wayne A. (1983) *The First Urban Christians: The Social World of the Apostle Paul*. New Haven: Yale University Press.

Millar, Fergus (1966) Review of W.H.C. Frend, *Martyrdom and Persecution in the Early Church* in *Journal of Roman Studies* LVI: 231-236.

Mitten, D.G. (1966) "A New Look at Ancient Sardis" *The Biblical Archaeologist* 29: 38-68.

Molland, E. (1954) "The Heretics Combatted by Ignatius of Antioch" *Journal of Ecclesiastical History* 5: 1-6.

Monceaux, Paul (1966) *Histoire littéraire de L'Afrique chrétienne depuis les origines jusqu'a l'invasion Arabe*. Tome premier: Tertullien et les origines. Bruxelles.

Moore, George, Foot (1921) "Christian Writers on Judaism" *Harvard Theological Review* XIV: 197ff.

——, (1927) *Judaism in the First Centuries of the Christian Era: The Age of the Tannaim*. Vol. 1. Cambridge: Harvard University Press.

Musurillo, Herbert (1972) *The Acts of the Christian Martyrs*. Oxford: Clarendon Press.

Neusner, Jacob (1971) *Aphrahat and Judaism. The Christian-Jewish Argument in Fourth Century Iran*. Leiden: Brill.

Neusner, J. and Ernest S. Frerichs, eds. (1985) "*To See Ourselves as Others See Us*" *Christians, Jews and 'Others' in Late Antiquity*. Chico, California: Scholars Press.

Neusner, Jacob (1987) *Judaism and Christianity in the Age of Constantine*. Chicago and London: University of Chicago Press.

Noakes, K.W. (1975) "Melito of Sardis and the Jews" *Studia Patristica* XIII, *Texte und Untersuchungen* 116. Berlin: Verlag, pp. 244-249.

Nolland, J (1979) "Do Romans Observe Jewish Customs (Tert. Ad.Nat. 1.13; *Apology* 16)" *Vigilae Christianae* 33: 1-11.

Norris, Frederick W. (1986) "Melito's Motivation" *Anglican Theological Review* LXVIII.1: 16-25.

North, John (1979) "Religious Toleration in Republican Rome" *Proceedings of the Cambridge Philological Society* n.s. 25: 85-103.

Oesterreicher, John, M. (1970) "Deicide as a Theological Problem" in John M. Oesterreicher, ed. *Brothers in Hope: The Bridge*. Judaeo-Christian Studies, vol. 5. New York: Herder & Herder: 190-204.

——, (1975) *Anatomy of Contempt: A Critique of R.R. Ruether's "Faith and Fratricide"*. New Jersey: Seton Hall University Press.

Parkes, James (1963) "The Christian Roots of Antisemitism" in *Antisemitism*. Chicago: Quadrangle Books: 57-73.

Parkes, James (1969) *The Conflict of Church and Synagogue: a study in the origins of antisemitism*. New York: Athenaeum.

Pearson, Birger (1971) "I Thessalonians 2:13-16: A Deutero-Pauline Interpolation" *Harvard Theological Review* 64: 79-94.

Pelikan, Jaroslav (1970) "De-Judaization and Hellenization: The Ambiguities of Christian Identity" in Joseph Papin, ed. *The Dynamic in Christian Thought*. Villanova: Villlanova University Press.

Perler, Othmar (1966) *Meliton de Sardes: Sur la Paque et Fragments*. Paris: Editions du Cerf.

Poliakov, Léon. (1965) *Histoire de L'Antisémitisme*. Du Christ aux Juifs de cours. Paris: Calmann-Lévy.

Prigent, Pierre (1964) *Justin et L'Ancien Testament*. Paris: Gabalda.

Rajak, Tessa (1985) "Jews and Christians as Groups in a Pagan World" in J. Neusner and E. Frerichs, eds. "*To See Ourselves as Others See Us*": *Christians, Jews and "Others" in Late Antiquity*. Chico, California:Scholars Press, pp. 247-262.

Remus, Harold E. (1982) "Sociology of Knowledge and the Study of Early Christianity" *Sciences Religieuses* 11: 45-56.

——, (1986) "Justin Martyr's Argument with Judaism" in Stephen Wilson, ed. *Anti-Judaism in Early Christianity*. Vol. 2. Waterloo: Wilfrid Laurier.

Rengstorf, K.H. & S.von Kortzfleisch (1968) Kirche und Synagoge: Handbuch zur Geschichte von Christen und Juden. Stuttgart: E. Klett.

Riley, Matilda, White (1963) *Sociological Research*. New York: Harcourt.

Rokeah, David (1982) *Jews, Pagans and Christians in Conflict*. Jerusalem: Magnes.

Rokeah, David (1983) "Anti-Judaism in Early Christianity" *Immanuel* 16: 50-64.

Ruether, Rosemary, Radford (1972) "Judaism and Christianity: Two Fourth-Century Religions" *Sciences Religieuses/ Studies in Religion* 2: 1-10.

Ruether, Rosemary Radford (1974) *Faith and Fratricide*: The Theological Roots of Anti-Semitism. New York: Seabury Press.

Ruether, Rosemary Radford (1979) "The Faith and Fratricide Discussion: Old Problems and New Dimensions" in Alan Davies, ed. *Antisemitism and the Foundations of Christianity*. New York: Paulist Press, pp. 230-256.

Sanders, E.P. (1976) "The Covenant as Soteriological Category and the Nature of Slavation in Palestinian and Hellenistic Judaism" in Robert Hamilton-Kelly and Robin Scroggs, eds. *Jews, Greeks and Christians in Late Antiquity*. Leiden: Brill, pp. 11-44.

Sanders, E.P. (1977) *Paul and Palestinian Judaism: A Comparison of Patterns of Religion*. London: SCM.

Schreckenberg, Heinz (1982) *Die Christlichen Adversus-Judaeos Texte und ihr literarisches, historisches Umfeld*. Frankfurt.

Schürer, E. (1973-87) *The History of the Jewish People in the Age of Jesus Christ* (175 B.C. - A.D. 135). Revised & edited by Geza Vermes, M. Black, F. Millar, M. Goodman, and P. Vermes. 3 Vols. Edinburgh: T & T Clark.

Scroggs, Robin (1980) "The Sociological Interpretation of the New Testament: The Present State of Research" *New Testament Studies* 26: 164-79.

Seager, Andrew R., and A. Thomas Kraabel (1983) "The Jewish Synagogue and the Jewish Community" in George M.A. Hanfmann, ed., *Sardis from Prehistoric to Roman Times*. Cambridge, Mass: Harvard University Press, pp. 168-191.

Shukster, Martin B. & Peter Richardson (1986) "Temple and Bet Ha-Midrash in the Epistle of Barnabas" in Stephen G. Wilson, ed., *Anti-Judaism in Early Christianity*. Vol. 2. Waterloo: Wilfrid Laurier, pp. 17-32.

Simon, Marcel (1986) *Verus Israel: A Study of Relations between Christians and Jews in the Roman Empire (135-425)*. Transl. H. Mckeating. Oxford: Oxford University Press.

Simonetti, M. (1955) *Studi Agiografici*. Roma: Signorella.

Smallwood, Mary E. (1976) *The Jews Under Roman Rule: From Pompey to Diocletian*. Leiden: Brill.

Smith, Johnathan Z. (1975) "The Social Description of Early Christianity" *Religious Studies Review*. vol. 1, no. 1: 19-25.

Smith, Robert W. (1974) *The Art of Rhetoric in Alexandria: Its Theological Practice in the Ancient World*. The Hague: Martinus Nijhoff.

Sordi, M. (1961) "I nuovi decreti di Marco Aurelio contro i Cristiani" *Studi Romani* 9.

Stanton, G.N. (1985) "Aspects of Early Christian-Jewish Polemic and Apologetic" *New Testament Studies* 31: 377-392.

Stern, Menahem, ed. (1974-84) *Greek and Latin Authors on Jews and Judaism*. Jerusalem: Israel Adademy of Sciences. 3 Vols.

Strecker, G. (1971) "On the Problem of Jewish-Christianity" in W. Bauer, *Orthodoxy and Heresy in Earliest Christianity*. Ed. by R. Kraft and G. Krodel. Philadelphia.

Stylianopoulos, Theodore (1975) *Justin Martyr and the Mosaic Law*. Missoula, Montana: Society of Biblical Literature.

Theissen, Gerd (1982) *The Social Setting of Pauline Christianity: Essays on Corinth*. Ed. and transl. by John H. Schuetz. Philadelphia: Fortress.

Thornton, T.C.G. (1987) "Christian Understanding of the Birkath Ha-Minim in the Eastern Empire" *Journal of Theological Studies* n.s. 38: 419-431.

Townsend, John T. (1979) "The Gospel of John and the Jews: The Story of a Religious Divorce" in Alan T. Davies, ed. *Antisemitism and the Foundations of Christianity*. New York: Paulist Press.

Trebilco, Paul R. (1991) *Jewish Communities in Asia Minor*. Cambridge: Cambridge University Press.

Trigg, Joseph Wilson (1983) *Origen: The Bible and Philosophy in the Third Century Church*. Atlanta: John Knox Press.

Turner, Johnathan H. (1986) *The Structure of Sociological Theory*. Chicago, Dorsey.

Weber, Max (1968) *The Methodology of the Social Sciences*. New York: The Free Press.

Werner, E. (1966) "Melito of Sardis, the First Poet of Deicide" *Hebrew Union College Annual* 37: 191-210.

Wilde, Robert (1949) *Treatment of the Jews in the Greek Christian Writers of the First Three Centuries*. Washington.

Wilken, Robert L. (1967) "Judaism in Roman and Christian Society" *Journal of Religion* 47: 313-30.

——, (1971) *Judaism and the Early Christian Mind: A Study of Cyril of Alexandria's Exegesis and Theology*. New Haven and London: Yale University Press.

——, (1976) "Melito, the Jewish Community at Sardis, and the Sacrifice of Isaac" *Theological Studies* 37: 53-69.

——, (1980) "The Jews and Christian Apologetics after Theodosius I Cunctos Populos" *Harvard Theological Review* 73: 451-71.

Williamson, Clark, M. (1982*) Has God Rejected His People? Anti-Judaism in the Christian Church*. Nashville: Abingdon.

Wilson, Stephen G. (1985) "Passover, Easter and Anti-Judaism in Melito of Sardis and Others" in Jacob Neusner and Ernest S. Frerichs, eds. "To See Ourselves as Others See Us" *Christians, Jews and 'Others' in Late Antiquity*. Chico, California: Scholars Press.

——, (1986a) "Introduction" in Stephen G. Wilson, ed. *Anti-Judaism in Early Christianity*. Vol.2. Waterloo: Wilfrid Laurier, pp. ix-xi.

——, (1986b) "Marcion and the Jews" in Wilson, ed. *Anti-Judaism in Early Christianity*. Vol. 2, Waterloo: Wilfrid Laurier, pp. 81-102.

——, (1986c) "Melito and Israel" in Stephen Wilson, ed. *Anti-Judaism in Early Christianity*. Vol. 2, Waterloo: Wilfrid Laurier, pp. 45-58.. New York: Paulist Press, pp. 230-256.

INDEX

STUDIA POST-BIBLICA

1. KOSMALA, H. *Hebräer – Essener – Christen*. Studien zur Vorgeschichte der frühchristlichen Verkündigung. 1959. ISBN 90 04 02135 3
3. WEISE, M. *Kultzeiten und kultischer Bundesschluß in der 'Ordensregel' vom Toten Meer*. 1961. ISBN 90 04 02136 1
4. VERMES, G. *Scripture and Tradition in Judaism*. Haggadic Studies. Reprint. 1983. ISBN 90 04 07096 6
5. CLARKE, E.G. *The Selected Questions of Isho bar Nūn on the Pentateuch*. Edited and Translated from Ms Cambridge Add. 2017. With a Study of the Relationship of Isho'dādh of Merv, Theodore bar Konī and Isho bar Nūn on Genesis. 1962. ISBN 90 04 03141 3
6. NEUSNER, J. *A Life of Joḥanan ben Zakkai (ca. 1-80 C.E.)*. 2nd rev. ed. 1970. ISBN 90 04 02138 8
7. WEIL, G.E. *Élie Lévita, humaniste et massorète (1469-1549)*. 1963. ISBN 90 04 02139 6
8. BOWMAN, J. *The Gospel of Mark*. The New Christian Jewish Passover Haggadah. 1965. ISBN 90 04 03142 1
11. NEUSNER, J. *A History of the Jews in Babylonia*. Part 2. The Early Sasanian Period. ISBN 90 04 02143 4
12. NEUSNER, J. Part 3. From Shahpur I to Shahpur II. 1968. ISBN 90 04 02144 2
14. NEUSNER, J. Part 4. The Age of Shahpur II. 1969. ISBN 90 04 02146 9
15. NEUSNER, J. Part 5. Later Sasanian Times. 1970. ISBN 90 04 02147 7
16. NEUSNER, J. *Development of a Legend*. Studies on the Traditions Concerning Joḥanan ben Zakkai. 1970. ISBN 90 04 02148 5
17. NEUSNER, J. (ed.). *The Formation of the Babylonian Talmud*. Studies in the Achievements of the Late Nineteenth and Twentieth Century Historical and Literary-Critical Research. 1970. ISBN 90 04 02149 3
18. CATCHPOLE, D.R. *The Trial of Jesus*. A Study in the Gospels and Jewish Historiography from 1770 to the Present Day. 1971. ISBN 90 04 02599 5
19. NEUSNER, J. *Aphrahat and Judaism*. The Christian-Jewish Argument in Fourth-Century Iran. 1971. ISBN 90 04 02150 7
20. DAVENPORT, G.L. *The Eschatology of the Book of Jubilees*. 1971. ISBN 90 04 02600 2
21. FISCHEL, H.A. *Rabbinic Literature and Greco-Roman Philosophy*. A Study of Epicurea and Rhetorica in Early Midrashic Writings. 1973. ISBN 90 04 03720 9
22. TOWNER, W.S. *The Rabbinic 'Enumeration of Scriptural Examples'*. A Study of a Rabbinic Pattern of Discourse with Special Reference to *Mekhilta d'Rabbi Ishmael*. 1973. ISBN 90 04 03744 6
23. NEUSNER, J. (ed.). *The Modern Study of the Mishna*. 1973. ISBN 90 04 03669 5
24. ASMUSSEN, J.P. *Studies in Judeo-Persian Literature*. [Tr. from the Danish]. (Homages et Opera Minora, 12). 1973. ISBN 90 04 03827 2
25. BARZILAY, I. *Yoseph Shlomo Delmedigo (Yashar of Candia)*. His Life, Works and Times. 1974. ISBN 90 04 03972 4

26. PSEUDO-JEROME. *Quaestiones on the Book of Samuel*. Edited with an Introduction by A. Saltman. 1975. ISBN 90 04 04195 8

27. BERGER, K. *Die griechische Daniel-Exegese*. Eine altkirchliche Apokalypse. Text, Übersetzung und Kommentar. 1976. ISBN 90 04 04756 5

28. LOWY, S. *The Principles of Samaritan Bible Exegesis*. 1977. ISBN 90 04 04925 8

29. DEXINGER, F. *Henochs Zehnwochenapokalypse und offene Probleme der Apokalyptikforschung*. 1977. ISBN 90 04 05428 6

30. COHEN, J.M. *A Samaritan Chronicle*. A Source-Critical Analysis of the Life and Times of the Great Samaritan Reformer, Baba Rabbah. 1981. ISBN 90 04 06215 7

31. BROADIE, A. *A Samaritan Philosophy*. A Study of the Hellenistic Cultural Ethos of the Memar Marqah. 1981. ISBN 90 04 06312 9

32. HEIDE, A. VAN DER. *The Yemenite Tradition of the Targum of Lamentations*. Critical Text and Analysis of the Variant Readings. 1981. ISBN 90 04 06560 1

33. ROKEAH, D. *Jews, Pagans and Christians in Conflict*. 1982. ISBN 90 04 07025 7

35. EISENMAN, R.H. *James the Just in the Habakkuk* Pesher. 1986. ISBN 90 04 07587 9

36. HENTEN, J.W. VAN, H.J. DE JONGE, P.T. VAN ROODEN & J.W. WEESELIUS (eds.). *Tradition and Re-Interpretation in Jewish and Early Christian Literature*. Essays in Honour of Jürgen C.H. Lebram. 1986. ISBN 90 04 07752 9

37. PRITZ, R.A. *Nazarene Jewish Christianity*. From the End of the New Testament Period until its Disappearance in the Fourth Century. 1988. ISBN 90 04 08108 9

38. HENTEN, J.W. VAN, B.A.G.M. DEHANDSCHUTTER & H.W. VAN DER KLAAUW. *Die Entstehung der jüdischen Martyrologie*. 1989. ISBN 90 04 08978 0

39. MASON, S. *Flavius Josephus on the Pharisees*. A Composition-Critical Study. 1991. ISBN 90 04 09181 5

40. OHRENSTEIN, R.A. & B. GORDON. *Economic Analysis in Talmudic Literature*. Rabbinic Thought in the Light of Modern Economics. 1992. ISBN 90 04 09540 3

41. PARENTE, F. & J. SIEVERS (eds.). *Josephus and the History of the Greco-Roman Period*. Essays in Memory of Morton Smith. 1994. ISBN 90 04 10114 4

42. ATTRIDGE, H.W. & G. HATA (eds.). *Eusebius, Christianity, and Judaism*. 1992. ISBN 90 04 09688 4

43. TOAFF, A. *The Jews in Umbria*. Vol. I: 1245-1435. 1993. ISBN 90 04 09695 7

44. TOAFF, A. *The Jews in Umbria*. Vol. II: 1435-1484. 1994. ISBN 90 04 09979 4

45. TOAFF, A. *The Jews in Umbria*. Vol. III: 1484-1736. 1994. ISBN 90 04 10165 9

46. TAYLOR, M.S. *Anti-Judaism and Early Christian Identity*. A Critique of the Scholarly Consensus. 1995. ISBN 90 04 10186 1